Octavian Capatina

The Spirit of Europe

europe books

europe books

© 2025 **Europe Books**| London
www.europebooks.co.uk | info@europebooks.co.uk

ISBN 9791256971091
First edition: May 2025

Translated from Romanian into English by Rareș Călugăr

The Spirit of Europe

TABLE OF CONTENTS – SELECTIVE CHRONOLOGY

THE GENETIC HISTORY OF EUROPEANS
THE "NATIVES" AND THE INDO-EUROPEANS
THE GREEK DEMOCRACY. SOLON (640 -558 BC)
THE ROMAN REPUBLIC   509 BC
SINGULARIZING EUROPE
THE LAWS OF THE TWELVE TABLES   449 BC
THE PRESOCRATIC PHILOSOPHY
SOCRATES, DEMOCRITUS, PLATO, ARISTOTLE
HELLENISM. EPICUREANISM. STOICISM.
EUCLID
THE HELIOCENTRIC MODEL AND ITS
CONFIRMATION
THE ASCENSION OF ROME (218-201 BC)
THE GRACCHI BROTHERS
DEMAGOGY AND POPULISM
THE CELTS
CONQUERING THE CELTS   58 BC
A NEW ERA DAWNS   33
APOSTLE PAUL. THE EVANGELISATION   46
PERSECUTING THE CHRISTIANS   66
MERITOCRACY. THE APEX OF THE ROMAN EMPIRE   98
THE QUESTION OF KNOWLEDGE
THE LONG ROAD TO KNOWLEDGE IN MEDICINE
THE DACIANS AND DACO-ROMANS
THE JEWS UNTIL THE AGE OF ENLIGHTENMENT   135
NEOPLATONISM
OTHER CHRISTIAN IDEAS AND HERESIES
MEDIEVAL THINKING - PATRISTIC
THE REFORM OF THE EMPIRE   293
MONASTICISM. THE RELIGIOUS ORDERS   300
FLAVIUS CONSTANTINE THE GREAT   324
HALF A MILLENNIUM OF IDEOLOGICAL WARS   325
BAPTISM OF THE LEADERS   337
SAINT AUGUSTINE (354-430)
TRANSLATING THE BIBLE   383
CHRISTIANITY – THE RELIGION OF THE EMPIRE   391

PAGAN TRADITIONS ADOPTED BY CHRISTIANITY
SAINTS, YET STILL HUMAN
FROM PERSECUTED TO PERSECUTORS   409
THE GOTHS. THE BURGUNDIANS. THE FRANKS
THE FALL OF THE WESTERN ROMAN EMPIRE   476
THE THREE FAMOUS THRACIANS. FLAVII   527
THE KINGDOM OF LOMBARDS   572
THE BISHOP OF ROME   590
THE ROMAN EMPIRE BEFORE THE ARAB EXPANSION   610
THE ARAB ADVANCE AND RETREAT   674
THE KHAGANATE OF THE VOLGA TURANIAN   681
THE ICONOCLASM   730
THE FRANKS AND THE PAPAL STATES   751
CHARLEMAGNE (768-814)   768
THE DIVISION OF THE FRANKISH EMPIRE   843
THE VIKINGS   845
THE VIKINGS FROM THE RUSS TRIBE AMONG THE SLAVS   859
BYZANTIUM UNDER THE MACEDONIAN DYNASTY   867
SCHOLASTICISM
THE GOLDEN AGE OF SLAVIC CULTURE   870
THE HUNGARIAN TRIBES AND THE CATHOLIC KINGDOM.   903
THE CALIPHATE OF CORDOBA   929
THE HOLY ROMAN EMPIRE   962
THE CAPETIANS   987
IBERIA. RECONQUISTA   1010
THE MILITARY ORDERS   1048
THE GREAT SCHISM OF THE CHURCH   1054
INDULGENCES   1063
THE CRUSADES   1096
THE CONCORDAT BETWEEN THE POPE AND THE EMPEROR   1122
AVERROES. THE UNIVERSAL INTELLECT
THE UNION BETWEEN CATALONIA AND ARAGON   1137
THE INDIVIDUALIZATION OF PORTUGAL   1139
THE PLANTAGENETS. IRELAND UNDER THE ENGLISH   1154
THE AUTONOMY OF ITALIAN CITIES   1183
THE INQUISITION   1184
THE ROMANIAN-BULGARIAN EMPIRE   1186
INTOLERANCE, CRIMES, GENOCIDES   1204

MAGNA CARTA LIBERTATUM   1215
THE TATAR INVASION   1241
THE SEPARATION OF THE EASTERN SLAVIC PEOPLES
RESUMING "SCIENTIFIC" RESEARCH
THOMAS AQUINAS
THE GEOGRAPHICAL DISCOVERIES   1271
THE SWISS CONFEDERATION   1291
THE PAPACY IN AVIGNON   1309
THE GHIBELLINES AND THE GUIELFS. PAPAL   1328
SUPREMACY
THE HUNDRED YEARS' WAR   1337
THE TSARS OF THE ROMANS AND SERBS   1346
THE PLAGUE   1348
THE REORGANIZATION OF THE HOLY ROMAN EMPIRE   1356
THE GRAND DUCHY OF LITHUANIA   1362
THE RENAISSANCE
THE REFORMATION, A RELIGIOUS AND SOCIAL MOVEMENT   1377
THE INTERNAL SCHISM OF CATHOLICISM   1378
THE EAST SLAVS, STILL UNDER THE TATAR YOKE   1380
THE BALKANS UNDER OTTOMAN RULE. THE   1389
ROMANIAN WALL
THE SCANDINAVIAN UNION   1397
THE RISE OF POLAND AND LITHUANIA   1410
THE POPE OR THE COUNCIL?   1415
UNIO TRIUM NATIONUM   1437
SOMETIMES THE PRACTICE PRECEDES THE CONCEPT   1438
THE COUNCIL OF FERRARA-FLORENCE   1439
THE SLAVE TRADE   1441
THE FALL OF CONSTANTINOPLE   1453
TU FELIX AUSTRIAE NUBE   1477
THE END OF THE RECONQUISTA   1492
CHARLES V   1519
THE RISE OF SWEDEN   1523
THE GERMAN PEASANTS' WAR   1524
FRANCE FORCED TO GIVE UP ITALY   1525
THE UNION OF BRETAGNE WITH THE FRENCH KINGDOM   1532
THE SEPARATION OF THE ENGLISH CHURCH FROM ROME   1534
THE PASHALIK OF BUDA   1541

9

THE COUNCIL OF TRENT, THE COUNTER REFORMATION 1545
CUJUS REGIO, EJUS RELIGIO 1555
THE UNION OF LUBLIN 1569
THE RELIGIOUS WARS IN FRANCE 1572
THE PEOPLE TAKE ON THE TOLL OF SOVEREIGNTY 1581
SPAIN SETS, ENGLAND RISES 1588
MODERN THINKING
THE EVOLUTION OF PUBLIC LAW
THE FIRST UNION OF ROMANIAN PRINCIPALITIES 1601
THE LIBERATION OF MOSCOW 1612
THE THIRTY YEARS' WAR. THE PEACE OF WESTPHALIA 1618
THE THIRD ROME 1634
THE IRISH REBELLION 1641
THE ENGLISH CIVIL WAR AND SUCCESSION 1642
DIVIDE ET IMPERA: A NEW DENOMINATION 1646
CHANGING LORDS. 1654
A LOST OPPORTUNITY 1683
THE ENLIGHTENMENT
MUSKOVIA'S AWAKENING 1700
THE RISE OF PRUSSIA 1701
THE UNION OF SCOTLAND AND ENGLAND 1707
THE TREATIES OF UTRECHT AND RASTADT 1713
THE PRAGMATIC SANCTION AND SUCCESSION 1713
AN UNPARALLELED MARTYR 1714
THE DIVISION OF STATES 1772
THE ERA OF SCIENCE AND TECHNOLOGY
KANT. GERMAN CLASSICAL IDEALISM. HEGEL
FROM FORCED MAGYARIZATION TO GENOCIDE
THE REVOLUTION 1789
A SHOCK DELIVERED TO OLD EUROPE 1799
THE RESTORATION 1815
CHANGES IN THE POLITICAL GEOGRAPHY 1817
EXISTENTIALISM
A CATASTROPHE CAUSED BY FAMINE 1846
THE REVOLUTIONARY WAVE 1848
THE EUROPEAN BALANCE – THE CRIMEAN WAR 1856
EVOLUTIONISM
NEW NATION STATES 1859

THE GERMAN WARS   1863
THE FINAL STAGE OF AN ABSURD EMPIRE   1867
"DAS CAPITAL" BY KARL MARX
THE SCIENCES UNTIL THE 19TH CENTURY
THE RUSSO-TURKISH WAR, WON BY ROMANIANS   1877
NIETZSCHE. THE TOTAL BREAK
THE SCRAMBLE FOR AFRICA
THE FIRST ZIONIST CONGRESS   1897
NORWAY'S INDEPENDENCE   1905
BULGARIA'S INDEPENDENCE. THE YOUNG TURKS   1908
THE BALKAN WARS   1912
STEPPING BEYOND THE BORDER
THE GREAT WAR   1914
INTELLECTUALS AND ATROCITIES. THE PEACE
AMONG SOLDIERS   1914
SOLDIERS OR POLITICAL LEADERS?
SELF-DETERMINATION, FROM DECLARATIONS   1917
TO STRICT VOTING
THE BOLSHEVIK-GERMAN REVOLUTION   1917
TERRORISM, COMMUNISM, FASCISM, NAZISM
NEW STATES ON THE MAP OF EUROPE   1918
THE SPREAD AND REBUTTAL OF BOLSHEVISM   1919
THE PEACE TREATIES   1920
THE UNCHANGING CHURCH. TWO DIFFERENT CHURCHES   1920
EUROASIANISM
A NEW IDEOLOGY – POLITICAL CORRECTNESS   1921
TERRITORIAL RECTIFICATIONS   1925
A NEW SPIRIT WITH NEW TREATIES
THE GREAT DEPRESSION   1929
THE SPANISH CIVIL WAR   1931
THE NATIONAL – SOCIALISTS IN POWER   1933
IRELAND'S INDEPENDENCE   1937
THE END OF EUROPE?
WORLD WAR II   1939
THE ANTI-COMMUNISM RESISTANCE IN ROMANIA   1944
THE MYTH OF THE DICTATORSHIP OF THE PROLETARIAT   1953
THE EUROPEAN COMMUNITY   1957
THE BUCHAREST SPRING   1964
KONRAD LORENZ – A LUCID MIND

11

REVIVAL AND REGRESSION 1968
THE FALL OF COMMUNISM 1989
NEW STATES ON THE MAP OF EUROPE. 1991
THE BLOODY SPLIT OF YUGOSLAVIA 1991
MOLDOVA'S STRUGGLE FOR UNITY 1992
THE AMICABLE SEPARATION 1993
THE RUSSIAN WORLD – A WORLD WITHOUT MORAL
AFTER MOLDOVA, CHECHNYA, GEORGIA – 2014
CRIMEA AND DONBASS
THE INVASION OF UKRAINE. THE GENOCIDE 2022
THE EUROPEAN WORLD OUTSIDE EUROPE AND THE UNITED NATIONS
A NEW WORLD ORGANIZATION BASED ON ETHICS
NATURE AS AN INDIVISIBLE WHOLE (THE ECO-HUMANISM)

BIBLIOGRAPHY
LIST OF FIGURES
INDEX

THE GENETIC HISTORY OF EUROPEANS

The methods for extracting DNA from fossilized bones were perfected about twenty years ago. This has since enabled a more objective approach to history, starting with the origin of humankind. As a result of these new methods of DNA extraction/reconstruction from the fossilized bones of creatures that lived hundreds of thousands of years ago, it was discovered that present-day Europeans are genetically composed, with insignificant variations, of ~1.5% Neanderthals, ~0.8% Denisovans, who were only discovered approximately 10 years ago, and about ~97.7% *Homo sapiens*. Precise knowledge of the genetics of European populations allows for many emendations, as well as dispelling numerous confusions that still persist in the European historiography to this day.

The Neanderthals, who were hunter-gatherers, roamed Europe around 700.000 years ago. As for the symbiosis with Denisovans, we still lack sufficient and pertinent data, but the symbiosis did occur, as is evident in our genes. Three waves of the *Homo sapiens* migration followed. Between these waves, which spanned many millennia, after each of the individual migrating waves, the genetic mix that had formed appeared "autochthonous" to the next. In the Paleolithic era, approximately 50.000 years ago, other hunter-gatherers from the Near East, belonging to *Homo sapiens*, arrived and were somewhat more adaptable and perhaps more fertile than the "hosts". This migration occurred slowly and peacefully, it spread from one valley to the next. Those *Homo sapiens* who remained in the Near East, in the region known as the Fertile Crescent (today's Iraq, Syria, Lebanon and Israel), discovered agriculture and domesticated animals. As a consequence, the population grew to such an extent that a new migration towards Europe began, through Anatolia. This second wave of *Homo sapiens*, consisting of Neolithic farmers, entered Europe through the Danube Valley slowly and peacefully

13

around 10.000 to 8.000 years ago (8,000-6,000 BC). These newcomers created great European Neolithic civilizations such as Vinča, Turdaș, Hamangia, Boian-Gumelnița, culminating with the astonishing Cucuteni civilization. As a result of the genetic symbiosis, the genetic composition about 6.000 years ago (4.000 BC) was around 37.5% Paleolithic genes and 62.5% Neolithic genes.

This was the genetic portrait of "Europeans" when the third wave of *Homo sapiens* arrived in Europe, the Indo-Europeans (the Yamnaya populations), from the northern shores of the Black and Caspian Sea.

Genetics of Europeans (Romanians): 97,5% sapiens, 2,5% neanderthal & denisovan

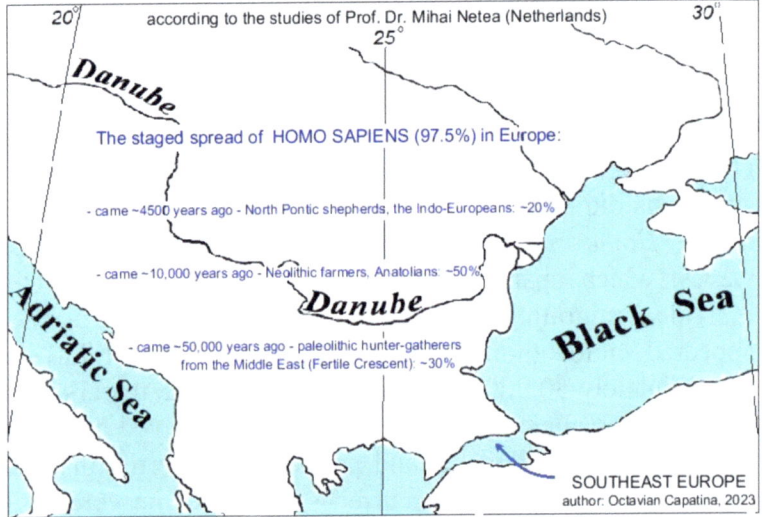

Fig. 1. The gradual advance of HOMO SAPIENS (97,5%) in Europe

The Indo-Europeans were shepherds and had domesticated the horse, which allowed them to migrate at a much faster pace than the previous waves. The Indo-Europeans, including the Thracians, Celts, Germans, and Slavs from the Bronze Age, established themselves as the ruling and warrior elites, surpassing the previous symbiosis. The language of the Indo-

Europeans became intertwined with the language of the natives. From this perspective, there is a single cultural curiosity in the mosaic of today's European languages – the Basques. Although genetically identical to all Europeans, they continue to speak a Neolithic language predating the arrival of the Celtic Indo-Europeans. The only known genetic exception are the Laplanders – the Sami people.

THE "NATIVES" AND THE INDO-EUROPEANS

In the Neolithic period, in Eastern, Central, and Southeastern Europe, a civilization developed (around 6000-3500 BC), a civilization which is deemed "palpable" through a multitude of artifacts discovered relatively recently. The main known centers are Vinca, Criş, Turdaş, Boian, Vădastra, Gumelniţa and Cucuteni. These artifacts indicate sedentary, organized populations, initially matriarchal, reverential towards *a primordial mother figure*. These populations prospered, being preoccupied with prestige and valuable goods – notably, the astonishing pottery adorned with geometric motifs. Artifacts from Boian, Sălcuţa, Turdaş, and Cucuteni:

2a) Boian, Sălcuţa, Turdaş

2b) Cucuteni

2c) Cucuteni

Fig. 2. Neolithic artifacts from the Lower Danube. Cucuteni culture. Sources: Muzeul Arh. Cucuteni, Muzeul de Istorie Iași, Muzeul de Istorie Națională București.

The stylistic matrix of the Indo-European populations proposed by the philosopher Lucian Blaga (1895-1961) was further developed through the research of M.P. Nilsson and Mircea Eliade. More recently, Maria Gimbutas and Adrian Poruciuc have continued the research that traces the evolution of Europeans in prehistoric times. The geometric forms of the Thracians and the subdued geometry of the Celts appear to originate in the Neolithic period.

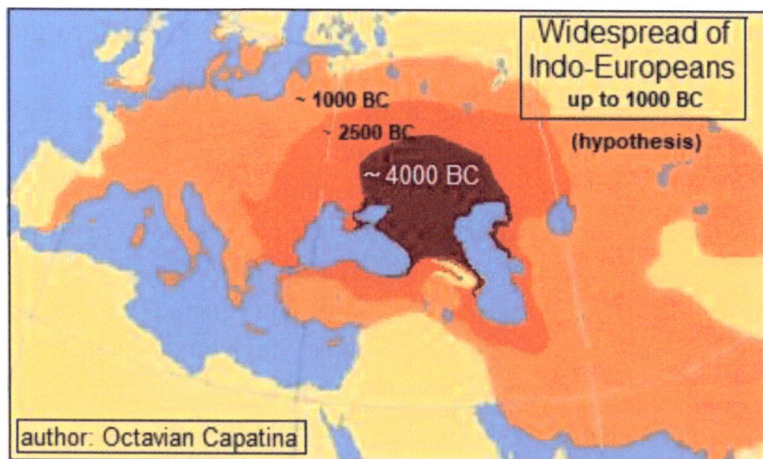
Fig. 3. The gradual advance of Indo-Europeans

Indo-Europeans, the Thracians and partially the Celts appear to have assimilated, to varying degrees, the culture of the indigenous people or "natives" in Central and Eastern Europe, even though the Celts ventured further towards the western edge of the continent. The "mismatch" between the theory of stylistic matrices proposed by Blaga and the new approaches intuited by Mircea Eliade and demonstrated by Gimbutas and Poruciuc arises from the philosopher's focus solely on the stylistic "output" of the Thracians rather than its roots. The observation that the Thracians should be understood as the symbiosis of the indigenous Vinca-Turdaș-Cucuteni civilization with the newcomers strengthens Blaga's theory of the stylistic matrix, relating to the ornamentation. The distinct stylistic "coloration" of Thracian Indo-Europeans compared to other Indo-Europeans stems from the texture provided by local populations. The imprint of the Boian-Vinca-Turdaș-Cucuteni culture – the geometric ornamentation seen today in the Carpathians, Balkans and Anatolia, the Thracian region – is particularly observable among the "indigenous" people of this

17

region. The same phenomenon happened with regard to the Indo-Europeans in the West, whom we call Celts or Gauls.

They are not merely a branch of Indo-Europeans; they represent a symbiosis with the indigenous populations encountered along their path, especially in the places where they settled. This symbiosis with the "natives" also explains the significant linguistic differences between Thracians (Dacians, Getae, Moesi, Bissenians, Phrygians, Bithynians, Illyrians and so on), Celts, Germans, Slavs, and Balts. Their prolonged isolation in distinct geographic areas alone could not wholly justify such differences. Only the symbiosis with the natives, with the locals, can explain the profound linguistic differences between them.

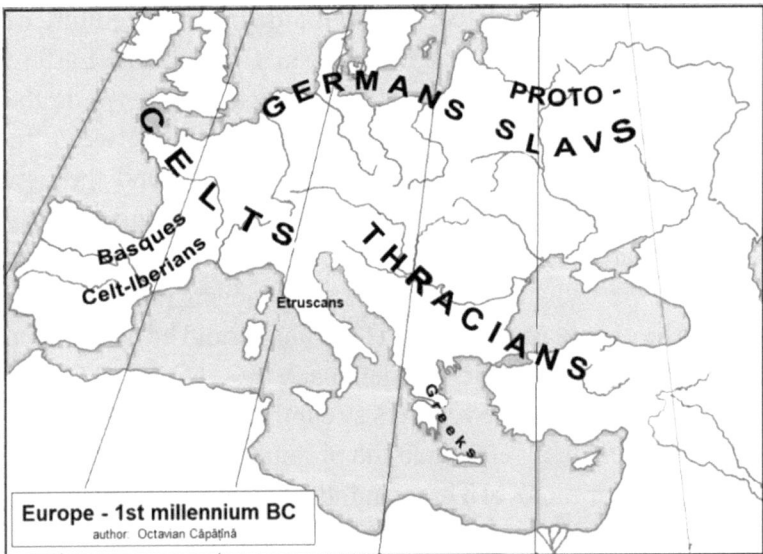

Fig. 4. Europe, 1000 BC. Between the Thracians and Celts there existed an area of interference outside that of origin.

PROTO-SLAVS

In the north-east of Europe, between the natives and the Indo-Europeans who came there in the first millennium before Christ, a population was formed which we can call proto-Slavic. According to the latest archaeological and linguistic research, today's Slavs were formed much, much later (in the second part of the first millennium AD). The Slavic languages has a Baltic, an Iranian and a Thracian component (Fl. Curta, S. Paliga, etc.). Thus, many words from the Romanian language that were considered to come from the Slavic language turned out to be from the Thracian language.

THE GREEK DEMOCRACY. SOLON (640 BC-558 BC)

Solon, considered one of the Seven Sages of Ancient Greece, was a renowned Athenian statesman and legislator. His reforms halted economic and moral decline, laying the foundations for Athenian democracy. He restored the importance of the *Citizen's Assembly (ecclesia)*, which held the primary governing function in the city-state at that time. He reconstructed the social base of the city, which had been eroded by turning small and medium landowners into slaves, due to debt. Those who had been turned into slaves due were freed, and he curbed property concentration by setting a limit on property ownership. He replaced the right to participate in magistracy based on one's birth in a noble family (Eupatridae) with the census (wealth).

Four census classes were created which had obligations proportional to their respective wealth. However, all classes had equal voting power in the Citizen's Assembly. Solon's legislation laid the groundwork for Athens' progress, allowing Athenian citizens to work, unlike the Spartan or Theban custom.

CLEISTHENES (565 BC - 492 BC) continued, in the last decade of the 6th century BC, the reforming endeavours of Solon. Through a new territorial division, he broke the stronghold and power of the nobles, definitively eliminating the old privileges of the Athenian clans. He had a decisive contribution to the development of the democratic system. The Athenians made a significant discovery – they didn't belong to the city because they themselves were the city.

THE ROMAN REPUBLIC (509 BC)

In 509 BC, following a rebellion carried out by the patricians and plebeians against the autocracy of the Etruscan king Lucius Tarquinius Superbus, the Roman Republic was established. In this system, two consuls were elected annually. Access to political offices followed a *cursus honorum*: a sequence of administrative positions had to be undertaken before one could run for the supreme office of *consul*. The Republic lasted until 27 BC, when the Roman Senate granted Octavian the title of *Augustus*, following the civil war that ended with Antony's defeat in 31 BC.

SINGULARIZING EUROPE (500-479 BC)

After the Persian Wars (Marathon, 490 BC, Thermopylae, 480 BC, Salamis, 480 BC, Plataea, and Mycale, 479 BC), the Persian autocracies relinquished Greece and Europe. This was followed by the golden age of ancient Greek culture, the era of Pericles (495-429 BC). Pericles, a democratic leader, came from the highest aristocracy. He abolished the veto power of the Areopagus, the aristocracy, leaving all power to the

Citizen's Assembly (*Ecclesia*). As democratic as he appeared in Athens, he was autocratic and profiteering with the allied cities, forming the *Delian League* in 477 BC. He collected a tax for the League, which benefitted Athens. Athenian civilization flourished and influenced Roman civilization and, through it, modern civilization.

THE LAWS OF THE TWELVE TABLES (449 BC)

Following endless disputes between patricians and plebeians, in 451 BC, the tribune Terentilius Arsa called for the codification and publication of customary law. In 449 BC, a commission of ten men published the codified customary laws on twelve bronze tables (*the Decemviral Code*). *The Twelve Tables*, an impressive code, contained provisions of public and private law. Among the civil provisions were those regarding the regime of private and public property, succession matters, and family organization, which were of significant importance. The legal norms concerning contractual obligations were relatively few. The Laws of the Twelve Tables were based on three principles: *to live honorably, not to harm another, and to give each their due.* These principles formed the core on which Roman law later developed, evolving in relation to the social, economic, and political life of the Roman state. From ancient Roman law, through repeated additions, emerged the following: Justinian's *Corpus Juris Civilis* (527-565), Napoleon's Code and today's civil codes.

THE PRESOCRATIC PHILOSOPHY

Thales of Miletus, Heraclitus (*everything flows*), Anaximenes, Anaximander, Anaxagoras, Parmenides (*immobility: everything that exists must necessarily be, everything that doesn't exist must necessarily not be*), Empedocles and others established a philosophy based on nature, a philosophy of things. For them, there was not

21

knowledge, but rather things that needed to be analyzed more thoroughly, more closely.

SOCRATES (circa 470–399 BC) did not leave anything written; all that has come down to us from him is thanks to the writings of Plato and Xenophon. Socrates preferred to discuss "pragmatic" issues related to city life and the moral life of individuals, instead of issues related to the positive knowledge of nature. Socrates resolved the crisis in *natural philosophy* by making two significant shifts: he changed the focus of philosophy from *the natural* to *the human* and, in contradiction to the sophists, posited that *truth* exists. He conceptualized "knowledge" as the understanding of the general within the particular, as finding the common denominator among particulars. Starting from the principle "*I know that I know nothing*", he arrived at knowledge through questions and answers, through reason (dia-logos). He preferred debating topics with his disciples in a dialectical manner, rather than laying down rules, truths, laws or solutions. Through this method of dialogue, he drew out truth from the depths of the human soul, a truth that individuals were not yet aware of. The dialogues were conducted in such a way that, as they progressed, the interlocutor would eventually contradict themselves and accept the opposing position. According to Socrates, the goal of humanity, the ultimate good, refers to the love of wisdom and the love of truth – *philosophy*. Goodness or the love of truth, and wisdom, would bring the individual to a state of inner happiness. Perhaps Socrates' most precious legacy can be summarized in the following: *the well-being of a person depends on themselves*. We find this idea in various

forms in the Eastern Church, in the writings of Thomas Aquinas, in the Catholic faith after the Council of Trent, and in Lutheran Kierkegaard's work. For this reason, a person must be moderate and just, must respect their neighbor, as well as the laws of the city and the laws of the gods. Socrates starts philosophy with ethics. According to him, the soul has a pre-existence and, therefore, it also has a post-existence (an afterlife). When his friends wanted to save him from death, he refused, choosing instead to submit to the laws of the city. Plato, his spiritual successor, saw him as a pinnacle of the Greek world. In *Magna Moralia*, Aristotle asserts that Socrates was preoccupied with the search for moral virtues, being the first to look for universal definitions to encapsulate them.

DEMOCRITUS (c. 460 BC – c. 370 BC)

Democritus of Abdera (a Greek colony in Thrace) continued the theory of his teacher Leucippus, which based on indivisible particles, developing it into a fully-fleshed philosophical system. According to this system, the foundation of all things consists of atoms and also of voids; atoms correspond to the tangible – the solid, while void corresponds to the intangible – that which is empty. Atoms are solid, indivisible, imperceptible and indestructible particles. They differ from each other in size, color and through their motion; in fact, they are in constant motion. By combining them, all things that make up the universe (both material bodies and the human soul) come into existence. Only fragments on topics like geometry, physics, technology, agriculture, medicine, poetry, and military art have survived from his extensive works. Democritus was the first to assert that the driving force of human history is constituted by the needs of people. The thinking of Democritus, the foremost materialist philosopher of the ancient world, exerted a strong influence on many thinkers: from Epicurus and Lucretius to Francis Bacon, Galileo Galilei, and Leibniz.

PLATO (circa 427 BC – circa 347 BC) was a philosopher, a disciple of Socrates and a teacher of Aristotle. Plato was interested in mathematics, wrote philosophical dialogues and established the foundations of the *Academy* in Athens, the first institution of "higher" education in the world. Plato continued the ideas of Socrates regarding the *pre- and post-existence of the soul*, asserting that we live both in a sensible and in a supersensible world (the other realm). This notion was later embraced by Christianity. From the doctrine of the two worlds, the world of ideas and the world of things, *the doctrine of Ideas*, derives the struggle between the sensible and the supersensible world, which takes place within us. To reconcile the worlds, a common denominator must be found – there has to be a process of *mediation*. The idea of mediation is a pillar of European culture (Vasile Muscă). The two worlds, *the world of changing things*, and *the world of ideas*, which are unborn and immortal (Plato's theory of forms), homogeneous and indivisible, are not only separate but also opposing. Here we have not only the resolution of the crisis of pre-Socratic philosophy but also a mediation between extreme positions, between the idea of *constant change* (Heraclitus) and the *idea of absolute immobility* (Parmenides). For all things and beings of the same kind, we have an idea, which represents their perfect archetype. Ideas are perfect uniques, while things are imperfect copies. It's not the idea of beauty that stems from beautiful things or beings; rather, the other way around:

we have the *idea* of beauty, and we see beautiful things and beings. A person who reaches the world of ideas will continue their ascent to the idea of the good. Plato envisioned an ideal form of governance, the *Republic*, in which there are three classes: rulers, defenders (guardians), and workers (farmers and artisans). Rulers were selected based on merit, with a demonstrated interest in the welfare of the community (meritocracy). To prevent the temptation of belonging to the ruling class, citizens were not allowed to possess gold, land, or houses. Instead, they received a fixed but not excessively large salary. Furthermore, they were not allowed to start a family. They were compensated through the honor of fulfilling public service. Women and men were to have equal chances to enter the ranks of rulers. For real equality of opportunity, the state was to take charge of educating children. Children were to undergo physical training and also study mathematics, philosophy and music. At the age of 35, after mastering the theoretical principles, they would undergo fifteen years of practical training before joining the ranks of rulers. Those who didn't pass the theoretical exam would be directed towards economic activity. Plato's model of governance in the *Republic* was not followed by any civil government in the world, except for the organization of the Catholic Church. The influence of Plato's *ideas* was indirect.

ARISTOTLE (384-322 BC)

Aristotle was born in Macedonia in the year 384 BC, and, at the age of 17, he went to study at Plato's *Academy* in Athens. He then remained in Athens for 20 years, until the death of Plato, after which he emigrated to Assos (the western coast of Anatolia) and later to Mytilene (in Lesbos), where he studied zoology and marine biology, achieving astonishingly accurate results for that time.

He returned home and became the tutor of the son of King Philip II of Macedonia, the future Alexander the Great. After Alexander ascended the throne of Macedonia in 335 BC, Aristotle returned to Athens. He declined to take over Plato's *Academy* and instead opened his own school, the *Lyceum*, which was financially supported by public funds through Alexander's generosity. The establishment of this new school, running in parallel with the *Academy*, also meant Aristotle's departure from Plato's speculations. Here, he wrote his works and disseminated many of his ideas for twelve years, until the death of Alexander the Great. After Alexander's death in Babylon, in 323 BC, the Macedonians were no longer safe in the "democratic" Athens, and so Aristotle emigrated to Euboea, where he passed away the following year. Aristotle believed that Plato had put the cart before the horses, that he had turned everything upside down. He demonstrated that nothing exists in our consciousness that did not previously exist in our senses; and that humans have an innate capacity to reason, to order, to classify. According to Aristotle's philosophy, reason represents the most significant trait of humans – yet this reason grinds to a halt if the senses do not feed it. Therefore, a person does not have innate ideas. Furthermore, Aristotle believes that reality consists of different individual entities (objects, beings) that represent a unity: *{form, matter}*. Form is therefore the sum of the attributes of the respective entity. Aristotle's form exists only in the specific case of the form of one respective entity. The distinction between matter and form is essential when humans are to know and recognize the concrete entities of the world. Some of Aristotle's ideas no longer hold today, but the rational approach to all the problems that we dealt with has remained, proving a definitive influence on the European world. This rational approach singularized Europe, enabling its great advancement over all other peoples in the rest of the world, until the 20th century, when all were "Europeanized" in one way or another. Aristotle left us with the conviction that, on the one hand, the universe is not controlled by chance or magic, but by rational laws, and on the other hand, that human beings have the right to investigate every aspect of the natural world. He also believed that, to clarify unknown aspects, both direct observations and logical reasoning must be used equally. Where theory is contradicted by practical observation and experiment, precedence is given to the experiment. In ethics, he believed in the middle path: *one should neither be cowardly nor reckless, but only courageous; one should neither be greedy nor wasteful, but only generous; eating too much or too little is dangerous, and only through balance and moderation do you become harmonious and happy.* His open system of thinking, without mysticism, without superstition, decisively influenced thought in Europe, even if at some point certain ideas of Aristotle were dogmatized. These dogmatizers of Aristotle's thinking became anti-Aristotelians without realizing it. But this deviation could not hamper the strength of line of thinking and his rational methods, which ultimately prevailed. It was precisely his logical thinking that allowed him to successfully engage in many fields of knowledge, including astronomy, geography, geology, physics, zoology, anatomy, physiology, ethics, metaphysics, logic, aesthetics, economics, politics and more. Aristotle's most well-known work pertains to logic. All ancient thought, including Aristotle's, was oriented toward the static aspect of existence. Movement was regarded with caution, something to be largely ignored; only the final, fixed, immutable state was to be studied and analyzed. For the Greeks, time was an eternal continuous present. In the early Middle Ages, Averroes (1126-1198) attempted a synthesis between Aristotle's rationalism and the new Islamic theology. Maimonides (1135-1204) achieved a similar synthesis in Judaism. Thomas Aquinas (1225-1274) did the same thing in *Summa Theologica*, but from a Christian perspective. Among Aristotle's ideas contradicted by life we can find: "slavery is part of the natural order of the world" and "women are inferior to men".

If we were to put ancient Greek philosophy into extremely simple formulas, we could say that: Democrit reduced the infinite world to a brick construction, Plato reduced philosophy to *hide-and-seek in the dark,* and Aristotle reduced reality to its ordering through two-dimensional vectors *{form, matter}*.

Fig. 5. The Provinces of Asia Minor

HELLENISM

From the perspective of European history, it's not the great strategist Alexander the Great (356-323 BC) that is actually important, but his political sense and cultural legacy – the Hellenistic kingdoms, where a symbiosis occurred between the European, Thracian and Greek spirits and the Asian, Persian,

Assyrian, Egyptian and Jewish spirits. Through this symbiosis, the ancient Thracians and Greeks brought Asian diversity, enriching Europe. In fact, Alexander did not aim for hardcore military occupation, but rather a cultural dominance. His political genius allowed him to see that his universal empire would survive only if all Oriental peoples, the Greeks and Thracians were treated as equals. This was inconceivable for the Greek spirit of the time, embodied by Aristotle (see Vasile Muscă). Through this intuition, by breaking away from the Greek mentality and the narrow vision of the *polis*, Alexander the Great universalized the ancient world. The empire led to the disappearance of city-state governments, of which the citizen felt he or she was a part of and consequently protected. In the Empire, the individual lost the security he was accustomed to in the *polis*. The collapse of the *polis* and the failure to adapt to the new condition of being a citizen of the Empire had an ontological effect, with individuals feeling uprooted and purposeless. Existence without purpose is a political death that precedes natural death. Hellenism, i.e., the new philosophical currents, was illustrated by the Cynics, Epicureans, Stoics, Skeptics, Neo-Pythagoreans, and Neoplatonists. All these currents of thought are philosophies of salvation, of redemption for the uprooted citizen. These new philosophical currents were contemporary with the advent of Christianity. Hellenism brought a change in the philosophical formula: while classical Greek philosophy aimed at preparing a person for how to die with dignity, as seen in *Phaedo, Socrates' Apology*, the philosophy of the Hellenistic era served as a *Manual*, a guide on how to prepare for life. Through Alexandria, the new spiritual capital of the world, the spiritual treasures of the ancient world and the new synthesis were transmitted to the Roman world, then to the Byzantine and Arab worlds, which ultimately shaped Europe as we inherited it. Religious ideas from Asia, especially the monotheistic ones, spread among the

29

various Thracians and declining Greek city-states, paving the way for what was to come: Christianity.

EPICUREANISM

The philosopher Epicurus of Samos (341 – 270 BC) had his own philosophical school in Athens called *The Garden*, where both men and women participated. He advocated for moderation, simplicity, and prudence – virtues that allowed for the selection of pleasures based on their consequences. Like the Stoics, the Epicureans also divided philosophy into three branches: Logic, Physics, and Ethics. In Logic, everything stems from the senses, marking the initial form of empiricism. Sensation, being the foundation of knowledge, is also the guide that leads us to pursue moderate pleasures and not to shy away from pain. In Physics (the explanation of nature), Epicureanism is rooted in Democritus' atomism, although atoms possess individuality, meaning a certain personality. The soul is composed of atoms; hence, there is no fear regarding its journey into the realm of death. Epicurean ethics are based on happiness and ataraxia, wherein the tranquility of the soul constitutes the goal of ethics. The pleasures to be sought after are wisdom and friendship. To achieve serenity and happiness, Epicurus argued that a person must recognize five essential truths: i) divinity – which should not inspire fear, ii) reality is apprehended through perceptions, iii) death should not be feared, iv) goodness is easily attainable, and v) pain can be endured. The wise person attains the serenity of the gods by freeing themselves from false fears, avoiding excesses and vain ambitions, and leading a simple life. Epicureanism was adopted and made known to the Roman world by the poets Lucretius and Ovid.

STOICISM

Stoicism is a philosophical school founded in Athens by Zeno of Citium, around 300 BC.

Fig. 6 Marc Aurelius

It lasted for centuries, encompassing both a pre-Christian and a post-Christian Stoicism. Among the Stoics, there were individuals from various backgrounds, including a slave (Epictetus) and an emperor (Marcus Aurelius). Stoicism did not pursue a goal in the form of knowledge for its own sake, not even self-knowledge. Instead, Stoicism pursued a pragmatic goal: attaining happiness through virtue. The ethics of the Stoics were rooted in virtue, which meant living in harmony with nature. According to them, virtue was rational, in contrast to passion, which was irrational. In the realm of Logic, their contribution was significant. In addition to Aristotle's logic of substance, Stoicism introduced the logic of relations. In the domain of Physics, Stoicism worked with a Heraclitean concept – fire, which they identified with divinity. According to the Stoics, "nothing is immaterial", a statement derived from sensory knowledge. They rejected the dualism of matter and spirit present in Plato's philosophy, believing that the world would not have been possible if it had not been composed of the same substance. The body and the soul, the divinity and the world were pairs in which the parts acted upon each other. Thus, the body generated thoughts through the senses, which then influenced the body's movements. All things were material, constituted from the fundamental substance of fire. Fire, in its primordial form, was represented by Divinity. Divinity was in relationship with the world, just as the soul was in relationship with the body. As such, Stoicism is both monist and pantheistic. The human spirit originated from the divine fire, which had a rational character. Therefore, the world was governed by

31

reason. From this, two significations arose: i) in the world, there was a purpose – a tendency toward harmony, beauty, and balance, and ii) because reason implies law, it followed that the world was governed by the absolute relationship between cause and effect. Therefore, a person could not be entirely and arbitrarily free; they had to follow the laws of nature.

EUCLID (approximately 330–270 BC). No biographical details are known about him; we only know that he was younger than Aristotle and a contemporary of Archimedes. We also know that he taught in Alexandria between 323 and 285 BC. One of his works, entitled *Elements*, one of five preserved writings, is a treatise on plane and spatial geometry, mostly a compilation of mathematical knowledge from the Eastern Mediterranean region. It includes the most eminent scholars, such as Pythagoras (570–495 BC), Hippocrates of Chios (approx. 460 BC), Theaetetus (approx. 417–369 BC), Eudoxus (408–355 BC), and Theodius of Magnesia (approx. 340 BC). The *Elements* is organized into 13 "books". A perfectly logically organized compilation, comprising 467 demonstrated theorems. Problems of plane and spatial geometry, arithmetic, the foundations of geometric algebra, the theory of proportions and whole numbers, the classification of irrational numbers – all of these are presented with remarkable clarity, precision and rigor. Euclid started from definitions and postulates – axioms, from which he deduced the proofs – the theorems. Each new theorem derives from the previous one. The importance of Euclid's work lies not so much in the novelty of the theorems as in the perfectly logical presentation of the sum of mathematical knowledge of

his time. This work served as a mathematics manual for two thousand years. But Euclid's main contribution was disciplining generations of European scholars through logical rationalism. Thus, for modern Europeans, the existence of a few physical principles from which all others derive is self-evident, not a threshold to be "conquered", assimilated as a foreign element. The work *Elements* had numerous Arabic versions from the 9th century onwards. In fact, the first Latin translation comes from Arabic, in the year 1120; the first direct translation from Greek was made by Zamberti in 1505, in Vienna. Johannes Kepler (1571–1630) used the tenth book of the *Elements*, which deals with incommensurable lines and surfaces, for his cosmological model. René Descartes (1596–1650) and Pierre de Fermat (1601–1665) based their works on Euclid's ideas and methods. Newton (1642–1727) wrote his fundamental work, *Principia*, following the same patterns employed in Euclid's work. The Indian, Chinese or Japanese cultures were for a long time not aware of the Euclidean method and so it did not have a significant impact on modern science until the 20th century. This leads us to a self-evident truth: it is only natural to recognize and place Euclid at the foundation of modern science.

THE HELIOCENTRIC MODEL AND ITS CONFIRMATION

Aristarchus of Samos (310-230 BC), a Greek astronomer and mathematician, calculated the diameters of the Sun, Earth and the Moon, as well as the distances between them. Although his estimations were rough, he reached a rational conclusion – Earth revolves around the Sun and not the other way around. But his hypothesis was rejected. Eratosthenes (276-195 BC) calculated the Earth's circumference and axial tilt with remarkable accuracy. The idea that the Earth is round and at the center of the universe remained popular among sailors. As a result, navigator Christopher Columbus

(1451-1506), in August 1492, set sail with three ships westward to reach the East, aiming for Japan and India. Arriving in the Caribbean in October 1492, he was convinced he had reached India. Nicolaus Copernicus (1473-1543), while in Italy in 1497, became acquainted with Aristarchus and Eratosthenes's ideas, as well as Columbus's achievement. For fifteen years, he continued making his observations and calculations to transition from the Earth-centered model to placing the Sun at the center of the universe. He compiled the logical and mathematical evidence in his book *De revolutionibus orbium coelestium*. Logically deduced arguments played a significant role; Copernicus's great merit was reintroducing the heliocentric theory. The Danish astronomer Tycho Brahe (1546-1601), the last major astronomer before the discovery of the telescope, made significant contributions to observing and precisely measuring planetary motion. He also cataloged over 800 stars. Johannes Kepler (1571-1630), using Tycho Brahe's empirically gathered, precise data, mathematically formulated the laws governing planetary rotations. He performed what we could call today *mathematical regression* and deduced the three laws of planetary motion around the Sun – even though this was achieved by deducing these laws from the proportionalities he verified using Tycho Brahe's data.

THE ASCENSION OF ROME (218-202 BC)

However, the democratic course was not a linear one: "*the people's obligations were that of military service and poverty*" (Sallustius). To alleviate tensions between patricians and plebeians, Rome's genius established the tribunate in 287 BC.

The final victory of Rome, the small republic, over the powerful Carthage in the Second Punic War, after a prolonged period of conflict, asserted the advantage of moral strength and the freely embraced sense of patriotism over professional mercenarism. It affirmed the superiority of a united people who never lost sight of liberty and justice, as the foundation of life and harmony within the community was seen to be justice: *without justice, there can be no agreement.*

THE GRACCHI BROTHERS

Romans were conquering new territories in the peninsula, building cities and bringing settlers to whom arable land was given; uncultivated land could be occupied by anyone who could work it by paying a tax (a tenth of the harvest). This would have led to an increase the number of Italic men. However, the result was quite the opposite. The wealthy, not the citizens, seized these immense land surfaces and worked them with numerous slaves. The small holdings of the citizens who served Rome for sixteen years as legionaries dwindled and were bought up by large landowners. The number of slaves exempt from military obligations increased while the number of Italic descends continued to decrease. Veterans whose fields disappeared swelled the ranks of Rome's poor and lazy plebeians. They lacked perspective and were easily manipulated by demagogues and adventurers. With the disappearance of free peasants, Rome would have been doomed, a fact which was taken into consideration by Tiberius Gracchus (163-133 BC). As a tribune, he updated the Licinian laws and limited latifundia to 500-1000 jugera (250 hectares) per family. Any excess was divided into plots of 30 jugera and given to the peasants. Tiberius was assassinated, but the fight was carried on by Gaius Gracchus (154-121 BC), who granted Roman citizenship to all Italians, reduced the Senate's prerogatives and revisited the agrarian issue. He too was treacherously assassinated. Their reforms, though only partially implemented, increased the number of small rural properties in Italy by 30%, thus revitalizing the republic.

LUCRETIUS (98-55 BC)

From Lucretius, a poet and philosopher, we have the poem *De Rerum Natura* (On the Nature of Things), which bears the imprint of the philosopher Epicurus, himself influenced by the materialistic concepts of Democritus. Lucretius brought back to Europe Epicurean thought and the atomism of Democritus. From the poem, organized into 6 chapters, emerge several surprisingly innovative ideas that influenced the European Enlightenment itself: i) the world, as well as the universe, had a beginning and will end at some point; ii) things are composed of atoms, but different atoms that are in continuous motion; iii) the mind and body are distinct entities; iv) the mind is born and dies; there is no life after death; v) hell is the product of imagination and the projection of experienced suffering; vi) superstitions are the result of ignorance. Lucretius' non-theological and non-dogmatic approach to existence was a cornerstone of the European way of thinking.

THE DICTATOR RELINQUISHES POWER

Lucius Cornelius Sulla (138-78 BC), a general, politician, power-hungry individual, confronted the *populares* faction led by the power-hungry general Gaius Marius (157-86 BC). As the leader of the *optimates*, he seized Rome, proclaimed himself dictator in 82 BC and triggered waves of deportations and assassinations among Marius' supporters. He limited the power of the plebeian tribunes, abolished the position of censor and restored the Senate's primacy. He established a cult of personality. After three years of dictatorship, he abruptly and without being forced by anyone, relinquished power and withdrew to his estate.

DEMAGOGY AND POPULISM.

Demagogy and populism have accompanied and continue to accompany the ascent to power. A few examples from Roman Republic history:

The adventurer Catiline, after looting Africa as governor, wanted to become consul. Losing three consecutive elections (65-63 BC), he changed his tactics: he promised the plebeians "a relief from debt" and adopted the tactic of political assassination as a means of gaining power. Suspected and accused of conspiracy, his hypocrisy reached a climax – he asked to be personally pursued and even offered to move into the house of the praetor.

To annihilate the tribune C. Gracchus, who granted land to the poor but also asked for a small tax for the public budget, his opponents, who violently opposed land distribution to said poor, outbid each other, through the tribune Livius Drusus, proposing that the tax owed by those who received land be reduced to zero.

While Pompey, Caesar and Crassus were in Spain, Gaul, and Syria respectively, a tribune, Clodius Pulcher (92-52 BC), remained in control of Rome with his bands of thugs. Since political assemblies were controlled by thugs, the Senate banned them. The tribune, who fancied himself the equal of Pompey, Caesar, or Crassus, distributed grain to the plebeians and proposed the restoration of "democracy", meaning the freedom of his gangs of thugs. Clodius proposed and obtained the restoration of public gatherings, of "democracy". Just what he needed to further control Rome. The Senate had to call upon Pompey to restore law.

Now, in the 21st century, populism is once again at the forefront of public affairs appropriated.

OVID (43 BC-16/17 AD)

In the poems collectively called *The Metamorphoses*, Ovid is surprisingly modern in relation to us, living two millennia later. Metamorphosis was a unifying theme among numerous ancient legends. The motives for transformations were often the envy and unjustified pride of the gods, and the method of transformation was usually violent and final. These

37

transformations were treated with humor and satire; they often ended in absurdity, so that the reader realized that both these metamorphoses and the deities themselves were seriously called into question and doubted.

THE CELTS

A group of Indo-European populations that initially settled between the upper Danube and the Alps, in the second millennium BC. Here they probably became individualized through symbiosis with the natives. During the next millennium they invaded Gaul, the Iberian Peninsula and the British Isles, and the southern Alps. They made incursions as far as the Balkans and Anatolia. Then they were pushed westward by the Germans.

CONQUERING THE CELTS

58 - 52BC The Roman wars of conquest against the Celts (Gauls, Suebi, Helvetii, Belgae, Britons etc.), known as the Gallic Wars, were incredibly harsh and lasted for years, concluding in 52 BC with the capture of Alesia and the surrender of the Gallic leader Vercingetorix.

A NEW ERA DAWNS

The fall of the *polis* and the emergence of the empire left thousands of people spiritually disoriented. The new atmosphere, the new reality demanded a new philosophy of salvation. Love for one's fellows and the equality of all before God – this was the new teaching of Jesus Christ, which primarily won over the impoverished. This teaching eventually captured the hearts of many pure souls, although never enough to eliminate the so-called *right of might*. The meanings of His life were understood by His disciples and spread from Judea to the edges of the known world as soon as apostle Paul became involved. Apostle Paul grasped the value of the life of the Savior from the very beginning. The institutionalization of faith created numerous problems and led to different opinions, giving rise to various cults and sects. One significant controversy, due to its consequences, was that of predestination. On one hand, humans are creations of God, made in His image and likeness, therefore, humans are the crowning achievement of Creation, but the choice of the path is theirs (the Orthodox denomination); on the other hand, humans are entirely subject to God's will (predestination – Evangelicals). The Catholic Church oscillated in its stance on this matter. In the Middle Ages, faith played a significant role, as medieval people dreaded to depart to the "realms beyond" without the blessing of a priest. This gave a tremendous advantage to the power of theologians over the faithful, unaided by secular power.

APOSTLE PAUL (4-66/67)

Known as Saul of Tarsus, from Cilicia, a province located in southeastern Anatolia, he was among the persecutors of the followers of the new religious doctrine immediately after the crucifixion of Jesus Christ. After a revelation on the road to Damascus, Saul converted to Christianity and became the most influential propagator of the new religion. He took his name from the Roman proconsul of Cyprus, Sergius Paulus, whom he converted. No other person played as important a role in the spread of Christianity. Apostle Paul's work was facilitated by the fact that all elites knew Greek. He was arrested in Jerusalem, released, and then arrested again in Epirus and taken to Rome. It is believed that he was executed. Among the apostles, only Paul had the intuition of the universality of the deeds of Jesus Christ. He is known as the Apostle of the Gentiles or, as a modern Socrates, Petre Tutea, said: *He's not a man, but the whole Mediterranean region.*

THE CHRISTIAN PEOPLES

Among the first peoples to be Christianized by the apostles, the former disciples of Jesus Christ, immediately after His ascension to heaven, were the Syrians, Phoenicians, Egyptians, Thracians and Greeks. Since the Romanians are a synthesis of Thracian (Dacian) and Roman elements, which took shape precisely during the early spread of Christianity, these new people of Latin expression were born Christian. Linguistic evidence thoroughly supports this assertion, including the fact that the Romanian language retained Latin forms related to worship, whereas the Neo-Latins adopted later Greek forms (see Vasile Pârvan – *Epigraphic Contributions to the History of Daco-Roman Christianity*).

PEDANIUS DIOSCORIDES (c. 40 - c. 90)

Pedanius Dioscorides, of uncertain origin, either Thracian or Greek, was born in Cilicia (Anatolia). As a physician, pharmacologist and botanist, he served as a surgeon in Nero's army. He accompanied Roman armies throughout the entire Empire, collecting information about plants and substances that could be used for treating various ailments. He wrote *De Materia Medica*, a five-volume book that is considered the precursor to all pharmacopoeias and the most significant botanical atlas in the world. This work remained the primary pharmacological reference for 1500 years in Europe, the Near East and the Arab world. The linguistic and historical value of the book lies in the recording of a series of local plant names from Dacia (60) and Egypt (20).

46 THE EVANGELIZATION

The disciples of Christ spread to all parts of the world: Paul preached to the Syrians, Thracians of Asia Minor and to Greeks; Andrew to the Dacian on the north-western coast of the Pontus; Peter to the Romans;

40

Thomas to the Persians and Indians; and Mark to the Egyptians.

The learned Gothic scholar Ulfila (310? - 381?), proficient in the Gothic language and converted to the Arian variant of Christianity in Cappadocia, preached Christianity to the Dacians and Goths along the Danube. He translated the Gospels into the Gothic language, becoming the apostle of the Goths. They imposed Arian Christianity in the conquered areas: northern Italy, the Rhine Valley, Iberia and northern Africa. 350

Nicetas (335-414), bishop of Remesiana (Dacia-Mediterranea), brought the gospel to "those wolves of the mountains", namely the Dacians south of the Danube. Nicetas's mission was successful, and the cult and religious services dedicated to Dionysus and other Thracian deities were gradually replaced with the Christian worship. ~370

St. Martin (316-397), a Daco-Roman from Pannonia, a Roman soldier in Gaul, who later became the bishop of Tours, organized the Christianization of the Gallo-Romans in the rural area. ~370

The Christianization of the province of Britannia was carried out gradually through missionaries from Gaul. Patrick (5th century) came from a Romanized and Christian family from Britannia, began his mission in Ireland. Ireland became a hotspot for Christian culture. Patrick was then made a saint. ~400

Augustine of Canterbury (?-604), sent by Pope Gregory I, Christianized the Anglo-Saxon tribes, established bishops in London and Rochester and founded the Canterbury monastery as well as many schools for priests. Charlemagne (768-814) waged wars for decades, brutally massacring the Saxons settled 597

772
-
804

settled between the Rhine and Elbe in order to Christianize them.

863 The brothers Constantine/Cyril (826-869) and Michael/Metodius (815-885), Greeks from Macedonia, are considered by the Slavs to be the inventors of the Cyrillic alphabet. They journeyed through Pannonia and Moravia, spreading Christianity among the Western Slavs, sent by Emperor Michael III at the request of Moravian prince Ratislav. Within

875 a few years, Slavic Christianity reached the shores of the Vistula.

The first attempt to Christianize the Baltic people

1186 was made by canon Meinhard. Hailing from the Hanover region, he built a stone church on the Daugava River in 1186.

Canon Albert of Buxhoeveden (1165-1229), arriving from the Bremen region at the head of an

1201 army, Christianized the Baltic regions in the style of crusaders, i.e., forcefully, and established the Diocese of Üxküll (Riga).

Teutonic Knights, reaching the shores of the Baltic Sea, clashed with pagan Prussians. After seven years

1242 of fighting, they had to forsake pagan customs, accept the Christian faith and acknowledge the Teutonic Order as the sole authority.

EUROPEAN THRACE, A ROMAN PROVINCE

46 The Kingdom of Thrace (between the Thracian Sea, now the Aegean Sea, and the Haemus Mountains) was transformed into a Roman province. The northern region of the Thracians, Moesia (between the Danube and the Haemus Mountains), had come under the rule of the Roman Empire during the time of Augustus, as early as 29 BC.

PERSECUTING THE CHRISTIANS

The Roman Empire was, generally speaking, tolerant of the religions of its subjects. However, after the fire in the year 64 that destroyed 10 out of the 14 districts of Rome, Nero (54-68) crucified and burned thousands of Christians as culprits. Among the victims were the apostles Paul and Peter. Other limited persecutions followed during the reigns of Emperors Domitian (81-96) and Trajan (98-117). Decius (249-251) initiated a conservative political program that included a return to the Roman polytheistic religion. In 250, Decius issued an edict against Christians. It marked the first empire-wide anti-Christian persecution; Christian clergy were ordered to renounce their faith and adopt the Roman religion. Many Christians chose to die as martyrs. This was followed by the persecution of 257-258 under Valerian (253-259). A period of relative peace for Christians began with Gallienus's edict in 260, lasting for 43 years. Emperor Diocletian (284-305), after a fire in Nicomedia, at his residence (in Bithynia, in Thrace, on the Anatolian coast of the Sea of Marmara) initiated the harshest persecutions against the followers of the new religion. Persecutions ceased after the second edict of tolerance issued by Licinius and Galerius. This was followed by the Edict of Milan in 313, under Constantine and Licinius, which guaranteed freedom and equality for all religions.

66

250 - 260

303 - 311

THE MERITOCRACY (98-180)

After Nero, after the Flavian dynasty, the dynastic principle was abandoned in favour of the principle of adopted emperors, i.e. those considered suitable to rule. The era of the "Five Good Emperors" - Nerva (96-98), Trajan (98-117), Hadrian (117-138), Antoninus Pius (138-161) and

Fig. 7. The 5 emperors chosen on merit

Marcus Aurelius (161-180) – marked a period of maximum development and expansion of the Roman Empire. The concept of meritocracy was acknowledged, but often forgotten in the political turmoil that characterized and still characterizes Europe.

THE APEX OF THE ROMAN EMPIRE

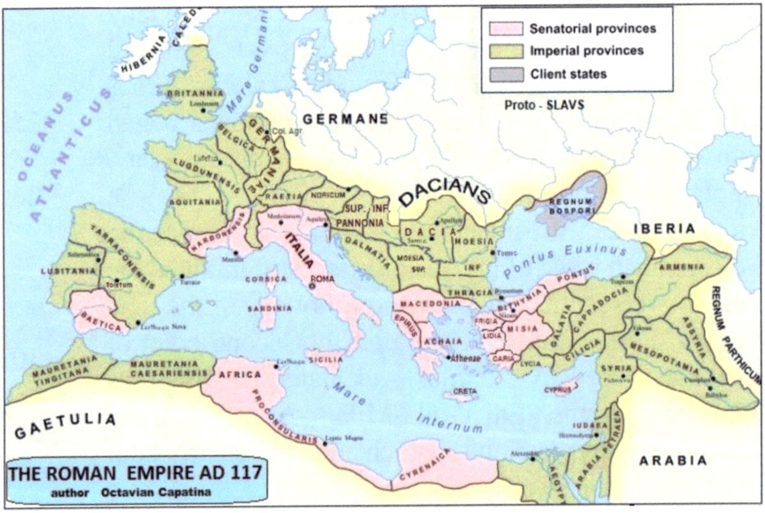

Fig. 8. The Roman Empire at the time of Trajan

Apolodorus of Damascus, with the assistance of the roman legions, designed and constructed the first stone bridge over the Danube in the year 106. The bridge was 1135 meters long. Trajan definitively defeated King Decebalus in the Second

Dacian War (105-106) and annexed Dacia. He stripped it of its riches, but also transformed it into a flourishing Roman province known as *Dacia Felix*. In 117, Trajan passed away. He had expanded the empire to its maximum extent, from the Iberian Peninsula to the Tigris, and from England and Dacia to the first cataract of the Nile. The succeeding emperor, Hadrian (117-138), halted territorial expansion, opting instead to consolidate and organize the empire. It is said that the happiest day of this great emperor's life was when he managed to convince some poor fishermen not to sell their fish to merchants but to form a cooperative and sell it directly in the markets. In 212, all free inhabitants of the empire were granted Roman citizenship. Due to frequent incursions by barbarian tribes from the east and north, Emperor Aurelian (270-275) withdrew the northern Dacian army in 274 to *Dacia Mediterranea*: the XIII (Gemina) Legion at Ratiaria and the V (Macedonica) Legion at Oescus.

THE QUESTION OF KNOWLEDGE

Ancient philosophy was predominantly ontological, while modern philosophy leans more towards the theory of knowledge. In general terms, and simplifying, knowledge involves an object and a subject; knowledge is the relationship between these terms. The Presocratics delved into understanding the nature of the world. For Socrates, the infinite nature of the world could not be known; hence, he shifted the focus of knowledge from nature to humanity. Socrates relinquished knowledge of the external world in favor of self-knowledge: *nosce te ipsum* (know thyself). Plato placed the object of knowledge in another realm, the world of ideas, leading to a complex and distinct relationship between object and subject. According to Plato, the soul is immortal, having a pre-existence in the world of ideas and descending into the human realm and undergoing a process of anamnesis; the soul also has a post-existence, involving an ascent to the world of ideas, an ascent that resembles forgetting or purification. The doctrine of the two worlds links Platonism to Christianity. In the Middle Ages, we encounter mystical knowledge, a connection between God and humanity, achievable only after the subject (the hermit or the saint) has achieved certain levels of purification. Knowledge, the direct contact between subject and God, is realized through unity with God – *unio mistica*. For Descartes (1596-1650), the subject and object of knowledge are two substances with an independent existence, impervious to external influence. Descartes' dualism fails to explain the *relationship*, namely knowledge, since the two substances, the material world and the rational world, are completely autonomous. Spinoza and Leibniz attempted to address this problem.

Spinoza's solution (1632-1677) is monism: he posits a single substance with two attributes – *extension* (the material aspect) and *reason* (the spiritual aspect). Since these two attributes belong to the same substance, they form a relationship, making knowledge possible. Things and ideas reciprocally influence each other. However, this monism of a single substance with two attributes leads to pantheism – God can be found in all things.

Leibniz's solution (1646-1716) is the pluralism of monads. He proposes an infinity of substances, monads, which have "neither doors nor windows", and knowledge requires an agreement between monads. Leibniz posits that the interaction of monads, their relationship, is governed by a pre-established harmony decreed by God.

Until Kant, rationalists and empiricists regarded the intellect merely as a mirror of reality. The intellect reproduced reality to a greater or lesser extent. Kant's (1724-1804) solution is simple, yet radical, stepping beyond the framework established by Descartes: *reason* is not passive; rather, it is active. *If God has given us reason, it is intended for our use.* Sapere aude. *Truth* is not a mere reproduction; it is a human creation. Kant settles the dispute between empiricists and rationalists in a simple manner: *concepts without intuitions are empty, while intuitions without concepts are blind.* The purpose of *knowledge* lies beyond it; the purpose of knowledge is to guide action – as Hegel said. This idea is embraced by Goethe in Faust.

THE LONG ROAD TO KNOWLEDGE IN MEDICINE

From prehistoric times until the time of Hippocrates (c. 460-370 BC), illness was seen as a parasitic influence of demons within the body, and, as such, *treatment* involved expelling these demons from the individual. The anatomist and physiologist Claudius Galen (129-201) studied the nervous, digestive and circulatory systems of various animals and described the therapeutic actions of hundreds of plants and substances. Many centuries passed before his anatomical descriptions were corrected by Andreas Vesalius (1578-1657).

A comparable period of time passed between the contributions of the physician Girolamo Fracastoro (1478-1553) to the understanding of contagious diseases, i.e. regarding them as caused by living pathogens, and the observation of bacteria by Louis Pasteur (1822-1895). Some of these bacteria were responsible for contagious diseases in animals and humans, while others caused food spoilage.

Subcutaneous inoculation of pus from smallpox pustules had been practiced for centuries in Africa and Asia. In the early 18th century, this method reached the British Isles from Constantinople. Over a century later, the method was accepted first by the British Parliament and then by the Royal Society of Medicine.

The studies of Robert Koch (1843-1910), demonstrating that anthrax is related to a microorganism, as well as his research on tuberculosis, paved the way for Pasteur. Pasteur conceived and developed the first vaccines by "weakening" the bacteria responsible for cholera in birds, and for rabies, respectively, laying the foundations of immunology.

Victor Babeş (1854-1926), who worked with both Koch and Pasteur, collaborated with Victor Cornil (1837–1908) to publish the first treatise on bacteriology in 1885: *Bacteria and their Role in the Anatomy and Pathology of Infectious Diseases*. Babeş also formulated the theoretical principle of antibiosis, explaining the antagonism between microorganisms through the secretion of substances with mutually inhibitory actions. He found that these substances could even halt the development of the species that secreted them.

Before Babeş, the Englishman John Burdon Sanderson (1828-1905) observed in 1871 that the fungus Penicillium inhibited the cholera bacillus. Much later, Alexander Fleming (1881-1955) reobserved what Burdon Sanderson had noted, but he did not reach the theoretical findings of Babeş. However, the synthesis of the first antibiotic, penicillin, was achieved only between 1939 and 1941 by Walter Florey and Ernst Chain.

In front of members of the Biology Society of Bucharest, on July 23, 1921, Nicolae Paulescu (1869-1931) presented his research results on the action of *pancreatic* extract in cases of diabetes. Paulescu described the separation of the active antidiabetic principle from the pancreas, which he named *pancrein*, on August 31, 1921 issue of the specialist journal *Archives Internationales de Physiologie*, which simultaneously appeared in France and Belgium. Pancrein, or insulin, has since saved hundreds of millions of lives.

George Emil Palade (1912-2008) laid the foundation for cellular biology, focusing on cell organelles. He isolated and studied mitochondria, the endoplasmic reticulum and ribosomes (particles of Palade), responsible for protein synthesis within cells. He established the pathways and mechanisms by which these cellular organelles membranes and various other cellular compartments.

THE DACIANS AND DACO-ROMAN POPULATION

Herodotus claimed that the Thracians (Dacians/Getae, Carpi, Pannonians, Odrysians, Triballi, Bessi, Moesians, Macedonians, Phrygians, Bithynians, Lydians etc.) were the second most numerous groups after the Indians. The Daco-Romans, a part of the Romanized Thracians, specifically the Dacians and the Romanized Moesians, never left their birthplaces despite various migratory pressures. They did not come from somewhere else, as humanist Aeneas Piccolomini, future Pope Pius II (1458-1464), observed over a millennium later in his *Hymn to the Danube*. They were born on both sides of the Danube, the European river *"which receives the swirling waters of the Inn, which beholds the splendors of Vienna, and spreads into the Pannonian plains, dividing the Romans into two."* This continuity is supported by pre-Christian and Christian evidence, such as linguistic, epigraphic, archaeological, documentary proofs, and the respective folklore and traditions. The traditions, customs and archaic pastoral songs encoded the struggle against the darkness of prehistory. The Romanian folklore and traditions today preserve not only traces of ritualistic, initiatory, hunting, pastoral and agrarian songs but also the forms of initiatory dances. The organization in groups, the chaining of young people in a circle or the so-called chain dance (hora), is typical of pagan rituals, reflecting their descent from prehistoric community expressions: the communion in the face of natural elements. The Daco-Romans were born Christians; the teachings of Jesus spread from person to person, beyond the legendary apostleship of St. Andrew among the Scythians. Material evidence of Christianity among the common people, the poor, the so-called *Christiania minora*, appeared in Trans-Danubian Dacia from the 2nd century (see N. Gudea). Another series of evidence was highlighted by the scholar V. Pârvan, who also focused on several Romanian words from the sphere of religion. These words have an older form compared to their equivalents in other Romance languages. Among these words, we can mention: *Dumnezeu (God), Duminică (Sunday), Crăciun (Christmas), drac (devil), Sânziana (fairy), zănatic (strange), sărbătoare (holiday), păgân (pagan)*. *The Lord's Prayer*, consisting of 60 words, has, depending on the version, 57-60 Latin words. In the Romanian language, there can also be found a series of Latin words related to religion, such as *biserică (church), botezare (baptism), credință (faith), iertare (forgiveness), suflet (soul), locaș (place of worship)*, etc., which have not been preserved in other Romance languages. These differences represent a remarkable history of the spread of the Christian faith in Europe: the Romanians converted from person to person, using Vulgar Latin, as early as the 1st and 2nd centuries, without the mediation of institutions, as in the West, where old Arianism was combated late by the Vatican. The Daco-Romans have always had a sense of their Roman identity. Here are a few historical accounts spanning centuries: the Byzantine Emperor, Constantine VII Porphyrogenitus (913-959), referred to Vulgars as Romans (Pω άνοι), because, as the emperor emphasized, that is how they referred to themselves.

Fig. 9. Fragment depicting the middle Danube region according to a Carolingian map.

50

Archbishop John of Sultanyeh (Persia), traveling through the regions inhabited by Romanians, from the Balkans to Braşov, in the summer of 1409, observed that *"the inhabitants of these lands consider themselves of Roman origin."* The scholar Nicolae de Modrusa, in his work *De bellis Gothorum* from 1474, wrote*: "The Romanians bring as an argument of their origin the fact ... that they speak from the cradle a common language, which is Latin, the use of which they have not abandoned."* In the nobility charter of Nicolaus Olahus, signed by Emperor Ferdinand I, it is written that the Vlachs are the descendants of the Romans, and "that is why even now they are called Romans in their own language." (see A. Armbruster).

THE JEWS IN EUROPE UNTIL THE AGE OF ENLIGHTENMENT

The Jewish revolt between 132-135 ended with the occupation of Jerusalem and their expulsion from Judea. The Jews spread to urban areas throughout the Roman Empire, as well as Persia. Under Caracalla, in 212, they obtained Roman citizenship, like all other inhabitants of the Empire. However, through the laws of Christian emperors Constantine, Theodosius, and Justinian, the Jews became second-class citizens. Pope Gregory I (590-604) rejected the forced baptism of Jews. Later, under Louis the Pious (814-840), they were placed under the king's personal protection. The First Crusade (1096-1099) brought the persecution of Jews and their expulsion to the east, in the triangle Vilna-Lublin-Kiev, within the Duchy of Lithuania. They were expelled from England in 1290, from France starting in 1306, and definitively in 1396 (what was known as France at that time being a small part of today's France). During the plague between 1347-1354, Jews were ghettoized, expelled or killed. Around 350 pogroms have been identified in the German region. There are exceptions, such as in the Kingdom of Sicily, under the Holy Roman Emperor Frederick II (1220-1250), Barbarossa, *stupor mundi,*

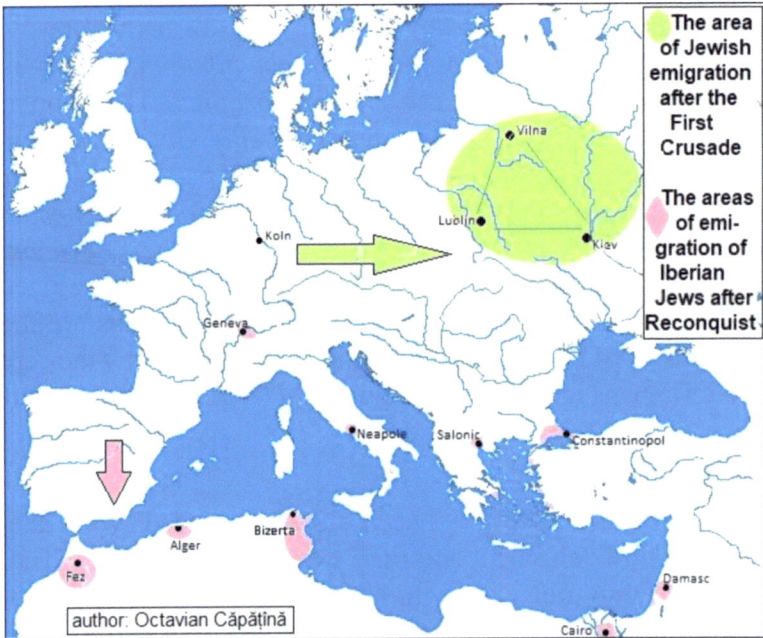

The area of Jewish emigration after the First Crusade

The areas of emigration of Iberian Jews after Reconquist.

author: Octavian Căpățînă

Fig.10. The expulsion of the Jews from Western Europe

where Jews were *servants of the royal house*. The conversion or expulsion of Jews from the Iberian Peninsula began with the expulsion of the last Moors; the main destinations for Sephardic Jews were the commercial areas of the Ottoman Empire.

NEOPLATONISM

Greek classical philosophy comes to an end with an important thinker, Plotinus (205-270), with an influence extending to Romanticism. Plotinus studied philosophy in Alexandria. He pondered over Aristotle, the Stoics and the Pythagoreans, as much as he did over Plato. He noticed the contradictions between Plato and Plato, between Plato and Aristotle, and wanted to extract something clear from their discrepancies. Thus, in *Phaedrus*, Plato sees the soul in the body as in a tomb, and in *Timaeus*, the soul is a gift from the Demiurge, meant to introduce intelligence into the universe. According to Plotinus, the soul was sent by God to perfect the world. The disagreement between Plato and Aristotle about the priority of consciousness or the senses was settled in favour of Plato. Plotinus and Neoplatonism see in *the Platonic ONE* the unique primal source from which every reality emerges, whatever that reality may be. From Aristotle, he retained the idea of *REASON*.

OTHER PAGAN AND CHRISTIAN IDEAS AND HERESIES

Gnosticism encompasses a collection of esoteric religious movements, consisting of various systems of beliefs united by the teaching that humans were divine souls trapped in a world created by a Demiurge, often identified with the God of Abraham.

Manichaeism, propagated by the Persian philosopher Mani (216-270), advocated the ontological dualism of Good and Evil, which opposed each other in an endless confrontation.

Arianism, originating in Alexandria and linked to the priest Arius (256-336), held that only God the Father is the uncreated and unbegotten principle, while Jesus Christ is created by the will of the Father, but not of the same essence with Him. This conception was declared heresy at the Council of Nicaea in 325 and reconfirmed as such at the Council of Constantinople in 381. However, Arianism did not die through this synodal condemnation, not even in Constantinople. Ulfila spread it among the Goths, so Arianism would be found among all the Goths. Moreover, the Catholic *filioque* controversy later originated from the Goths in the Iberian Peninsula. Even Emperor Flavius Constantine (324-337), who presided over the Council of Nicaea, was baptized by an Arian priest on his deathbed.

Donatism was a religious movement that emerged in 311 in the North African Church, in the province of Numidia, around the dispute about the validity of the sacraments when administered by an immoral officiant. This movement, led by Donatus Magnus (d. around 355), was considered heretical at the Council of Carthage in 411.

Nestorianism is an older Christian doctrine that experienced a revival through the teachings of Nestorius, who became the Patriarch of Constantinople between 428 and 431, during the reign of Emperor Flavius Theodosius (408-450). Nestorianism attempted to rationally explain and understand the incarnation of the Logos, the second person of the Holy Trinity, in the Savior. Nestorianism argued that the two natures of the Savior, divine and human, are separate, and thus there are two entities: Jesus Christ as a human and the Logos dwelling in him. In 431, Nestorius requested the emperor to convene a new Council, hoping that his thesis would prevail in the assembly. The Council was held in Ephesus, where Nestorianism was declared a heresy. Persecuted Nestorians sought refuge in Persia.

Monophysitism, preached by the monk Eutyches (378-454) from Constantinople, was a reaction to Nestorianism. Monophysitism claimed that Jesus Christ had only one nature, the divine one, as the human body was merely apparent. Monophysitism was practiced by Patriarch Cyril of Constantinople and was supported by Patriarch Dioscorus of Alexandria. Emperor Flavius Marcian (450-457) convened the Council of Chalcedon in 451, which condemned Monophysitism and upheld the complete reality of the Son's image, with two natures united in one person.

Filioque, a theological term that refers to the issue of the "procession" of the Holy Spirit from God the Father and from God the Son, was used by theologians like Ambrose, Augustine, Maximus the Confessor and John of Damascus, without any disputes arising regarding its dogmatic understanding. However, these thinkers used it to show that the Holy Spirit proceeds from the Father through the Son. Another meaning of *Filioque* was imposed in the Gothic kingdoms in the context of the fight against Arianism spread by the followers of Ulfilas. The emphasis on *Filioque* aimed to underline the Nicene-Constantinopolitan Creed, specifically that Christ doesn't *receive* the Spirit, but being God Himself, He participates alongside God the Father in the origin of the Holy Spirit. The *Filioque* clause was officially adopted first by the churches in Gothic areas, where Christianity had Arian roots. Officially, *Filioque* spread to Iberia after the Council of Toledo in 589, then to northern Italian peninsula after the Council of Aquileia in 796, and to Central Germanic Europe following the Council of Aachen in 809.

However, Pope Leo III (795-816) asserted that the Christian Creed's formula should be recited without the *Filioque* and demanded the use of its original version. Only Pope Benedict VIII (1012-1024) officially sanctioned *Filioque* in Rome, in 1014, by introducing it into the Creed. When Luther raised the issue of correct doctrine, he adhered to orthodoxy and didn't accept the addition introduced by Rome. Pope John Paul II (1920-2005) emphasized the unity of the Church's Trinitarian faith by renouncing the *Filioque*, which he claimed also resulted from a mistranslation.

The Pelagians were a small group of believers formed around a monk from Britain, Pelagius (354-420 or 440), who settled in Latin and Christian Africa. He came to Rome in 410 to argue that humans are not affected by the original sin, and therefore, through good deeds and virtuous behaviour, each individual can attain salvation. Pelagius and his disciples were excommunicated in 418. Like the Donatists, the Pelagians were considered heretical. The resurgence of Pelagianism, a much more significant strand of Christian thought, returned to Western Christian thinking through Thomas Aquinas.

The Paulicians, also known as *Bogomils* or *Cathars*, were brought by the Byzantine Emperor John Tzimiskes (969-976) from Armenia around 970 and settled near the city of Philippopolis in Thrace. They made converts among the locals, among the Daco-Romanians, that is, among the common people (*vulgars*). Spiritually, they descended from Manichaeans. The Bogomils believed that God had two sons. The elder, Satanail, rebelled against the Father. The younger son was the archangel Michael, whom they identified with Christ. Satanail, after his fall, created the earth and all of nature. Humanity represents a compromise between God and Satanail, owing the soul to the former and the body to the latter. The supremacy of the body over the soul, i.e., of Satanail over God, lasted until the incarnation of the archangel Michael, under the name of Christ. According to the Paulicians, most of the Old Testament is the apotheosis of Satanail. Satanail, not God, is the one Moses worshipped. Captured by Christ, Satanail was cast into Tartarus, leaving only Satan on Earth. Even the entire Church, with its icons, relics of saints, and hierarchy, according to them, was the work of Satan. By promoting disobedience against any ecclesiastical or civil authority, the Paulicians considered themselves the only true Christians. Besides the *Lord's Prayer*, they rejected other Christian prayers, replacing them with their own. The common people, the *vulgari*, as the Latin monks called them, spread Bogomilism as far as southern France, where they were known as Albigensians or Cathars. Creating significant problems for the papacy, the Cathars were viewed by the authorities of the time as vagabonds [bléche] with wicked customs [bougre] (see B.P.Haşdeu).

MEDIEVAL THINKING – PATRISTICS

Medieval thinking draws inspiration from two sources: the Bible and Nature. Both must be read like books, with *nature* also embodying biblical wisdom.

For Christianity to become universal, it needed the vision of Paul and the assistance of Greek philosophical thinking. Departing from the radical Platonian dualism – from this world, earthly, sensible, completely opposed to the world beyond, heavenly, supersensible – Christian philosophy had to bridge the gap between these two worlds. Christianity adopted the older idea of the divine-human, the *theos anthropos*, by which Jesus, with his dual nature, unites the earthly world with the heavenly realm. Christ's dual nature is of significance for Christians because they cannot establish a direct relationship with God.

THE REFORM OF THE EMPIRE

Emperor Aurelius Valerius Diocletian (284-305), a skilled general and organizer, carried out an administrative reform of the empire, in 293, by reorganizing it into 12 dioceses led by governors and assisted by vicars. Each diocese comprised around 100 provinces. He established the tetrarchy: each co-emperor administered a part of the empire – the west, by Marcus Aurelius Maximian, and the east, by himself, as *Augusti*, assisted by Flavius Constantius (Britannia, Gaul) and Galerius Valerius Maximian (Mediterranean Dacia, Greece, Pannonia) as *Caesars*.

293

THE MONASTIC LIFE AND ORDERS

Ascetic life began with Anthony the Great (251-356), who retreated to the Egyptian desert to lead a perfect life. Devout Pachomius the Great founded the first monastery in Egypt. Much later, Benedict of Nursia (480-543) established the first Western monastery, Monte Cassino, and the *Benedictine* order with simple rules: poverty and abstinence, obedience to the abbot, prayer, and work. Their motto was *ora et labora – pray and work.*

300

529

	Then, Irish monks established hundreds of
590	Christian monasteries in the Frankish and Lombard
-	kingdoms after 590. Over time, the Benedictines
717	indulged in luxury, leading to reactions, in the form
	the Cluniacs and the Cistercians.

The *Cistercian* Order developed around the Cistercium Abbey (Cîteaux, Beaune) in France and spread throughout Europe. Their motto remained *ora et labora.*

1156 The *Carmelite* Order (named after Mount Carmel) was composed of hermits who provided a place of solitude for pilgrims in their cells in the Holy Land.

1213 The *Franciscan* Order, the Order of Friars Minor, adhered to the rules of returning to the simple life of the apostles, established by Francis of Assisi. The order rapidly spread due to its stance in favor of the poor. In 1231, the *Franciscans* became an order of the Papal Inquisition.

1215 The *Dominican* Order was founded by the Spanish monk Dominic (1170-1221) in Toulouse with the goal of eradicating the Cathars from the northern Pyrenees. The Dominicans were itinerant priests and became the "learned" arm of the Catholic Church. Dominicans, alongside Franciscans and Carmelites, were mendicants (beggars).

1534 The *Jesuit* Order, the "Society of Jesus", was founded by the Basque noble Ignatius of Loyola at the University of Paris, who established four vows: obedience, poverty, chastity, and unconditional submission to the Pope. The Jesuits played a role in the spiritual renewal of the Catholic Church after the shock of the Reformation, implementing the decisions of the Council of Trent (1545-1563).

They established educational institutions, spread Catholicism across all continents, infiltrated Protestant territories, but with limited success. Their involvement in politics and their duplicitous behaviour, seen as pursuing their goals without scruples, led the term "Jesuit" to become synonymous with deceitful and hypocritical individuals. For this reason, Jesuits were expelled from Portugal, Spain, and Latin America between 1759 and 1773. At the insistence of the House of Bourbon, France and Spain sought the suppression of the Jesuit order, a request that Pope Clement XIV (1769-1774) fulfilled in 1773. After Napoleon's exile and the conservative restoration of Europe in 1815, the Jesuit order was reestablished by the Vatican.

FLAVIUS CONSTANTINE, THE GREAT (306-337)

Flavius Constantine was born in Naissus, in the Mediterranean Dacia, sometime between 280 and 285. In the tetrarchy established by Diocletian, after the abdication of the *Augusti* in 305, the *Caesars* took their place. They, in turn, appointed their own Caesars: Galerius Valerius Daza (Maximinus) in the East and Flavius Constantine in the West. Disagreements and civil wars arose among them. In the year 306, Constantine was proclaimed *Caesar* in Britain, replacing his father Flavius Constantius. He ruled over Britain and Gaul. In 312, Constantine defeated Maxentius, who had proclaimed himself co-emperor and governed Rome and the province of Italy since 306, leaving Constantine as the sole ruler in the West. In the East, similarly, Maximinus Daza (Syria, Mesopotamia, Asia Minor and Egypt) and Licinius (Mediterranean Dacia, Thrace, Macedonia, Greece) confronted each other, with Licinius emerging victorious. The empire was split into two parts. Through the Edict of Milan in 313, issued by Constantine and Licinius, Christianity was recognized as a religion of the empire. In 324, Constantine faced Licinius, who was a skilled leader and organizer. Constantine emerged victorious, and thus, after 40 years from the beginning of Diocletian's reign, the empire once again had a single emperor. To achieve this, Constantine did not shy away from committing crimes. He recaptured the southern part of Dacia (north of the Danube), reinforced the fortifications along the northern banks of the Danube, and constructed a defensive wall. In 328, he inaugurated the second Roman bridge over the Danube at Sucidava (Celei). In five years and six months, Constantine built the "New Rome" near Byzantium, in Thrace, endowing it with a Capitoline Hill, a Senate, a Praetorium, a Forum and a Sacred Way. He replaced the temple of Jupiter with the Basilica of St. Sophia. For Europe and the survival of Greco-Roman civilization, New Rome was of paramount importance, similar to Alexandria's role in preserving the Hellenistic culture.

Influenced by Christianity, Constantine reformed Roman civil law, deciding in 318 that imperial edicts had absolute authority and could annul laws. Sunday was declared an official holiday, during which no administrative acts were to be performed except for the liberation of slaves. Fortunately, this "legal" tendency did not continue; otherwise, not much would have remained of Roman jurisprudence. Nonetheless, in criminal law, Constantine introduced several commendable innovations. Premeditated killing of a slave, even by the master, was considered murder and punishable; separating a slave's family upon changing ownership was prohibited; abuse of power by a father over children was prohibited; child abduction and patricide were severely punished; he established the right of every prisoner to see the sunlight daily and so on. By imposing Christianity in the Empire, the emperor positioned himself at the top of the Christian hierarchy. He remained *pontifex maximus*, thus continuing the Roman imperial tradition within Christianity. Consequently, in the Orthodox

Church, the patriarch remains subordinate to the emperor. As secular power was fragmented in the West at that time, a paradigm arose in which atomized secular power depended on the goodwill of the bishops. This is why the struggle of separating secular power form the Church is to take centuries.

HALF A MILLENNIUM OF IDEOLOGICAL WARS

The first Council of Nicaea. At Nicaea (in Thracian Bithynia), where Emperor Constantine convened the patriarchs of the church to resolve the conflict with Arius, the dogmatic and canonical foundations of Christianity were laid. God the Son is of the same substance as God the Father (consubstantial). At that time, the date for Easter was also fixed as the first Sunday after the first full moon following the Spring Equinox. The decisions of the council became law and were imposed throughout the empire. The council rejected celibacy for priests. It established four equal spiritual patriarchates: Jerusalem, Antioch, Alexandria and Rome. The proceedings were conducted in the Greek language, as, on the one hand, all bishops were familiar with Greek, the language of the New Testament, and on the other hand, the overwhelming majority of bishops and Christians were in the East. Only Constantine addressed the bishops in Latin. Despite the council's decisions, Arianism persisted for a long time. Ulfila, the bishop of the Goths, promoted Arian Christianity. Even Constantine was baptized by an Arian priest. **325**

The Ecumenical Council of Constantinople confirmed the decisions of Nicaea and confessed that the One God in Essence is Three in Persons: the Father, the Son and the Holy Spirit. The Three Persons are equal **381** and consubstantial, differing only in their personal properties. The council also decided to reunite metropolitan provinces into patriarchal dioceses.

431 The *third Council of Ephesus* combated Nestorianism, which claimed that in Jesus Christ there are two distinct natures, and it established the terms of the Easter rituals. The council abandoned any tolerance towards other ideas or beliefs.

451 The *fourth Council of Chalcedon* combated Monophysitism, which asserted that the human nature assumed by Christ at the Incarnation was absorbed by His Divine nature (consubstantiality), so that the human nature entirely disappeared.

553 The *fifth council*, held in Constantinople, attempted, without any success, to reconcile with the Monophysites.

680 At *the sixth council*, also held in Constantinople, the Monothelites (masked Monophysitism) were combated. They tried to reconcile the official doctrine with Monophysitism, claiming that in Christ there are two natures, divine and human, but only one will, the divine will.

787 The *final council*, held in 787 at Nicaea, addressed the issue of iconoclasm. It decreed: *"It is permissible and even beneficial and pleasing to create icons and venerate them, but this veneration should only be honor, not worship."*

The *Studios Monastery Movement* (of the Studios Monastery in Constantinople), which lasted for 50 years, claimed the independence of the church in doctrinal matters from the emperor.

THE BAPTISM OF THE LEADERS
The baptism of military leaders often preceded the

baptism of their subjects. However, sometimes centuries passed between baptism and full Christianization, and Christianization did not always entail a complete abandonment of pagan customs. Emperor Constantine converted to Christianity in the year 312 after his victory against Maxentius, and, within a year, he accepted Christianity throughout the **337** empire, alongside other pagan cults. Emperor Constantin was baptized on his deathbed in 337. In the year 391, the old cults were banned, and Christianity became the official religion of the Empire.

After his victory at Tolbiac against the Alemanni 496 in 496, Clovis, the King of the Franks who was converted to Christianity by his wife Clotilda, was baptized in Reims.

The Visigothic King of Iberia, Recared (586-601), 586 renounced Arianism and converted to Catholicism. The Visigoths were Arians, and the Iberians had embraced Arianism.

Mojimir I, a leader from Great Moravia, was 831 baptized by the bishop of Passau in 831, but his successor Ratislav aligned himself with the Byzantine Church.

Boris, the Turanic Khan south of the Danube, 865 received baptism and compelled the pagans around him to convert to Christianity. The common people, known as *vulgari*, had been Christian for centuries.

Mieszko (960-992), the leader of the Poles, and his 966 court, were baptized through the intervention of the duke's wife, Dobrava, from Bohemia.

Vladimir I, the Viking, son of Sviatoslav and a descendant of Rurik, ruler of Kiev (980-1015), received 988 baptism in 988 in Cherson (in Crimea – Byzantium), where he married Anna, the sister of Emperor Basil II Volgar Slayer (976-1025). Upon returning to Kiev, Vladimir destroyed pagan temples and built churches. He was canonized.

995   Olaf I (Tryggveson), after being proclaimed king in 993, forcefully introduced Christianity to the shores of Norway. He had been baptized in exile on the English Isles of Scilly a few years earlier. Olaf I imposed the Christianization of Iceland, which was under his authority. The Christianization of Iceland occurred in a unique manner through a popular assembly (*Althing*), which decided to abandon the worship of Norse gods and adopt Christianity.

Pope Sylvester II and Emperor Otto III decided to establish two territories to the east of the Holy Roman Empire, creating two new bishoprics: one in Gran (Strigoniu) and another in Gniezno (Gniesen). The tribal leader Vaik, baptized as Stephen, was crowned in 1001 by the German monk Ascherick as the king of

1001   Hungarian clans in Pannonia (see I. Slavici). The crown was of Byzantine origin. The Germans, the organizers of the new kingdom, were Catholic. This marked the beginning of the gradual re-conversion of indigenous Romanians and Byzantine rite Slavs to the Catholic rite, as well as the conversion of the few remaining pagan Asians in Pannonia.

The Christianization of Sweden began with the baptism of King Olaf Skötkonung by the bishopric of

1008   Hamburg-Bremen. Furthermore, in 1014, Olaf laid the foundation for the bishopric of Skara and initiated the destruction of the pagan temple in Uppsala, where sacrifices to Norse gods were still being offered.

SAINT AUGUSTINE (354-430)

Augustine was born in Thagaste, on the northern coast of Africa, near Hippo (now Annaba, Algeria). At the age of 16, he went to Carthage to study, where he also fathered a child. At 19, he decided to study philosophy and converted to Manichaeism. At 29, he travelled to Rome and then to Milan, where he became a professor of rhetoric. Here, he listened to the sermons of Bishop Ambrose; at the age of 32, he converted and was baptized by Ambrose. He returned home. At the age of 42, he became the bishop of Hippo and quickly became one of the most respected clergymen. He wrote around 500 sermons and over 2000 letters. He shifted from a skeptical relativism, doubting any truth, to absolute beliefs. There was one absolute truth: the existence of God comes from outside of man, the other absolute truth being: the existence of the soul comes from within man. He was strongly influenced by Cicero. He drew extensively from Cicero's works for his own writings, including his work titled *The City of God*. He appropriated Cicero's ideas to fit into his theory. He justified religious intolerance and advocated armed coercion against heretics. For Augustine, the purpose of man was to achieve *good*, with *good* being connected to the knowledge of absolute truths, and *evil* being the result of their ignorance. From this point, he combated Manichaeism, Donatism and Pelagianism. He opposed Pelagius's ideas with the concept of predestination. Predestination was not adopted by the Eastern Church, only by Catholics. When later Thomas Aquinas challenged predestination, the Catholic authorities considered him a heretic. Predestination was upheld by Luther and Calvin but contested by Catholics after the Council of Trent (1545-1569).

TRANSLATING THE BIBLE

The Old Testament, which is an eclectic collection of books that includes the history and religion of the Jewish people, was written in Aramaic and Hebrew. The New Testament, which is dedicated to the life of the Savior and the Christian revelation, was written in Ancient Greek.

383 The bishop of the Goths, Ulfila, who received Arian Christian education in Cappadocia and Constantinople, translated the New Testament into Gothic (*Gotische Bibel*).

406 In the 5th century, Eusebius Sophronius Hieronymus (347-420), born in Stridonius, in *Dacia Mediterranea* (now Croatia), provided the Latin translation of the *Bible, the Vulgate*, which became the official version of the Catholic Church.

862 The brothers Constantine (Cyril) and Michael (Methodius), two Greeks from Thessaloniki, along with their disciples, began translating parts of the Bible into Old Slavonic.

1226 Jean Le Bon, of the University of Paris, started translating the *Bible* into French in 1226. The translation was continued in the 14th century by J. de Sy, J. Nicholas, G. Vivien and J. de Chambly.

1383 John Wycliffe (1320-1384), a scholastic philosopher and professor at the seminary in Oxford, an advocate of the use of vernacular languages and dissident against the Vatican, personally translated the *New Testament*. His associates translated the *Old Testament* into English.

1412 Jan Hus (1369-1415), who was familiar with the works of Wycliffe, continued the work of revising a *Bible* translation that had been started before 1412. *The Prague Bible* dates back to 1488.

142? King John I of Portugal (1385-1433), also a great scholar, personally translated the *Psalms* and the *New Testament*. However, a complete Bible only appeared in 1753.

In Spanish, early biblical fragments were translated by Spanish Jews; a Bible known as the *Alba Bible* appeared in 1430. The first complete *Bible* in Spanish appeared after the Reformation, in Basel, in 1569. 1430

In Polish, the first five books of the *Old Testament* appeared in 1455, while the complete *Bible* was published in 1563. 1455

The first translations into Romanian, in manuscript form, including the *Acts of the Apostles*, appeared sometime after 1460, under Hussite influence, in western Romania (characterized by rotacism and Latin words that now are out of use). This translation is partially preserved in late copies, on sheets dated between 1505 and 1560. The first printed text appeared in Sibiu, in 1553 – *the Gospel of Matthew* (in a bilingual Slavonic and Romanian edition) in the translation of Philip Moldovan. In Orăștie, the first five books of the *Old Testament* (the *Palia de la Orăștie*) appeared in Romanian in 1582. Some time after 1460

In Italian, the first translation by Nicolò Malermi according to the *Vulgate* appeared in 1471. Another translation by the Dominican Zaccaria from Florence appeared in 1542. 1471

Martin Luther (1483-1546) translated the *New Testament* into a lively, supra-dialectal *German* language in 1522 (based on Erasmus of Rotterdam's Latin version), and the *Old Testament* in 1534. 1522

Luther's *New Testament*, in a Danish-German version, circulated from 1524, both in Denmark and Norway, but in Danish it was translated by Bishop Hans Poulsen, in 1607. 1524

In Swedish, the *New Testament* was translated after a version by Luther, in 1526, and the *Old Testament* in 1541. 1526

67

	Gabor Pesti translated fragments from the *four*
1536	*Gospels* from Latin into Hungarian. This translation appeared in 1536, in Vienna.
1548	In Finnish, Mikael Agricola translated *the New Testament* in 1548.
158x	In Flemish, Philip of Marnix (1538-1598), a leader of the War of Independence, partially translated the *Bible*; this version was one to influence the first complete translation of the *Bible*, published at the request of the States General in 1637.
1820	In Norway, the Danish-German (1524) and Danish (1607) translations circulated at first. In 1816, the Norwegian Bible Society was established, and, through Olaus Nielsen, the first Norwegian translation of the *New Testament* was published in 1820.

CHRISTIANITY, THE RELIGION OF THE EMPIRE

391
In the year 391, Christianity becomes the official religion of the Roman Empire, and the pagan cults are prohibited by the last Roman emperor, Flavius Theodosius I (379-395). Theodosius I divided the Empire between his two sons, Flavius Honorius and Flavius Arcadius, into the Eastern Roman Empire, with its capital in New Rome, and the Western Roman Empire, with its capital in Milan. Rome had declined and was subjected to constant plundering.

PAGAN TRADITIONS ADOPTED BY CHRISTIANITY

We provide an account below of only three examples out of the multitude of such possible examples. Mircea Eliade thus observes:

"The conversion to Christianity led to religious symbioses and syncretisms that often brilliantly illustrate the specific creativity of agrarian or pastoral 'folk' cultures ... It is

important to present a few examples of pagan-Christian syncretism, illustrating both the resistance of traditional heritage and the process of Christianization. We chose, to begin with, the complex ritual of the Twelve Days, as it has roots in pre-historic times. Since we cannot present it in its entirety (ceremonies, games, songs, dances, processions of animal masks), we will focus on ritualistic Christmas songs. They are attested throughout Eastern Europe, even in Poland. The Romanian and Slavic name for these songs, 'colinde', derives from the Latin 'calendae Januarii'. For centuries, ecclesiastical authorities tried to eradicate them, but without success. (In 692, the Council of Constantinople reiterated the prohibition in very severe terms.) Finally, a certain number of carols were 'Christianized', in the sense that they borrowed mythological characters and themes from popular Christianity."

Another example can be seen in the celebration of Pentecost, dedicated to the Descent of the Holy Spirit, where we have three layers of beliefs. The last one, the Christian layer, was superimposed on *Rosalia* (the festival of roses) – a day dedicated to the Roman cult of the dead, which, in turn, was superimposed on the pagan ritual of protection from "iele" – beings believed to fly through the air and harm people they encounter.

Lastly, ordeals and judicial duels were pagan forms of "judgment". They came from pre-historic times; they were adopted by antiquity, then clothed in Christian belief, and are found until modern times. All of them were based on the belief that the divine would intervene to show the innocence or guilt of the person subjected to a trial by fire, to boiling water, red-hot irons, duels or other forms of ordeals. The judicial duel, as an indicator of guilt or innocence, seems to have originated in the areas populated by Germanic peoples and spread throughout medieval Europe. The Catholic Church only began

69

to have doubts in 1315, when a Council prohibited the blessing of ordeals by priests. The reformer Savonarola lost his authority among his followers in 1498 precisely because he rejected the trial by fire. The judicial duel was banned in the mid-19th century in England and in the early 20th century on the continent.

SAINTS, YET STILL HUMAN

The first saints, coming after the apostles, were the martyrs of the new faith. After Christianity became the sole religion of the Roman Empire, the new saints were chosen from among the ascetics, and later from those who laid the foundation of its doctrines. Among them is Cyril, Patriarch of Alexandria (412-444), considered one of the Fathers of Church, who successfully fought against Nestorianism. He is celebrated by Orthodox, Coptic, Catholic, Anglican and Protestant communities, despite his intolerance towards opponents, Jews, and free thinkers (such as Hypatia). The fourth wave and type of saints were pagan military leaders, many of them bloodthirsty, who accepted baptism and imposed Christianity on various peoples through fire and using the sword.

FROM PERSECUTED TO PERSECUTORS

When Christianity became the official religion of the empire in 391, other religions were officially banned and their followers were oppressed, often facing worse fates. Temples of pagan deities were demolished, valuable manuscripts were burned, individual liberties were lost; the destruction in Roman Constantinople began as early as 331.

After Augustine became the bishop of Hippo in 395, he got involved in the conflict with the Donatists and took a significant step towards intolerance by justifying the secular arm's intervention and repressive laws against heretics. His concept of the state justified the *unchristian* intolerance of Christians, of Catholics.

Then a series of popes, among whom Gregory I and VII excelled, cultivated intolerance.

During the First Crusade in the Rhine region, Jews were expelled or massacred. Suspicions about Jews are repeated during the Second Crusade. 1096

In 1204, when the Crusaders occupied Constantinople, we remember it as a pinnacle of religious intolerance: there weren't just persecutions, but also looting, crimes and mass killings, which we will come to again. 1204

Another pinnacle of Catholic persecutions against all non-Catholics was reached at the Provincial Council of Ofen (at Buda, in Pannonia), in 1279, which decreed the fight against Orthodox priests, called schismatics, in Pannonia: *"They are not allowed to hold divine worship, build chapels or other holy places, nor are the faithful allowed to participate in such divine worship or to enter such chapels. In case of necessity, the use of force against these priests is allowed."* In the kingdom, schismatics could no longer hold public office. Penalties were also provided for new converts if they attended schismatic services or received sacraments from schismatic priests. It was also decided that "Jews, Saracens, Ishmaelites and other unbaptized persons shall wear permanent distinctive signs on their chests." 1279

When the plague spread across Western Europe, minority groups, especially Jews, were accused of poisoning wells, which allegedly triggered the plague. Testimonies obtained through torture were followed by pogroms throughout Western Europe. 1350

After the fall of the last Moorish stronghold in 1492, the Spanish monarchs gave Jews four months to either convert or liquidate their properties and leave

1492 Spain. The converted, known as *conversos*, were often suspected of not completely renouncing the practices of their old faith. Based on a denunciation, they were judged and most often executed if they failed to flee the country. Between 1481 and 1525, over 5000 convictions were handed down, including Jewish families in exile. For them, fleeing was an irrefutable proof of "sin". Self-exiled individuals went to Portugal, the Netherlands, England, North Africa among Muslims, and Eastern Europe as well.

THE GOTHS

After several centuries of leaving the mouths of the Vistula and Elbe rivers and wandering through the east, a part of the Goth becomes distinct in historiography, based on their final geographical destinations – there are the Ostrogoths (in the Italian Peninsula) and the Visigoths (on shores of the ocean, the Iberian Peninsula). In their new kingdoms, they formed elites, both warrior and administrative, as well as religious (Arianism), within the local, Romance-speaking populations.

401 *The Visigoths.* After the Goths were accepted into the Roman Empire in 376, under Valens, they revolted in 378 and defeated the Romans at Adrianople. Under Alaric (370-410) from Illyria, they attacked Italy, where they were repeatedly defeated between 401 and 403, but, in 410, they managed to loot Rome. They crossed into the southern Gaul (Toulouse), under the name Visigoths, and established the Kingdom of Toulouse (419-507), which would fall to the blows of the Franks. They crossed the Pyrenees into Iberia and founded a new kingdom that fought against the Byzantines, but eventually disappeared under Arab rule, in 711.

The Ostrogoths. The Goths reached the northern shores of the Black Sea, and, from there, they went into Dacia and Pannonia. Led by Theodoric (471-526), they plundered the Balkans, prompting Emperor Zeno (474-491) to accept Theodoric as a federate and appoint him *magister militum and patricius* of Italian pars in 488. They made their way to Italian peninsula, where they battled against the mercenaries of Flavius Odoacer, the first barbarian king of Italy. In 493, Theodoric and Odoacer signed a treaty dividing northern Italy between them, but, later on, Theodoric killed Odoacer. Theodoric, a viceroy accepted by the emperor, established an Ostrogothic kingdom in northern peninsula (493-553), which soon disintegrated under the attacks of the Lombards.

488

533

THE BURGUNDIANS ON THE RHONE VALLEY

Coming from the east, the Burgundians, a Germanic tribe, settled in the Rhine-Main region. Pressured by the Romans, they left this area and settled along the valleys of the Rhone, where they founded a kingdom in 443. This kingdom was conquered by the Franks in 534. As in other parts, in these successive conquests, the warrior elites changed, not the local population, i.e., the tillers of the soil.

443

534

THE HUNS

The Huns, a nomadic tribe from Asia, who were as fierce as they were small, arrived in Europe in the early 5th and tribute. They were defeated by the general Flavius Aetius, the "last Roman", near Troyes, in 451.

451

The Roman army was aided by the Franks and the Visigoths. The Huns vanished, leaving only memories of their cruelty.

THE FALL OF THE WESTERN ROMAN EMPIRE

402 Due to scheming and corruption at the emperor's court, the Western Empire became a mere shadow. By 402, the Senate and the emperor had taken refuge to Ravenna. The Daco-Roman general Flavius Aetius, the "last Roman", fell victim to these political schemes. Flavius Odoacer, the leader of a legion of Germanic mercenaries in the service of the Eastern Roman Empire, occupied Ravenna and peacefully

476 removed Romulus Augustulus (aged 13), the last "emperor" in the West. Odoacer was proclaimed patrician and governor in the name of Rome by former emperor Julius Nepos, but he sent gifts to Constantinople, acknowledging the authority of the Eastern Roman Empire in Italy.

THE FRANKS

After the Battle of Soissons, in 486, Clovis (481-
486 511), the king of the Franks, conquered the last remnant of the Roman state in Gaul, situated between the rivers Loire and Somme, led by Syagrius, who called himself *dux*. With the assistance of the Burgundians, Clovis also conquered Aquitania from the Visigoths after the Battle of Vouillé, in 507. The small Burgundian territory between the Saône and Rhone rivers was annexed to the Frankish kingdom
537 after the Battle of Autun, in 532. Shortly after this, the territories of modern-day Switzerland (536) and Provence (537) were also annexed. The conquering Franks, founders of a state, gradually assimilated with the Gallo-Romans. *The Salic Law* was the Civil Code

of the Franks, a code compiled around the year 500, under Clovis. Recorded in Latin and an old Dutch dialect, the Salic Code formed the basis of Frankish laws throughout the early medieval period and had the merit of influencing future European legal systems. The Salic Code not only codified civil law (inheritance), but also criminal law (punishment for crime). The most well-known and referenced Salic rule is the exclusion of women from inheriting thrones and possessions.

THE THREE FAMOUS THRACIAN *FLAVII*

Under Flavius Iustinianus (527-565), a Thracian not unlike Constantine the Great, the Eastern Roman Empire reached its maximum expansion. However, the most significant event of his time was the rewriting of Roman law, led by jurists under the guidance of the empire's most renowned legislator, Flavius Tribonianus (485-542), originally from the province of Thracian Anatolia. The legal reform aimed to unify the law and eliminate contradictions by gathering the entire jurisprudence into a single code. All Roman laws from Emperor Hadrian onward were compiled, and the norms of Roman law (*ius vetum*) were updated, creating a collection known as *Corpus Iuris Civilis*. This collection consists of four parts:

Fig. 11. The 3 famous Flavius: Tribonian, Iustinian, Belisarius

75

1. *Codex Justinianus* (529), containing all imperial constitutions from Hadrian onwards. The code recognized the equality of individuals before the law and was sourced from *Codex Theodosianus, Codex Gregorianus, and Codex Hermogenianus*.
2. *Digestae* (533), which was a compilation of commentaries by major Roman jurists from the imperial period.
3. *Institutiones* (533), a legal manual for use in law schools, containing excerpts from the other two collections with updated legislation.
4. *Novellae*, published after the emperor's death, containing imperial constitutions issued by Justinian after 534.

General Flavius Belisarius (c. 505-565), originally from south of the Danube, recaptured North Africa and Sicily from the Vandals in 540. He reclaimed the southern half of the Italian Peninsula, including Rome (553), from the Ostrogoths, and the southeastern part of the Iberian Peninsula (554) from the Visigoths.

Fig. 12. The Roman Empire at the time of Justinian

76

The Mediterranean Sea once again became an internal Roman sea. Flavius Belisarius, a Thracian hailing from south of the Danube, was compared to Hannibal and Caesar; he was also referred to as the "last of the Romans". The significant achievement of Justinian lay primarily in finding and partially supporting these two figures, Belisarius and Tribonian.

THE KINGDOM OF THE LOMBARDS

The Lombards, members of a Germanic tribe originating from Northern Europe, pushed by the Avars, left Pannonia and occupied the northern part of the Italian Peninsula in 568, putting an end to the Ostrogothic kingdom. They established a kingdom with its capital in Pavia, in 572, which lasted until 774, when it was incorporated into the Carolingian Empire.

572

774

The Lombard Kingdom included Tuscany and the Po Valley, the latter being taken from the Byzantines. Ravenna, Venice and Istria remained under Byzantine control.

THE BISHOP OF ROME

In the year 590, Gregory I (590-604) was elected as the bishop of Rome. Gregory came from the ranks of the old Roman aristocracy; he had been a prefect of Rome before becoming a monk. Gregory was chosen as bishop by unanimous consent from the clergy, the Senate and the people. Despite considering himself unworthy of the position, he requested that Emperor Flavius Tiberius (582-602) in Constantinople not ratify his appointment.

590

However, due to circumstances, the emperor confirmed his appointment as the bishop of Rome. This pope became, by necessity, the *de facto* ruler of Rome, assuming the administrative functions of the defunct empire. This laid the groundwork for the organizational model of the Catholic Church. He cheerfully demolished many ancient pagan buildings. By the end of his life, the Western world acknowledged the Bishop of Rome as a leader.

THE ROMAN EMPIRE BEFORE THE ARAB EXPANSION

610

Under Emperor Flavius Heraclius (610-641), the Roman Empire adopted Greek as its administrative language, even though the majority of its inhabitants considered themselves to be Romans. The Roman Empire was in a dire situation at that time. The Persians had captured Jerusalem (614), Egypt (616), and, with the help of the Jews, Damascus (613). They were making incursions into Anatolia. In 621, Emperor Heraclius managed to drive the Persians out of Anatolia.

627

In the Battle of Nineveh (627), the Persians suffered a severe defeat and had to return all the conquered territories. In 626, the Avars and Slavs besieged Constantinople, but they were forced to retreat.

THE ADVANCE AND RETREAT OF THE ARABS

674 - 678

In the first siege of Constantinople, from 674 to 678, the Arabs suffered their first major defeat. A new technology, called the *Greek fire*, played a significant role in their defeat. The Arabs sought another route into Europe. The Visigothic Kingdom in Iberia was conquered by the Moors after the *Battle of Jerez de la Frontera* (711). The Iberian Peninsula, except for the

711

Basque region, and the northern kingdoms of Galicia and Asturias, fell into the hands of the Moors for centuries. In the eastern Mediterranean, the Arabs attacked the Roman Empire once again.

Emperor Leo III the Isaurian (717-741) faced the brother of Caliph Omar II. The Arabs suffered an unprecedented disaster. Fourteen years later, in 732, the Franks, led by Charles Martel near Poitiers, defeated an "Arab" army, thus defending Western Christianity.

Why the term "Arab" between quotation marks? Because both "Muslim" and "Christian" armies had many mercenaries from the opposing religious side. The forces that operated in the Iberian Peninsula had more Berbers than Arabs. Later, in the armies of the Cordoba emirs, thousands of local Christians were enlisted. In the 10th century, mercenary soldiers from Gascony, Languedoc, Provence, and Aquitaine appeared under the crescent moon. However, the use of mercenary armies was not an exclusively Muslim concept. Emperor Heraclius (610-641) had under his command 40.000 "pagans": Khazars, Turks, Kurds, and Arabs, alongside local Vlachs (Daco-Romans), Greeks and new Slavic arrivals. It's important to note that such inexactness leads to confusion, which unfortunately has become common in both historical narratives of the past and the present.

THE KAGANATE OF THE VOLGA TURANIANS

This was a state founded by Turanian-Turkic warriors who came from the Volga region to northeastern Balkans, around the year 681. The Volgarian warriors (sometimes referred to as Proto-Bulgarians in historiography) ruled over the majority of Daco-Romans in southern Danube, along with the new Slavic arrivals. At its height, the Volgarian Empire extended from Pannonia to the Black Sea and from the Dnieper to the Adriatic Sea. It became the main rival of Byzantium in Balkan engaging in numerous wars.

717

732

681
-
1014

During the Second Arab Siege of Constantinople, the Volgarian army aided Byzantium. Byzantium had a strong cultural influence on the Slavs, and, through Khan Boris (852-889), in 864, Bulgaria adopted Christianity. The collapse of the Avar Khanate due to Frankish attacks allowed the Volgarian Khanate to extend its control north of the Danube into the Pannonian Plain and up to the Dnieper. The rule of the Volgarians during Boris's reign also covered the area between the Danube and Tisza rivers (the Voivodeship of Zalan) and southern Transylvania. Their control was nominal, often involving the collection of tributes from the native populations. The Khanate besieged Constantinople in 923-924, but, in 1014, Byzantium, under Basil II, finally ended the Turanian-Turkic Khanate.

THE ICONOCLASM

730

In the declining and increasingly threatened Eastern Roman Empire, a religious dispute arose regarding the veneration of images depicting saints and Christ, on the grounds that it could lead to a return to pagan idolatry. Iconoclasts only accepted the crucifix. Iconoclasm became official in 730, under Emperor Leo III the Isaurian. Irene, the daughter of Leo III, regent from 780 and empress between 797 and 802, convened the Seventh Ecumenical Council in 787 to settle the dispute.

787

Iconoclasm was based on an Old Testament text: *"Thou shalt not make unto thee any graven image ... Thou shalt not bow down thyself to them, nor serve them: for I the Lord thy God am a jealous God."*

FRANKS AND THE PAPAL STATES

Pepin (751-768), the son of Charles Martel and the majordomo of the last Merovingian king, Childeric, sought the advice of the Pope regarding the division of power, as the sovereign was indifferent to the fate of the kingdom. Pope Zachary (741-752) responded that *"power belongs to the one who exercises it."* Pepin understood and convinced his sovereign to take religious vows, thereby proclaiming himself the king of the Franks in 751. Pope Stephen II (752-757) then placed Rome under the protection of the Franks. In return, Pepin gifted the Pope properties that were part of the Exarchate of Ravenna. This marked the formation of the Papal States, the Domains of St. Peter, which lasted until 1870.

751

CHARLEMAGNE (768-814)

Following Pepin, his son Charlemagne took over the leadership of the Franks. He conquered northern Italy from the Lombards and declared himself king of the Franks and Lombards. He defeated the Avars in Pannonia. The nomadic Avar warriors, like all Turco-Mongol nomads, became extinct. Charlemagne failed to occupy the Iberian Peninsula, which was under Moorish rule, but he established a small *march* in the southern Pyrenees. Charlemagne's coronation as Emperor of the West by Pope Leo III took place in Rome on Christmas Day, in the year 800. This title was recognized by Emperor Michael I (811-813) of Constantinople through the Treaty of Aix-la-Chapelle in 812. As a gesture of goodwill, Charlemagne returned Venice to the Eastern Roman Empire, which he had just wrested from it. He also conquered Saxony and built cities and monasteries. In terms of finance, Charlemagne prohibited usury in his empire. Some view Charlemagne's construction efforts as a reconstitution of the Western Roman Empire, albeith with a "German engine".

768

800

812

DIVIDING THE THE FRANKISH EMPIRE

843
    The grandsons of Charlemagne divided the empire through the Treaty of Verdun, in 843. Lothair took the middle part (known as Lotharingia): Italy, Burgundy, Lorraine and the Low Countries. His brother, Louis the German, received all the possessions east of the Rhine, while their half-brother Charles the Bald got the western part, delimited in the east by the rivers Rhone, Saône,

880
Scheldt and Meuse. In 880, through the Treaty of Ribemont between the heirs of Louis the German and Charles the Bald, the boundary was established that would separate France and the German lands in the medieval period. Centuries after Charlemagne, the Byzantines referred to all Westerners as "Franks".

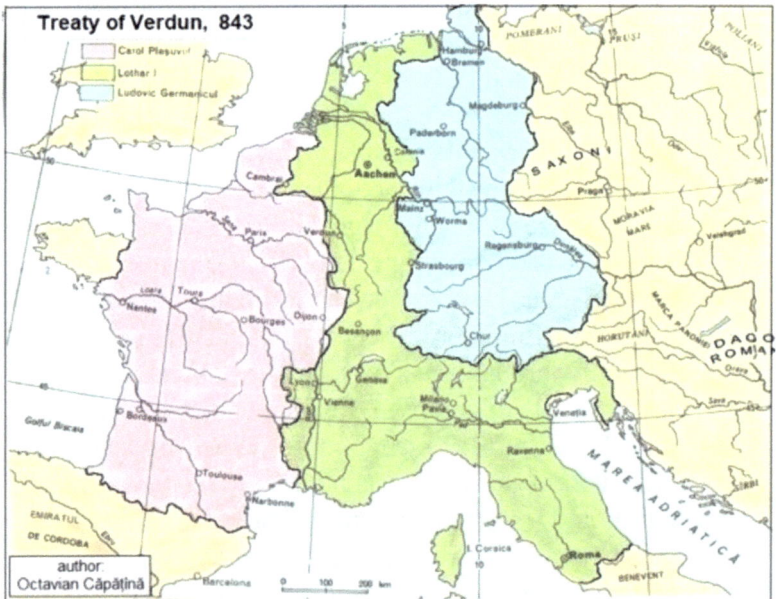

Fig. 13. The division of the Frankish Empire

THE VIKINGS

The Vikings, growing in strength, made expeditions along the coasts of Iceland, Greenland, America, France, Africa and the Black Sea. In 845, the Vikings reached West Francia, and in 885/886, they besieged Paris, having arrived in the British Isles a few decades earlier. **845**

Harald I united the small groups along the Atlantic coast and founded Norway. The Viking Rollo received Neustria (Normandy) from the Frankish King Charles III, a region already 872 controlled by the Vikings. Rollo's great-grandson 911 William, Duke of Normandy, landed in southern England, defeated the Anglo-Saxons in the Battle of Hastings and was crowned King of England at 1066 Westminster. The Vikings also reached Sicily in 860, but they did not stay. The rising Arabs occupied the island in 965. However, over a century later, in 1068, 1068 Normandy Vikings returned and conquered the island. Viking Roger I founded a kingdom in Sicily in 1091, which lasted for a century.

THE STATE OF THE VIKINGS (RUS TRIBE) IN NORTHEASTERN EUROPE

The Vikings from the "Rus" tribe, led by Rurik, established a state between Slavs and Finns on the Volkhov River, at Novgorod, around the year 859. **859** Olaf (Oleg), Rurik's son, moved the capital to Kiev on - the Dnieper around 882. Under Vladimir the Great 1057 (980-1015), the Slavs of Kiev were Christianized by the Byzantines. This Viking-based state among the Slavs is considered the precursor to the three Slavic nations: Belarusians, Ukrainians and Russians. The naming of this state as "Kievan Rus" creates both intentional and unintentional confusion.

THE EMPIRE UNDER THE MACEDONIAN DYNASTY

The Roman Empire experienced its last period of prosperity during the Macedonian dynasty. Fierce battles were fought against the Arabs in both the East and the West. While Malta, Syracuse and Palermo were gradually lost in the West, Emperor Nikephoros II Phokas (963-969) subjugated the Emirate of Aleppo (Syria) in the East. Emperor John Tzimiskes (969-976) halted the Russians and the Volga Vikings (also known as Proto-Bulgarians) at the Danube. The Slavic-Volga army led by Sviatoslav, the Prince of Kiev, was defeated in 971 at Dorostolon (Silistra, Bulgaria). Emperor Basil II Volgaroktonos (976-1025) crushed the Volga Vikings and recaptured the entire Balkan Peninsula. Historiographies often confuse the nomadic Turanian people from the Volga with the Volga Vikings and the Romanized Thracian natives referred to as *vulgari* in Latin sources, which meant common people. The Volga Vikings, a small Asiatic Turanian population, were influential only as military leaders, with the majority of the population being the Romanized Thracians (*vulgari*) and Slavs. At the death of Basil II, the empire stretched from Armenia to the Adriatic and from the Danube to the Euphrates. However, 50 years later, in 1071, the Byzantines were defeated by the Turks at the Battle of Manzikert.

867
-
1057

1071

SCHOLASTICISM

Scholasticism is the movement whose followers engaged in a significant intellectual endeavour, seeking to reconcile faith with reason. Anselm of Canterbury (1033-1109) aimed to rationally prove the existence of God. Anselm's ontological argument was: *the existence of God is deduced from the concept of God.* Centuries later, Kant's retort was: *"The notion of a dog doesn't bark."* Impossible and unnecessary, for if you are strong in faith, you need no rational demonstration (from the philosopher Vasile Muscă). Another great dilemma that troubled *scholasticism* was the problem of *universals* (Aristotle's concepts), which was raised by Porphyry the Phoenician, a student of Plotinus. Scholasticism reached its pinnacle in the 13th century through: i) the discovery and utilization of Aristotle's writings, ii) the rivalry between Franciscans and Dominicans, and iii) the emergence of universities in Bologna and Paris. The most prominent representatives of scholasticism are Albert the Great (1195-1280) and his celebrated disciple, Thomas Aquinas (1224-1274).

THE GOLDEN AGE OF SLAVIC CULTURE

Byzantium recognized the autocephaly of the Patriarchy of the Slavs at Preslav as early as the reign of Khan Boris (852-889), when the Christianization of the Slavs began. Under the rule of Simeon (893-927), the region of Thrace and Moesia, inhabited by the common people (vulgari) and Slavs, led by a warrior class of Turanian origin (Volgarian), or what was left of it, experienced a remarkable flourishing of Slavic religious culture. This era is rightfully referred to as the Golden Age today. Slavonic was acknowledged as a liturgical language; it established itself as a language of liturgical worship among all Eastern Slavs, as well as among the Daco-Romanians. Russian also evolved from this Slavonic language.

870

85

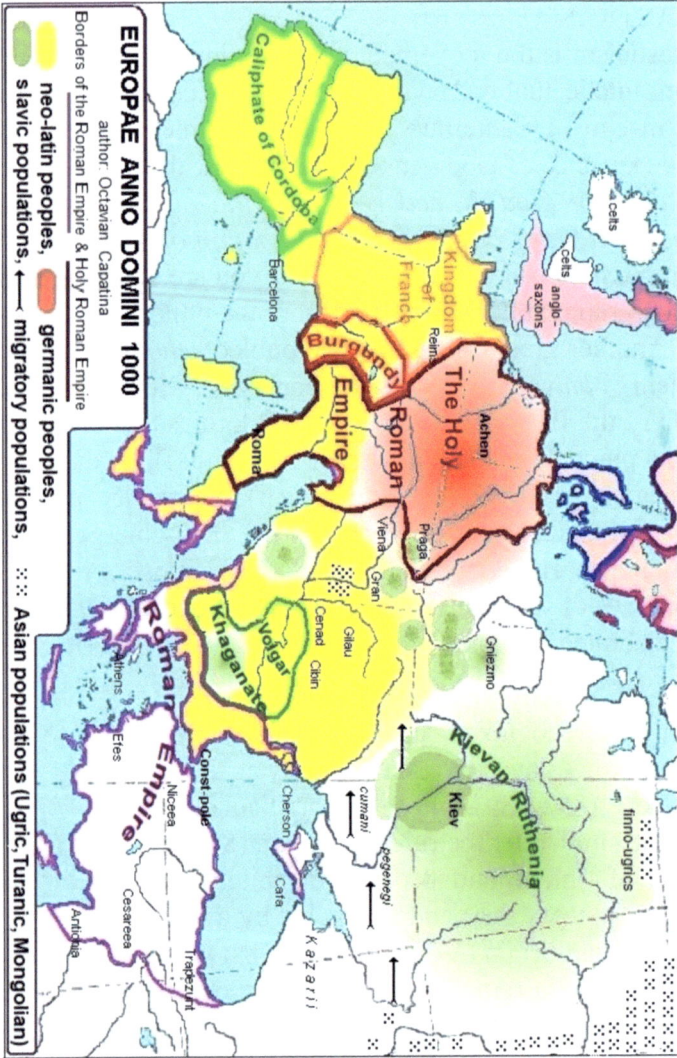

Fig. 14. Map of Europe in the year 1000

THE HUNGARIAN TRIBES AND THE CATHOLIC KINGDOM

As early as the second half of the 9th century, the Turanian tribes of Hungarians were involved both in raiding expeditions and as mercenaries in conflicts across Europe. They arrived on Csepel Island on the middle Danube (Pannonia) sometime after 903. The plundering campaigns of these nomads in the west were halted at Merseburg (933) and then decisively stopped by the Saxon King Otto the Great (936-973), with a crushing victory on the Lech River (near Augsburg) in 955. Weakened, the tribes no longer dared to raid in the west. Practically speaking, they disappeared after this battle, given that around the year 1000, about 7% of Hungarian ancestry was still present in Pannonia, according to genetic studies by the Hungarian Academy (*Culture, Confession, Ethnicity, and Race in the Middle of Danube Basin*). In 1000, the Vatican established a bishopric in Gran (Esztergom) in northern Pannonia and, through German monks, organized a Catholic kingdom with an *apostolic* mission, aiming to convert the locals of Byzantine rite and the very few remaining pagan Asian warriors grouped in 16-17 clans. This Catholic kingdom was named Hungary, probably due to a naive admiration for the Huns, whom the Latin monks of the Middle Ages associated with the Hungarian nomads. In those times, Catholicism, and not just it, relied on and admired brute force if it served its purpose. This new kingdom was neither Hungarian nor Hun, as proven by historical facts and confirmed by genetics. The northern expansion of the Catholic kingdom was halted by the Bohemian King Ottokar the Great (1253-1278), who was also the Duke of Austria and Styria, in the Battle of Kressenbrunn in 1260.

After **903**

933

955

1260

1330   The eastern and southern expansion of the Catholic kingdom was slowed down by the still powerful empire of the Asanesti south of the Danube. The southward expansion of the Catholic kingdom was halted at Posada (1330), in the *Terra Romanorum*, through the brilliant victory of a Basarab (1310-1352) over Charles of Anjou (Kingdom of Naples), the new king of Hungary. Charles was brought to "Hungaria" by the Vatican after suppressing the Cuman resurgence in the Pannonian Kingdom. Basarab had ancestors documented in chronicles dating back to 1241, which speak of the great Tatar invasion. Charles of Anjou's soldiers were primarily Romanians from northwest of the Carpathians.

1394   Stephen I of Moldavia (1394-1399) also halted the expansion of Catholicism with an important victory in 1394 near Târgu Neamț against Sigismund of Luxembourg (1368-1437), then only the King of Croatia and Hungary, later the Holy Roman Emperor.

CALIPHATE OF CORDOBA

929   In the 10th century, Cordoba became a caliphate under Prince Rahman III (912-961). At that time, Cordoba had 700 mosques, 400 public baths and the largest library in the world, consisting of 400.000 volumes. This is the period when ambassadors from Constantinople were received with great ceremony and brought the text of Pedanius Dioscorides' *De Materia Medica* as a gift to the culture-hungry prince. The prince had sought the manuscript in Cairo and Baghdad, where Dioscorides' book, along with many other works of antiquity, was translated into Arabic and preserved from

1031   destruction. The caliphate collapsed in 1031, and in its place, four major Moorish Kingdom emerged in Malaga, Seville, Toledo and Valencia, along with several smaller vassal states.

THE HOLY ROMAN EMPIRE

Otto the Great (936-973), Duke of the Saxons, King of the Germans, and the first Emperor of the Holy Roman Empire of German Nation, was called upon by Pope John XII (955-963) to restore order in Rome, which was under attack by King Berengar II of the Lombards. Otto came to the Pope's aid. As a reward, the Pope anointed him Emperor. The eastern half of the Carolingian Empire thus became *The Holy Roman Empire*. Seeing the Emperor's increased power, the Pope asked the Byzantines and Hungarians to fight against the Saxons. Otto learned of this and came to Rome twice, replacing two popes and making the Romans swear they would never name a pontiff without the Emperor's approval.

962

THE CAPETIANS

With the extinction of the last Carolingian and the election and coronation of Hugh Capet (987-996) in the former West Frankish Empire, a dynasty was born whose kings self-styled themselves as "emperors", thereby rejecting the sovereignty of the Holy Roman Empire. The Capetian dynasty ended in 1328 with the death of Charles VI (1322-1328).

987

IBERIA, RECONQUISTA

The expulsion of the Moors began from Asturias, which had not been occupied by the Arabs. The division among the Moorish kingdom encouraged Christians to start the reconquest of the peninsula. In 1035, Sancho the Great, King of Navarre, established two separate kingdoms for his sons: Aragon and Castile, which, along with Portugal, embarked on the reconquest of the peninsula. In 1212, the northern Christian kingdoms united and achieved a victory filled with hope.

**1010
-
1212**

THE MILITARY ORDERS

The Order of Saint John (the Knights Hospitallers). In 1048, an Amalfitan (from Italy) established the Order of the Knights Hospitallers on the Holy Land with the purpose of providing medical assistance to pilgrims at the Holy Sepulchre. In 1113, it became an independent order within the hierarchy of the Church in Jerusalem, directly dependent on Rome. After the fall of Acre, the last Christian stronghold in 1291, the Knights retreated to Cyprus (1291-1310), then to Rhodes (1310-1523), and finally to Malta (1530-1798).

1048

The Order of the Templars. Hugues de Payens, along with other volunteers, organized to provide military protection for pilgrims at the Holy Sepulchre. Officially recognized by Pope Innocent II in 1139, the order grew in power and membership.

1118 - 1307

It comprised both warrior monks and chaplain monks. Members of the Order, who were not warriors, established a strong financial infrastructure in Europe, introducing methods of territorial value transfer, from which the European banking system emerged. Philip IV, known as Philip the Fair (1285-1314), confiscated their immense wealth in 1307, accusing the Templars of heresy; he imprisoned them, where they were tortured and burned at the stake (about 2000 monks). Pope Clement V (1305-1314), pressured by the French king, declared the Templars heretics in 1312.

The Teutonic Order. Pope Celestine III (1191-1198) ordered the knights of the Hospitallers Order to take care of a hospital in Acre (Palestine), where the wounded soldiers of German origin who had fought in the Crusades were cared for. This hospital was formed based on linguistic criteria. Skilled fighters, the Germans were directly dependent on the Pope and became one of

1190

the most feared military orders. The Vatican brought them to the Land of Bârsa (Transylvania, 1211) as an outpost of Catholicism and to save the Latin Kingdom in Constantinople. A kingdom struck by Romanians led by Cumans warriors. Due to the fears of Andrew II of Hungary regarding the power of the Teutonic Order, the German knights left Transylvania for the Baltic shores (1225) to impose Catholicism among the pagan tribes of Prussians and Lithuanians.

THE SCHISM OF THE CHURCH

The epilogue of the schism between Constantinople and the Vatican: Patriarch Michael I (1043-1059) and Pope Leo IX (1049-1054) excommunicated each other. **1054** The historical foundations of the schism were two: the understanding of *Pontifex Maximus* and the fight against *Arianism*: i) With the disappearance of the Emperor, that is, of Pontifex Maximus, the former prefect of Rome, who became Pope Gregory I, assimilated the priestly function and the civil administration of Rome; Gregory saw himself as the Emperor. Hence the claim of universality of the Catholic Church. In the East, the Emperor remained Pontifex Maximus, and the Patriarch continued to be subordinate to him. ii) Christianization in the East, beyond the apostles, was done from person to person.

In the West, the Goths undertook popular Christianization in the Arian variant. By the time Rome woke up, the West was already Arian. To combat Arianism, Rome exaggerated what was self-evident in the East, chiefly that the Holy Spirit proceeds from the Son, emphasizing the *filioque* idea. The irony was that Rome's goal was to maintain the Nicene-Constantinopolitan faith.

INDULGENCES

1063 During the pontificate of Alexander II (1062-1073), the practice of indulgences emerged. The Church, popes, bishops, who considered themselves *vicarius Dei*, offered forgiveness of sins in exchange for favours, initially spiritual – the fight for holy places, but over time, more and more material. Pope Urban II (1088-1099) extended this unfortunate practice, which plagued Catholicism until the Reformation. The practice of indulgences did not remain a Catholic exclusive. It is worth noting the case of the Patriarch of Jerusalem, who in 1601 visited all three Romanian countries to sell "pardons for sins" for money.

THE CRUSADES

The first "holy" wars were waged by Emperor Flavius Heraclius against the Persians, between 621 and 627, with the aim of reclaiming Syria, Palestine and Egypt. He also recovered the Holy Cross from the Persians, which he returned to the Church of the Holy Sepulchre in 629. Out of the numerous crusades carried out by the Vatican in the name of the "true faith", six were aimed at the liberation of the holy places, while the rest were against "heretics". Heretics were considered all those who did not pay tithes to the Catholic Church, whether believers or pagans. There were six crusades conducted as expeditions to free the holy places and punish paganism, not seven. The so-called Fourth Crusade was not actually related to the holy places. However, to avoid confusing the reader after a millennium of inaccurate historiography, I have kept the commonly known numbering.

1095 - 1096 *The First Crusade.* Responding to the call of Byzantine Emperor Alexios Komnenos, Pope Urban II organized a crusade for the liberation of the holy places during the Council of Clermont in 1095.

Urban delivered a memorable speech before the Council, which was attended by knights as well: *"...this land in which you dwell is too small, ...it provides too little sustenance... That's why you're killing each other. So let hate depart from among you... Set out for the Holy Sepulchre... Begin this journey for the forgiveness of your sins..."* The first wave, the "peasants, crusade", consisting of disorganized peasants, did not get far. Some of the crusaders in Pannonia were killed and scattered, while others were completely massacred by Turks when they reached Anatolia. The second wave, in 1096, composed of knights, captured Jerusalem from the infidels and slaughtered them in 1099.

The Second Crusade. Upon news of the fall of Edessa, a new crusade was launched by Bishop Bernard of Clairvaux and led by Conrad III of the Hohenstaufen dynasty and King Louis VII of France. Jerusalem had not even been threatened. Crusaders wanted Damascus as well but were defeated. The crusaders retreated, but they stirred the Arabs' anger. By 1177, the Levant had become "Frankish", and Egypt had become their protectorate. A bold adventurer, Renaud de Châtillon, provoked the Arabs. In 1187, Muslims led by the Kurd Saladin (1171-1193) reclaimed Tyre, Edessa, Jaffa, Jerusalem, and Acre, massacring the crusaders in turn.

1147
-
1149

The Third Crusade. The third crusade, led by Frederick I Barbarossa, Richard the Lionheart of England, and Philip II of France, engaged the entire western world. After a major victory at Iconium, Frederick Barbarossa died by drowning in a river in Anatolia. The crusaders continued and captured Acre, concluding a truce with the powerful Saladin,

1189
-
1192

self-proclaimed Sultan of Egypt, in which Christians received a coastal strip for pilgrims to travel to Jerusalem.

1204   *The Fourth Crusade.* The fourth crusade was limited to the atrocities and looting of Constantinople (see *Intolerance*).

1209 - 1229   *The Crusade Against the Cathars.* The crusade against the Cathars, perhaps the bloodiest of all crusades, was initiated by the Vicar of God on Earth, Pope Innocent III (see *Intolerance*).

1212   *The Children's Crusade.* The crusade of the youth – tens of thousands of young boys and girls – were taken to Marseille, Ancona and Genoa by various fanatics and scammers. In Italy, local bishops prevented the boarding of the youth. However, from Marseille, the young people were taken by merchants with the destination of Alexandria, where they were sold as slaves.

1228 - 1229   *The Fifth Crusade.* The fifth crusade, a diplomatic crusade, unique in its own way, was led by Frederick II (1220-1250), Emperor of the Holy Roman Empire and King of Sicily, a very learned man with anti-papal sentiments. He set out on this "crusade" with 5 ships and 100 knights, his entourage. They reached Acre, where he concluded a treaty with the Sultan of Egypt, in which the Crusaders were ceded Jerusalem, Nazareth, and Bethlehem. The emperor and the sultan agreed that Jerusalem was a holy city for both faiths.

1248 - 1254   *The Sixth Crusade.* The sixth crusade was directed against Egypt to weaken the material base of the Muslims.

The Muslims had recaptured Jerusalem in 1244. Louis IX, the King of France (1226-1270), after a minor victory (at Damietta, Egypt), was defeated and taken prisoner along with his entire army. He was ransomed and returned to France after 5 years.

The Seventh Crusade. The seventh crusade was also led by Louis IX of France. He and 3.000 knights landed on the shores of Tunisia with the aim of converting the sovereign and establishing a base against Egypt. After disembarking from Cartagena, Louis IX died.

1270

In 1291, Acre, the last Christian stronghold, fell into the hands of the Mamluks, and Tyre, Beirut and Sidon were also abandoned. Cyprus resisted the Muslims until 1489, and Rhodes held out until 1523.

THE CONCORDAT BETWEEN THE POPE AND THE EMPEROR

The Concordat of Worms between Pope Calixtus II (1119-1124) and the Holy Roman Emperor Henry V (1111-1125) ended the investiture controversy of bishops within the empire, which had lasted since 1075. The Concordat made a distinction between "temporal", secular power, and "spiritual" power. The emperor had the right to appoint bishops within the German realm, while the pope only invested them. It marked a defeat for papal claims.

1122

AVERROES AND THE UNIVERSAL INTELLECT

The Spanish philosopher of Arab origin, Averroes, studied theology, jurisprudence, medicine, mathematics, and philosophy, while also serving as a judge in Cordoba. His commentaries on Aristotle's texts sparked intense debates among scholars of his time. The Latin theologians, who sought a Christian Aristotle, either didn't understand Averroes or couldn't comprehend him, associating him with heresy. Averroes posited an absolute truth accessible only to the *Universal Intellect*, whereas an individual's mind possesses only a secondary, partial truth useful for practicing faith. This view led to speculations about the double truth. Initially, his ideas found followers among Christian scholars, but later they caused significant disturbance. Thomas Aquinas settled the dispute by admitting a certain kind of "rationalism", in the sense that, if rationalism leads to a truth different from theological truth, then either the premises are wrong, or even the reasoning itself is flawed. And the reasoning must be repeated until the rational truth aligns with Christian truth.

THE UNION BETWEEN CATALONIA AND ARAGON

1137

The Count of Barcelona became the king of Aragon, a small kingdom at the southern foothills of the Pyrenees. Together, Catalonia and Aragon grew stronger, increasing pressure on the Moors. Louis VII of Aragon formally relinquished sovereignty over Catalonia over a century later.

THE INDIVIDUALIZATION OF PORTUGAL

1139

1249

In 1139, the north of Portugal asserted its independence from the Kingdom of León. In 1147, with the assistance of Crusaders (from the Second Crusade), Lisbon was liberated from the Moors. In 1249, the southern province of Algarve was freed. The borders from then are the same as those today. Under King Alfonso III, in 1254, the first session of the Cortes took place in the city of Leiria, an assembly composed of representatives of the nobility, middle class and all municipalities.

THE PLANTAGENETS

Henry II (1154-1189), King of England, Duke of Normandy, and Count of Anjou, Main and Touraine, by marrying Eleanor of Aquitaine in 1154, became more powerful on the continent than the French kings.

IRELAND UNDER THE ENGLISH

After experiencing flourishing development in the 5th to 8th centuries, the fragmentation of Ireland allowed its occupation by the Anglo-Normans in 1171. In 1175, Henry II of England proclaimed English sovereignty over the island. The English nobles sent to the island gradually assimilated into the local population.

THE AUTONOMY OF ITALIAN CITIES

Defeated by Verona and the Lombard League at Legnano in 1176, the Holy Roman Emperor Frederick I Barbarossa (1155-1190) signed the Treaty of Constance (Switzerland) in 1183. This treaty recognized the right of self-governance for representatives of Italian cities, elected by the citizens.

THE INQUISITION

Faced with the Cathars, who had organized themselves along the lower course of the Rhône River, Pope Lucius III (1181-1185) and Emperor Frederick I Barbarossa (1155-1190) devised a special investigative procedure called *the Episcopal Inquisition*, in 1184. Pope Gregory IX (1227-1241) appointed the inquisitor Conrad von Marburg to eradicate heretics in the German territory in 1227. Four years later, the same pope established *the Papal Inquisition* with more punitive legislation and entrusted it to extraordinary judges among the Dominicans.

The Spanish Inquisition was fundamentally different from both the Papal and Episcopal Inquisitions. It was a monarchical institution established by the rulers Isabella and Ferdinand, serving the monarchy. Additionally, Spain didn't experience the clerical corruption seen in German, French and Italian lands and cities. The Spanish Inquisition was rigorous and significantly more "humane" than the other Inquisitions or the feudal "civil" tribunals of France, Germany or Italy. For instance, while the burning of "witches" was a commonplace occurrence on the continent, likely resulting in thousands of victims, such accusations were not taken seriously by the Spanish Inquisition. Spanish inquisitors acknowledged that only God could perform miracles, rendering witchcraft accusations inconsistent. The Spanish Inquisition was not uniform; it underwent four distinct phases of manifestation.

1478

THE ROMANIAN-BULGARIAN EMPIRE

The Thracian-Roman peoples, the Romanians, were referred to by foreigners using terms initially coined by the Germans for Latins – "volochi", "valachi", "vlahi" or "olahi". The Thracian-Romanians from the southern Danube region were also called "vulgari" by Latin monks, meaning common people. These people rose against the Byzantine Empire under the leadership of the brothers Petru and Asan. With the help of Romanians and Cuman warriors from the northern Danube region, they defeated the Byzantines led by Emperor Isaac II Angelos (1185-1195, 1203-1204) and formed a kingdom between the Danube and the Balkan Mountains. Ioniță Caloian (1197-1207), the youngest of the Asan brothers, was courted by both the Byzantine emperor and the Pope. Emperor Alexios III recognized the imperial title for Ioniță. The Vlacho-Bulgarian empire under the Asan dynasty included Macedonia and territories extending to the Adriatic Sea. However, Ioniță did not acknowledge the authority of the

Constantinople Patriarchy over his country and turned to Pope Innocent III (1198-1216) for the consecration of bishops. A papal legate crowned Ioniță, and the bishop of Târnovo was appointed as a metropolitan. But Ioniță's relations with the Vatican soured due to the so-called Fourth Crusade. A war for supremacy in the Balkans began between Ioniță Caloian and the Latin Empire of the East (1204-1282). Ioniță emerged victorious, capturing the Latin emperor Baldwin of Flanders. Due to this war, Ioniță's previously strained relations with the Vatican deteriorated. The potential preservation of the ethnic identity of the Daco-Romanians, the "vulgarii", through adopting the Latin confession, was missed. After the death of King Ioan Asan II (1218-1241), the Romanian dynasty waned, with the throne being occupied by representatives of the Slavic elite and those undergoing Slavic influence through the Slavic cult. This continued until 1393, when the capital, Târnovo, was captured by the Turks, and the "Bulgarian" synthesis was also suppressed.

INTOLERANCE, CRIMES AND GENOCIDE

In 1204, the armies of the Fourth Crusade no longer fought for the liberation of the holy places; instead, they looted Constantinople and its inhabitants, shattering icons, devastating churches and stripping them of all tradeable valuables – gold and silver. The Byzantine chronicler Nicetas Choniates recalls that *"the Muslims did not violate our wives... they did not throw our people into misery, did not strip them naked to walk them through the streets, did not let them die of hunger, and did not throw them into the fire... However, these Christian peoples, who make the sign of the cross in the name of the Lord and share the same religion as us, behaved this way towards us."*

1204

1207

99

Pope Innocent III, who considered himself *vicarius Christi*, was the most powerful pontiff. He equated heresy with the Byzantine rite.

He declared that schismatics, from sovereigns to nobles to peasants, were unjust possessors and should be dispossessed through looting and plundering (*dati fuerint in direptionem et praedam*). Therefore, Romanians in Pannonia, the Tisza Plain, and Transylvania, of the Byzantine confession, were no longer just schismatics but heretics; they could be killed just like Muslim infidels or Jews.

1209   The Cathars (Albigensians, Bogomils) considered the material world as a prison where souls (belonging to God) were trapped. This Cathar thesis was deemed heresy by the Vatican and was combated, leading to the extermination of its adherents. The first measures against the Cathars date back to 1147 and were initiated by Pope Eugenius III. The crusade against the Albigensians (1209-1229) was launched by Innocent III (1198-1216). The extinction of the Cathar sect occurred around 1244 at the fortress of Montségur. The number of victims of the "crusade" is estimated at around one million people.

1279   The Catholic provincial council of Buda in 1279, during the reign of King Ladislaus the Cuman (1272-1290), decided, with regard to the Orthodox believers, that they could no longer hold divine worship, build churches and chapels. The faithful were prohibited from participating in Byzantine divine services or entering Byzantine chapels. Schismatics were also barred from holding public offices in the new kingdom. Penalties were established for Christians recently converted to Catholicism, if they continued to participate in schismatic services or received the sacraments from schismatic priests. Additionally, it was decreed that *Jews, Saracens, Ishmaelites and other unbaptized individuals should wear permanent distinctive signs on their chests.*

Jan Hus (1369-1415), the rector of the University of Prague, was burned at the stake as a heretic. Pope Martin V, through a bull issued on March 1, 1420, authorized the killing of Hus and Wycliffes supporters and initiated the Crusade against the Hussites.

Pope Innocent VIII (1484-1492), convinced of the existence of witches, issued a papal bull granting inquisitors full powers to eradicate witches. Thousands of "witches" were burned at the stake. The entire Catholic Europe, under this noble impulse, was engulfed in madness, except for the Iberian Peninsula. 1484

Jean Calvin terrorized Geneva, both spiritually and politically. He imprisoned or burned at the stake as "heretics" all those who did not obey him. Between 1562 and 1598, during the conflicts in France against the followers of Jean Calvin, called Huguenots, around 3 million people died. In Paris alone, during one night, the St. Bartholomew's Day massacre, 2.000 Huguenots were assassinated by Catholic partisans. 1541

1562

Giordano Bruno (1548-1600), a theologian and philosopher, was condemned and burned at the stake for his pantheistic views and his belief in the infinity of the universe, ideas considered heretical at that time. 1600

The Thirty Years' War (1618-1648), erroneously called a religious war, pitted Catholics allied with Protestants against Protestants allied with Catholics. The image of this terrible war in a hypothetical painting: *"starving peasants fighting over horse carcasses with packs of wolves"*. The number of direct and indirect victims was staggering around 7 million. 1618 - 1648

1642 - 1652	The human toll in the English Civil War, between 1642 and 1649, between Anglicans and Catholics, was estimated at 190.000 lives. In Ireland, from the outset of the Irish forces' rebellion until 1652, when Catholic royalists surrendered, another 300.000 victims fell.
1685	Louis XIV (1661-1715) expelled the Huguenots from France by revoking the Edict of Nantes in 1685. To save their lives, around 200.000 Huguenots fled to neighboring Protestant countries, many to Prussia.
1700	The accelerated "awakening" of the northeastern Slavs under Tsar Peter the Great (1689-1725), including the transformation of the Russian Church into a branch of the tsar's civil services, cost approximately 3 million lives.
1761	Orthodox monasteries in Transylvania, along with their monks, were set on fire and demolished by the Austrian army in the name of the true faith.
1793	*The Jacobin Terror.* After filling the prisons, the "revolutionaries" ended up slaughtering the prisoners – approximately 40.000 people. Each butcher received 6 francs/day, food, and unlimited wine. According to a testimony: *"The butchers are cheerful, playing and singing around each corpse."* The subsequent civil wars cost the lives of several million people.
1848	*The first genocide of modern Europe.* The Hungarian-speaking individuals, who were still an insignificant minority in the eastern part of the Habsburg Empire, where the *"forced Magyarization"* of the Romanian-German-Slovak majority (see Johann Weidlein) had been going on for over half a century, saw an opportunity in the revolutionary year of 1848. In Transylvania, the most primitive form of feudalism was alive. Here, the vast majority of the population was

Romanian and Saxon, dominated by Magyarized feudal lords throughout history. The Romanian was *at the mercy* of the nobleman. The Magyarized Slovak L. Kossuth felt a shiver from the precedent of 1846 – the uprising of Ruthenian peasants in Galicia against Polish feudal lords. Therefore, for the "revolutionaries" in Pest, the movement of 1848 was the perfect occasion to erase the Romanian individuality of Transylvania, for its ethnic purification. The civil war was the Hungarian solution for exterminating those who did not want to unite with Hungary or accept Magyarization. The savagery that followed, unparalleled in modern Europe, resulted in at least 53.000 victims, of which 89,9% were Romanians, 6,7% were Germans and other ethnicities. The remaining 3,4% belonged to the "revolutionaries", as Hungarian historiography puts it, or "the rebels", according to Austrian and Romanian accounts. Only that "revolutionary" force was recruited from non-Hungarians: Romanians (from Banat, Bihor, Maramureș, and Transylvania), Swabians, Slovaks, Poles, Italians, Germans. Young individuals from Europe, Germans, Austrians, Italians, Poles, joined the "revolution" against the monarchy. The Germans saw the Habsburg Empire as an obstacle to German unity, while Italians and Poles saw it as a prison for their peoples.

The first extermination camps in Europe. The Battle of Verdun, the great German hope, began in February 1916, and, despite enormous losses, the Germans led by Erich von Falkenhayn barely gained a few villages by the end of the year. Romania's entry into the war on the side of the Entente on August 15, 1916 (Julian calendar), was a heavy blow to the Germans. A blow for which the Germans sought revenge in the most unworthy manner possible. During the winter of 1916/17, German soldiers

1917

103

established the first extermination camps in Alsace and Lorraine – without food and without warmth, for Romanian prisoners (violating international norms, the 1907 Hague Convention ratified by Germany in 1909). In the summer of 1917, Bolshevikized Russians were leaving the front. Nothing would have stood in the way of the Germans in the east anymore. However, the generals August von Mackensen and Erich von Falkenhayn were stopped at the gates of Moldova by the bravery of the Romanian armies at Mărășești, Oituz, and Mărăști. An additional humiliation that led to the extermination of Romanian prisoners in Alsace at the hands of the Germans (see Jean Nouzille).

The Bolshevik Genocide – The number of people directly killed through shooting, starvation and cold is hard to calculate, because, first of all, the figures are on the order of tens of millions, second, because in Soviet Russia, the authorities no longer cared about evidence, as they themselves practiced assassination in political struggles; third, because a clear distinction cannot be made between those killed in the revolution, in the civil war with weapons in hand, or in class struggle, and the "collateral" deaths; fourth, because one can no longer dissociate between the tens of millions of victims who died from "natural" causes (cold, disease) and those who died from induced causes. Just as one cannot discriminate between a suicide and an orchestrated murder committed by secret police. A Bolshevik writer, Roy Medvedev, who analyzed Stalin's crimes between 1962 and 1988, referring to the class struggle of 1937-1938, speaks of over 700.000 high-level communist activists "murdered with evidence", activists "exposed" in "public" trials. Most of these activists murdered by Stalin went through a sham trial, thus they could be counted. Many more hundreds of

1917
-
1991

thousands of communists were simply liquidated. Millions of "enemies" never returned from the Gulag.

Holodomor – the Soviet genocide by starvation. It was carried out in the Ukrainian Soviet Republic and the Moldavian Autonomous Soviet Republic (Transnistria) between 1932 and 1933. The goal was to crush the resistance of the local population with European aspirations to Sovietization. According to recent estimates, around 4 million people died directly. The birth deficit during this period for Ukraine and the Moldavian Autonomous Soviet Republic was approximately 6.5 million. In addition to those who died of starvation, there were thousands of Moldovan families who, in an attempt to escape to Romania, were shot on the Dniester River. `1932 - 1933`

The First Genocide in Bessarabia. The occupation of Bessarabia according to the pact between Stalin and Hitler, between June 28, 1940, and June 22, 1941, also marked the first genocide carried out by Soviet NKVD troops supported by communist Jews. The genocide consisted of the assassination and deportation of over 300.000 Romanians, representing more than 12.23% of the population (see Anton Moraru). `1940 - 1941`

The second genocide in Bessarabia. This genocide begins with military alterations on the front in August 1944 and the occupation of Bessarabia by the Soviets, when thousands of people were executed for "collaborating" with the Romanian "bourgeois-landowning" class, as traitors of the Soviets, and hundreds of thousands were deported in waves under conditions that most often led to death. In this genocide, a separate chapter was dedicated to the victims of the planned famine in 1946/47. `1944 - 1989`

Figure 15. The Soviet deportations in Besserabia
between 1940-41 and 1944-52

Here, the horrors surpassed those of the Thirty Years'
War (1618-1648), when it was said that wolves and
survivors fought over the corpses of dead horses; here,
young children were killed so that the adults could
survive. The total number of those assassinated and
deported exceeded one million.

The second genocide in Transylvania. In addition to the Holocaust unleashed by the German National Socialists in Europe, a distinct and unimaginably cruel genocide stands out, perpetrated by Hungarians in northwest Romania and historic Maramureș. Thousands of children, pregnant women, the elderly, along with adults, were assassinated solely because they weren't Magyarized, didn't accept Magyarization, or because they were Jews. Churches and synagogues were demolished and set on fire. Romanian priests and intellectuals were expelled. Young individuals without military training were sent to the frontline for mine clearance and placed at the frontlines. Some were shot in the back. A provisional and limited total, confined to the regions of Romania and Slovakia under Hungarian occupation, counts 500.000 Romanians, Jews, Slovaks and Ruthenians killed directly or indirectly: i) by units of the Hungarian army in the occupied territories (Ip, Trăznea, Lazuri, Huedin, Sati-Mare, Mureșenii de Câmpie, Sărmaș, Moisei, etc), ii) through civilian groups everywhere in the occupied areas, iii) by sending them to the front with the aim of ethnic cleansing, iv) in forced labor camps (in Hungary and occupied territories), v) in extermination camps (Kamenets-Podolsk-1941, Dorošići-1943, Auschwitz-Birkenau-Dachau-1943-44).

1940 - 1945

The Holocaust. Prelude. In the 1920s, in the first fascist country in Europe, Jews were exterminated in a camp near Lake Balaton (see the diary of Eva Heyman). Through the Nuremberg Laws (1935), Jews in Germany were deprived of German citizenship. Between November 9 and 13, 1938, during the so-called *Kristallnacht*, Jewish properties were destroyed

1920 - 1938

in numerous German and Austrian towns (around 7.500 Jewish shops). As German troops advanced westward, special units called *Einsatzgruppen* hunted down and concentrated left-wing communists and intellectuals, Jews and non-Jews, Roma, homosexuals, mentally ill individuals, and even people with various physical disabilities behind the frontlines. At the Wannsee Conference (1942), *the Final Solution - Die Endlösung der Judenfrage* was adopted. Jews, as well as other "undesirables", were confined to ghettos, labor camps, and extermination camps. In some areas of occupied Europe, networks for crossing borders into less exposed countries like Romania were established.

1942
-
1945

The Final Solution was implemented most extensively in the territories held by the Horthy regime (see Oliver Lustig, a survivor from Birkenau). According to some estimates, up to 12 million people were killed, including communists, socialists, disabled individuals, Slavs, Jews and Romani people.

1945
-
1946

The expulsion of Germans, about 16 million people, after World War II from Prussia, Poland, Czechoslovakia, Yugoslavia, and Hungary – only their "movement" cost 2 million German lives.

1992
-
2025

The War in Moldova was the first of Moscow's new imperial wars. This initial war was organized by the KGB, GRU with Transnistrian militias, Cossacks and Ukrainians, individuals from Kamchatka (Smirnov) or China (Galina Andreevna), and the Russian 14th Army. It resulted in the exodus of hundreds of thousands of people and the death of tens of thousands of others (see Ion Costaş). It was followed by Georgia in 2008, Ukraine in 2014, and most recently, the genocide in Ukraine in 2022.

MAGNA CARTA LIBERTATUM

After the defeat of King John I of England (1199-1216) by King Philip II Augustus of France (1180-1223), after the loss of Plantagenet territories north of the Loire and in conflict with English barons, these barons imposed *Magna Carta* and its laws on the king, in 1215. The document, in its initial form, was drafted by the Archbishop of Canterbury, Stephen Langton, to make peace between the unpopular king and a group of rebel barons. *Magna Carta* represented a major political reform, emphasizing the rights of the barons, as well as the London community, an act against the arbitrary authority of the despot and in favour of the rights of communities. An act from which the rights of free people emerged. Innocent III, who considered himself the vicar of Jesus Christ on Earth, declared the document null and void. This was followed by a two-year civil war that ended with the victory of the barons and the *de facto* acceptance of *Magna Carta* by nine-year-old King John's son, Henry III, who had just passed away. In 1265, the barons also obtained the convening of a parliament to approve the taxes set by the king.

Jun 15
1215

THE TATAR INVASION

The Tatars crushed the Cumans and the Russians at Kalka, in 1223. Then, led by Khan Subutai, they set their sights on Europe; in 1240, they occupied Kiev, and then, in the spring of 1241, the Tatars divided their horde into several detachments, which swiftly struck Eastern Europe, in the north, centre and south. The Turco-Mongols, always small in number, had the habit of terrifying the local population through violence to control them easily and extract their labour with very few "occupational" forces. Suddenly, in March 1242, the bulk of the hordes withdrew from

1223

1241

Central Europe due to the succession issue after the death of Great Khan Ogedei (1186-1241). The Tatars did not withdraw from the eastern European steppes; the Slavs here would identify as Muscovites and later as Russians (reminiscent of the Viking elite of the 9th century). The other eastern Slavs split into Ruthenians (under the Poles) and Belarusians (under the Lithuanians). The Tatars remained rulers for many centuries, from the northern Black Sea region to Siberia, under the name of the Golden Horde. The Slavic formations in the north paid tribute to the Tatars. In 1243, Prince Vladimir of Suzdal was appointed by Khan Batu (1205-1255) as the representative of the Russian leaders, responsible for their actions and for collecting taxes. In the 1440s and 1450s, the Horde was ravaged by a new tribal war and split into seven Khanates: Qasim, Kazakh, Uzbek, Crimean, Kazan, Astrakhan and Siberia. In 1783, the last Tatar entity, the Crimean Khanate, transitioned from Ottoman suzerainty to Russian suzerainty, which the Russians did not observe.

THE SEPARATION OF THE EASTERN SLAVIC PEOPLES

After the Mongol invasion, the destiny of the Eastern Slavs changed for good, even on the improbable hypothesis that the autochthonous overrun Indo-European Slavs would not have mattered. But the autochthonous mattered, nonetheless. Therefore, the symbiosis around Lake Ilmen, the upper Volga, and the symbiosis on the upper Dnieper are somewhat different. Over the millennia, after the Mongol rule, the symbiosis on the Dnieper (the future Ukrainians and Belarusians) entered the Lithuanian-Polish orbit; the symbiosis of the upper Volga region remained in the Mongol orbit for centuries to come, but in the end, the Volga Slavs were no longer Slavs, but a new Slavic-Mongolian mixture.

RESUMING "SCIENTIFIC" RESEARCH

"With the collapse of the ancient world and as the framework of the Roman Empire became infused with Christianity, many changes occurred that adversely affected the course of 'scientific' thinking, which had, however, established such serious foundations during Antiquity. The Christian orientation towards the transcendent world, towards 'transcendence', influenced, at least initially, the pursuits of a 'scientific' nature in an almost catastrophic manner. Tertullian's words are symptomatic of the rejection of any interest in the investigation of nature: 'Investigation is no longer necessary after reading the Gospels'" – noted the philosopher, Lucian Blaga. The reservoirs of Byzantine and Arab knowledge were needed, which preserved Hellenistic thought for a millennium, until Western Europeans awakened and were willing to adopt it. But also, to take it further, through experimentation. After the first pillar of modern science laid by Euclid (~330-270 BC), the second pillar was now placed by Peter Peregrinus of Maricourt. Living in the 13th century, he studied and experimented with magnetism and wrote about the properties of magnets. His disciple, Roger Bacon (1214-1294) introduced the concept of experimental science. Bacon wrote: *"Without experience, nothing can be known thoroughly. There are two ways to attain knowledge: through reasoning and through experience."* These two, P. Peregrinus and R. Bacon, considered mathematics as the key to other sciences. Parisian Nicolas Oresme (1323-1382) described the motion mathematically, laying the foundation for analytical geometry in the line of Descartes and infinitesimal calculus in the line of Newton and Leibniz. Oresme first mathematized the concept of time, just as German Nicholas of Cusa (1401-1464), theologian, philosopher, astronomer and mathematician, secularized the notion of infinity, extending it from theological to cosmological domains. In the atmosphere of the Renaissance, Leonardo da Vinci (1452-1519), Nicolaus Copernicus (1473-1543) acted as

bridges to modern science. Giovanni Benedetti (1530-1590) and Galileo Galilei (1564-1642) sought to verify, to doubt. They took on Aristotle, an unquestioned authority until them – questioning, for example, the Aristotelian claim that heavier objects fall faster than lighter ones. They found that Aristotle was mistaken and that objects, regardless of their weight, fall at the same rate if not for air resistance, if not for friction. Galileo also discovered inertia, the law of motion composition, and defined the notions of velocity and acceleration. With the help of a telescope (1609), Galileo observed that Earth is just one of the planets in the solar system, and from this moment, everything would change for scientific and cultural elites. Experimental research can be considered to be constituted, in its orientation and methodology, of the works of Kepler, Galileo, Descartes, and Newton.

THOMAS AQUINAS (1224-1274)

A Benedictine and later a Dominican, a professor in Paris and Naples, a theological adviser and lecturer at the papal Curia, Thomas Aquinas attempted and succeeded in reconciling Aristotelianism with Christian doctrine, "harmonizing" philosophy with theology as they were in his time. He reintroduced the works of Aristotle into the European discourse, which greatly influenced him. He definitively departed from the theology of predestination of Augustine, arguing that human freedom and individual autonomy, far from being limited by the relationship with God, are actually ensured by that relationship. He accepted reason as a means of arguing in physics, separating theology from philosophy. Used correctly, philosophy and theology cannot deceive us, for there cannot be two truths – he responded to the objection raised by the Arab philosopher Averroes of Cordoba, who argued that the structure of religious beliefs makes them in total contradiction with rational knowledge. Starting from "absolute faith", Aquinas acknowledged that reason operates autonomously within the theological framework. His most important work, *Summa Theologiae*, was the result of his concerns generated by the need to address the questions and doubts of his time. *Summa* was primarily a systematic and comprehensive exposition of all the problems that theology and the world of scholars faced, an untouched synthesis from Aristotle up to his time. In the work *On the Governance of Princes – De Regimine Principum*, written in 1266, Thomas called for the abandonment of ordeals and "God's judgment", replacing them with investigations and procedures that today we call "civil". The resistance of old-fashioned theologians, Augustinians, and proponents of predestination was fierce. In 1270, along with the condemnation of Averroism, Thomas himself was discredited. Thomas's merits were recognized after his death; he was canonized in 1323, declared a Doctor of the Church in 1567, and in the 19th century, his views were considered part of official Catholic theology.

THE GEOGRAPHICAL DISCOVERIES

Marco Polo (1254-1324), a Venetian, crossed Asia in 1271, reaching Persia, Mongolia, China, Sumatra and Ceylon, which he described upon his return.

1271

The Portuguese sought the East Indies to the east, the Spanish, to the west. Christopher Columbus (1451-1506), a Catalan born in Genoa, acting on behalf of Castile, discovered "India", actually America, by sailing west in 1492.

1492

The Portuguese Vasco da Gama (1460?-1524) opened the route to India by circumnavigating Africa via the Cape of Good Hope. He discovered Mozambique and reached India in May 1498. The Portuguese Ferdinand Magellan (1480-1521) set out to circumnavigate the Earth leading a Spanish fleet of ships (1519). He crossed the Atlantic, entered the Pacific Ocean through the strait between Patagonia and Tierra del Fuego, reaching the Philippines, where

1498

He was killed. Sebastian del Cano (1476-1526), who took command of the expedition, crossed the Indian Ocean and then, circumnavigating Africa, returned to Spain aboard the ship Victoria in 1521. Trade with the "Indies" provided economic advantages to the Iberians for a century. The sailors of these risky expeditions in search of the Indies were often convicts who accepted the risk in exchange for regaining their freedom, but most died before returning. Through these geographical discoveries, European thinking assimilated a new dimension – the planet's vastness.

1519
-
1521

THE SWISS CONFEDERATION
On August 1, 1291, the Eternal Alliance (Dreiwaldstätterbund) was signed by the three cantons of Schwyz, Uri, and Unterwalden with the goal of self-defense against Austria, Burgundy and the Holy Roman Empire. The Confederation's victory over aggressive Austria in the Battle of Morgarten (1315) solidified the League, which became the nucleus of the Swiss Confederation.

1291
-
1315

THE PAPACY AT AVIGNON
In 1305, after the death of Boniface VIII and the short papacy of Benedict XI, a French pope, Clement V (1305-1314), was elected with the help of the French king, Philip IV (1285-1314). Clement V transferred the Papal Curia to Avignon in 1309 due to the disorder in Rome. The same pope, under pressure from Philip IV, accused the Knights Templar of heresy in 1312. The papal court remained in Avignon until 1378.

1309
-
1378

GHIBELLINES AND GUELFS.
PAPAL SUPREMACY

German elector princes decided not to wait for the Pope's approval. The Holy Roman Emperor, Louis IV of Bavaria (1328-1347), was crowned in Milan by the oldest dean of the Roman nobility in 1328. This event triggered a conflict that reverberated across life in the free Italian cities: some noble families supported the imperial cause, Ghibellines (Waiblingen), while others supported the pope's cause, Guelphs (Welfen). The engine of the battles between them was access to the cities' wealth.

1328

THE HUNDRED YEARS' WAR

As early as 1154, alongside Normandy, the English kings held significant domains on the continent. For these possessions and for the succession to the French throne after the death of the last Capetian, Charles IV (1322-1328), the English, waged wars against the French for over a hundred years. Edward III (1327-1377) of England, the maternal grandson of the last Capetian, supported his claim to the French throne by arguing that Salic law would prohibit inheritance through a female, but would not prohibit inheritance through a female line. According to this interpretation, Edward III would inherit the French throne. However, gatherings of French nobles and prelates and the University of Paris decided that Salic law excluded the right of inheritance through a maternal line, and they chose Philip VI (1328-1350) from the House of Valois, a distant male descendant of the penultimate Capetian, as king. Thus began the Hundred Years' War. Until 1429, the victories were mostly on the side of the English. After the Battle of Agincourt (1415),

1337
-
1453

the French were compelled, by the Treaty of Troyes (1420), to accept the Plantagenets' succession to the French throne. Joan of Arc emerged, leading a small army to lift the English siege of Orléans (1429); the tide turned in favor of the French. Duke Philip the Good of Burgundy (1419-1467) changed sides and, through the Treaty of Arras in 1435, no longer supported the claims of Henry VI of England to the French crown. The Hundred Years' War concluded after victories by the House of Valois at Formigny (1450) and Castillon (1453), when the King of England lost his last significant continental fief, leaving only Calais.

THE TSAR OF ROMANS AND SERBS

1346

Ştefan Duşan (1331-1355), who occupied neighboring Bulgarian and Byzantine possessions, proclaimed himself the Tsar of the Romans and Serbs in his residence in Skopje in 1346. He ruled over a large part of the Balkan Peninsula (Macedonia, Thessaly, Epirus, Serbia, Albania and Zeta - Montenegro) after many long battles with the Bulgarian Tsardom and the Byzantine Empire. After his death, his administrative construction fell apart. However, Ştefan Duşan had the insight to establish a Serbian Patriarchate, which maintained nationalism and hope for revival during the difficult times that followed.

THE PLAGUE

1348

The epidemic was brought from the East, from Crimea, by Genoese merchants on their trading vessels.

The pandemic quickly spread to Constantinople, northern Italy, France, southern England (1348), the German lands (1349), and Scandinavia (1350).

Millions of people died in the affected areas, roughly a third of the population.

The plague lasted for 4-5 years and was wrongly blamed on the Jews due to their exclusive religious practices.

THE REORGANIZATION OF THE HOLY ROMAN EMPIRE

After two hundred years of disputes and misunderstandings, through the *Golden Bull*, Emperor Charles IV – Wenceslaus (1355-1378), regulated the election of the emperor without the intervention of the pope. The "Emperor of the Romans" was to be elected **1356** in Frankfurt and crowned in Aachen by the 7 electors: the archbishops of Cologne, Trier, and Mainz, the Count Palatine of the Rhine, the Duke of Saxony, the Margrave of Brandenburg, and the King of Bohemia. From 1648, the Duke of Bavaria replaced the Count Palatine of the Rhine, but the 8th elector emerged – the heir of the Count Palatine, and from 1692, the 9th elector appeared.

THE GRAND DUCHY OF LITHUANIA

The Grand Duchy of Lithuania constantly gained ground in the south, occupying the territories of the Slavs, Brodniks (East Romanians) and the Tatar Horde. In 1362, the Lithuanian Duke Algirdas **1362** defeated the Tatars on the Southern Bug River and forced them to move their center of power further south, into Crimea.

THE RENAISSANCE

The Renaissance, as a historical phenomenon, unfolded from the 15th century to the 16th century, but it was prepared in the 14th century (by figures such as Dante, Wycliffe). The Renaissance transitioned Europe from the Middle Ages, from Scholasticism to Modernism. Before being a movement of cultural renewal in the broadest sense of the word, the

Renaissance established itself as a state of mind: people were trying to build a better life on Earth, they were weary of theology, of the fear of the afterlife. The Renaissance, with its three major dimensions of *Humanism, Renewal of the Arts and Religious Reform*, was primarily a rediscovery of life, of the joy of living in this world. The first two dimensions are secular and congruent. The discovery of *humanity and nature* is the essence, emphasized by the greatest interpreter of the Renaissance, Jacob Burckhardt. The Reformation also returned to the origins, to the biblical text, and to living individuals (vernacular languages), and, as such, it was a complex phenomenon. Not so for Friedrich Nietzsche, who saw Luther's Reformation as an anti-Renaissance phenomenon. Similarly, as Humanism returned to ancient texts, so the arts returned to Greco-Roman models. With the spirit of the Renaissance, individuals realized that individuality is irreducible, that they are unique and unrepeatable: man is the measure of all things. Through each unique individual, existence and nature are realized in a new and unprecedented way, enriching them. From this perspective, J. Burckhardt argued that the characteristic of the Renaissance individual is pride, the pride of uniqueness.

Fig.16. The detachment of Italian painting from the Byzantine hieratism took centuries. (author composition)

After Dante (1265-1321), figures like Petrarch (1304-1374) and Boccaccio (1313-1375) emerged, unafraid to write about nature, love and worldly sins. These scholars rejected scholasticism in favour of new literary forms centered on human existence. The rejuvenation in literature and philosophy served as the preparatory phase of the entire movement. The phenomenon began in Italy and gradually spread across the continent. Liberating the human spirit from scholastic confinement was a laborious process. With the fall of Constantinople, scholars proficient in Greek expression sought refuge in the West, bringing the Greek language and the treasures of ancient culture that catalyzed the Renaissance.

The center of European culture shifted from the "declining" Eastern Roman Empire to Italy. Scholars of the time began to take an interest in the ancient Greeks, in the manuscripts of Ovid, Lucretius, Virgil, Cicero, and in the human condition. The philologists of the Renaissance, through their exercise of comparing different sources of ancient authors to establish the correct version, contributed to the emergence of modern critical thinking. If scholasticism was dominated by Aristotle, the Renaissance rediscovered Plato and Plotinus. The Academy of Florence was a focal point. Platonism and Neoplatonism seemed more fertile and richer, spawning a range of philosophical currents from mystical to scientific. Aristotelianism also benefited. In Padua and Bologna, scholars focused on Aristotelian texts, and, through textual criticism, they managed to eliminate certain distortions introduced by scholasticism. The original ideas of Aristotle were reinstated. The Renaissance in religious terms (Marsilio Ficino – *The Platonic Theology*), distinct from the Lutheran and Calvinist Reformations, was more than just anti-scholastic; it aimed at a philosophical theology. Nietzsche saw the Renaissance as an anticlerical, antichristian movement, to

119

*Fig.17. Renaissance, Renewal of Europe - Venus
(drawing by **Lucian Şoit** inspired after S. Botticelli)*

which Germanic culture, through Luther's Reformation, did not respond adequately.

Luther's Reformation was a suppression of the gains of human spirit against religious dogmas, thus it was anti-Renaissance and anti-secularization of life – this is what Nietzsche referred to in *The Antichrist*. Some consequences of the Renaissance include critical thinking, heliocentrism, the concept of an infinite universe, autonomous value, pantheism, and, most importantly, the notion of historical time in relation to antiquity. The acceptance of heliocentrism was a victory of rational thought and sensory experience. Starting from the idea of an infinite universe, Nicolaus Cusanus deduced the uniqueness of the universe; he then logically argued that an infinite universe is a creation of an infinite Creator. As two infinites cannot coexist, the Creator God is identical to the universe, to the created world, leading to pantheism (G. Bruno).

Fig. 18. Renaissance, Renewal of Europe – Mars
*(drawing by **Lucian Șoit** after St. Catterson)*

The Renaissance also led to the search for an ideal world order – as seen in Thomas More's *Utopia*. The Renaissance manifested itself in technology and science, in the exploration of new continents. After the plague, there was a demographic increase across Europe; as the population grew, new methods and techniques emerged in mining, metalworking, milling, carpentry, mechanics, including printing and cadastral engineering. In other words, the Renaissance was both favoured by and favoured the economy. The results in arts and architecture: Giotto, Fra Angelico, Botticelli, van Eyck, van der Weyden, Raphael, Michelangelo, Dürer, H. Bosch, Donatello, Brunelleschi, Leonardo da Vinci; in literature alongside precursors (Dante, Petrarch, Boccaccio): Ariosto, Tasso, Rabelais, Shakespeare; in political philosophy – Thomas More, Machiavelli, Jean Bodin (anti-Machiavellian), Neagoe Basarab, John Milton. Additionally, the ideas of religious tolerance from Erasmus of Rotterdam. The Latin language and the printing press transformed Europe's scholars into a single, vibrant community. J. Gutenberg (1400-1468) greatly served both the Renaissance and the Reformation by democratizing the word of the Bible. Gutenberg introduced significant innovations to the printing process: movable type composition, an appropriate metal alloy, a precision matrix for casting sets of letters, oil-based ink and a more efficient press. All of these contributed to a much more efficient printing technology than what existed before. In 1455, the first *printed Bible* appeared, even in a vernacular language – the material support of religious reform.

THE REFORMATION, A RELIGIOUS AND SOCIAL MOVEMENT

1377 The English theologian John Wycliffe (1330-1384) was a formidable critic of Pope Gregory XI (1370-1378), of the papacy, and of the dogma that claimed the popes were nothing less than *Vicarius Dei* (Vicars of God). Initially, Wycliffe only argued that the Church was sinful and needed to give up its properties and return to the simplicity and poverty of the apostles. The Pope ordered his arrest. However, the outcome was different: Wycliffe began to attack the theory of transubstantiation – through which the Catholic hierarchy presented itself as an extension of Christ's.

122

authority. Wycliffe took up the task of translating the Bible into the language of the people.

Jan Hus, the rector of the University of Prague and a follower of Wycliffe's writings, also took a stand against the luxury and corruption of the Catholic hierarchy. Hus preached against the papal indulgence issued by Pope John XXII. Excommunicated in 1410, with a promise of impunity from Sigismund of Luxembourg (b. 1368 – d. 1437), who was then the king of Germany, Hungary, and Croatia, Hus appeared before the Council of Constance (Switzerland). He was condemned and burned at the stake as a heretic. His followers, the Hussites, launched a war of national emancipation from the German religious hierarchy (1419-1436). Rome launched a crusade (1420) against the Hussites and issued a bull authorizing the killing of all supporters of Wycliffe and Hus. The Czechs could not be defeated. Their ideas penetrated even to the east, into the Romanian territory. $\qquad$ 1410

Girolamo Savonarola (1452 - 1498), a Dominican friar, preached in Florence from as early as 1490, asserting that the church needed *reform: to be scourged and renewed*. In 1494, with popular support, he drove Piero II de' Medici out of the city and established a republic that lasted for 4 years. He fought against the most immoral and depraved pope of his time and against the Duke of Milan, who led an anti-French league. He attempted to establish a Christian republic throughout Italy. The excesses of his followers in their battle against frivolity and vanity also affected invaluable books and artistic values. He was captured by his enemies, tortured, hanged, and finally burned at the stake. Corruption had deeply $\qquad$ 1490 - 1498 penetrated the Catholic Church, (except for Spain), the limits of which were difficult and unimaginable.

1517 The reaction did not take long to appear. In Wittenberg, in February 1517, Martin Luther (1483-1546) published the 95 "theses" against corrupt practices. He rejected the Pope's primacy and infallibility, as well as corrupt Catholic customs and practices. What he proposed: *sola fide, sola scripta, et sola gratia*. He didn't intend to split the Church, but the Vatican's resistance to his attempt at moral cleansing pushed the reform further. His ideas, which democratized Christian faith, spread rapidly across northern Europe, from the Atlantic to the Carpathians.

1533 John Calvin, initially a supporter of Luther's ideas, left Paris and settled in Geneva. He asserted the sovereignty of God, the only savior of humanity through predestination. Calvin, somewhat contradictory, added that man's fate is his responsibility. More radical than Luther, he recognized only two sacraments: Baptism and Communion. He rejected the doctrine of the presence of the "body and blood of the Lord" in communion, as well as the invocation of saints and the institution of the episcopate. Instead, he argued that interest and usury, not explicitly condemned by the Bible, could be practiced. Not only preachers, but also the leadership of each Calvinist church should be chosen by the faithful. Calvin's ideas spread to Switzerland, Scotland, the Netherlands, France and Transylvania. Hungarian-speaking landowners were pushed in this direction by their Ottoman overlords in order to separate them from Catholic Austrians (the so-called "Hungarian" Calvinism-Turkism).

INTERNAL SCHISM OF CATHOLICISM

After the death of Pope Gregory XI (1370-1378), who had returned to Rome from Avignon in 1377, two popes were elected. The Roman Council, under popular pressure, chose an Italian, Urban VI, as Pope. The decision dissatisfied the French cardinals. They elected Pope Clement VII, who established himself in Avignon. The Catholic world split: Urban VI presided over the Holy Roman Empire, England, Ireland, Portugal and Northern Italy, while Clement VII had France, Spain, Scotland, Sardinia and Sicily. A unifying council convened in Pisa in 1409, which deposed the popes from Rome and Avignon and elected Alexander V as Pope. However, the deposed popes did not relinquish their positions, leading to three simultaneous popes. Another unifying council held in Constance (Switzerland) in 1415 yielded no results; only when the pope from Avignon lost support was Martin V (1417-1431) elected as the sole Pope.

1378 - 1417

THE EAST SLAVS, STILL UNDER TATAR RULE

After the Battle of Kalka, the Tatars dominated the Slavic and Romanian (brodnici) tribes in Eastern Europe. The victory of various Russian formations in the Battle of Kulikovo on the Don River, in 1380, against the Golden Horde, did not change their subordination to the Tatars. Only over a century later, the direct yoke of the Tatars over the northern Slavs was no longer felt, because the Grand Duke of Muscovy became their master. Paradoxically, the weakest Slavic formation in the region, chosen by the Tatar overlords to collect tribute from others, over time expanded its influence and strengthened itself.

1380

THE BALKANS UNDER OTTOMAN RULE

1389
-
1396

Indigenous Serbs and Romanians (Vlachs) were defeated by the Turks on the Câmpia Mierlei field in 1389. Following the defeat of crusaders and Romanians at Nicopolis by the Turks and Serbs in 1396, the Balkans, except for Constantinople, fell under Ottoman dominion.

THE ROMANIAN WALL

1395
1442
1456
1462
1469
1475

1574

1595

Mircea the Elder (1384-1418) successfully confronted Sultan Bayezid Ildirim in the first Ottoman expedition north of the Danube. For the first time, a sultan was defeated by a Christian prince on the battlefield, in 1395, at Rovine. Later, Mircea even dared to meddle in the succession of Ottoman sultans. Iancu de Hunedoara (1456) chased them away, Vlad the Impaler (1462) kept them beyond the Danube. Stephen III, known as Stephen the Great (1475), successfully faced Mehmed II, the conqueror of Constantinople. Stephen the Great was considered in Europe the most prominent Christian prince in the anti-Ottoman struggle. Ion Vodă, a true Hercules, in a series of lightning-fast actions, scattered the Turks and Tatars one after another. Michael the Brave (1593-1601) shook the Ottoman Empire to its foundations. Vlad the Impaler and Michael the Brave struck terror into the Turks to such an extent that they only felt safe after crossing the Bosporus into Asia. As a result, the Romanian lands were never transformed into pashaliks, as were the state formations of the Greeks, Bulgarians, Serbs and Hungarians.

THE SCANDINAVIAN UNION

Under the Danish crown, Norwegians, Danes and Swedes formed the Kalmar Union. This lasted for over a century, until the Swedes rejected Danish sovereignty in 1523.

1397

THE RISE OF POLAND AND LITHUANIA

The personal union between Jagiello, the Grand Duke of Lithuania, and Queen Jadwiga of Poland was based on the prenuptial act of Krewo (1385). Jadwiga baptized Jagiello, and in 1386, he was crowned King of Poland (1386-1434). One of the goals of the Union was also that of resisting the pressure of the Teutonic Knights. The Lithuanian king of the Union achieved victories against the Teutonic Knights at Tannenberg and Grunwald, in 1410, with significant Moldavian assistance provided by Alexander the Good (1400-1432). After the fall of Marienburg, long the capital of the Teutonic Order, the knights recognized the sovereignty of Poland through the Peace of Thorn in 1466. The Lithuanian-Polish Union gained access to the sea and secured the independence of Danzig and sovereignty over Prussia.

1410

THE POPE OR THE COUNCIL?

During the most acute period of the Catholic Schism in 1415, the Council of Constance (Switzerland) declared, through the decree *Sacrosancta*, the superiority of the decisions of a council over those of a pope. It couldn't have been otherwise, when the Catholic Church had two or three popes simultaneously. In a world completely disoriented, in 1492, Cardinal Borgia bought the papacy and ruled under the name Alexander VI (1492-1503). He "relaxed" the morals of the corrupted Vatican so much

1415

that if the *Reformation and Counter- Reformation* hadn't appeared, it would have truly been a catastrophe.

1870

Centuries later, and despite protests from many theologians, the First Vatican Council of 1869-1870, convened by Pius IX (1846-1878), adopted the dogma of papal infallibility, which directly contradicted the *Sacrosancta* bull – a return to the Middle Ages. This initiative went unnoticed by political factors as the day after its adoption, the Franco-Prussian War began, and two months later, Italian troops occupied Rome and abolished the Papal States, the *Patrimonium Petri*.

UNIO TRIUM NATIONUM

1437

After the Romanian peasant uprising in Transylvania against Catholic taxes, a pact of self-defense was signed among the Catholic guests (landowners granted property by the Hungarian kings, the Saxon patriciate and the Szekler Land leaders). This pact, known as the *Union of Three Nations (Unio trium nationum)*, significantly worsened the lives of the locals, who were reduced to the status of slaves, *viviarum rer* (see D. Prodan). Their lives were at the mercy of the feudal lords – *usque ad bene placitum principum ac regnicolarum*, as stipulated in the constitutional statute of the province for the status of the indigenous Romanian. This aberrant regime was somewhat ameliorated in 1852 after the revolutions of 1848/49, but effectively ended only in 1918. Austria covered up the unimaginable behaviour of the Transylvanian and Slovak feudal lords until the empire collapsed.

SOMETIMES PRACTICE PRECEDES CONCEPT

Philip IV of France (1285-1314) successfully confronted the papacy, particularly Boniface VIII and his bull *Unam Sanctam*, which stipulated the Pope's

superiority over secular power. Charles VII of France 1302
(1422-1461) established *gallicanism* as a state law,
meaning the French Church's independence from the
Pope. Papal bulls would only come into effect after the
king's approval. In the struggle between the theocracy
of the Vatican and earthly powers defending their **1438**
material interests, the idea of divine right dynasties
emerged – the power of kings no longer derived from
the Pope, but directly from God. Consequently, the
mission of kings was not only to organize civil society,
but also the life of churches, which became national.
This practice existed in the Eastern Roman Empire,
where the emperors had authority over both the
patriarchates and the patriarchs – a practice dating back
to Octavian Augustus, who was also the Pontifex
Maximus.

In the conflict for possessions in Italy between the
King of France and the Pope against Charles V (Quint), 1527
his army looted and committed mass killings in Rome,
treating Clement VII like an ordinary prisoner. Once
again, the papal threat of *excommunication* would
become increasingly faint. The kings saw themselves
as anointed by God.

Jean Bodin (1530-1596), an opponent of the
Machiavellian principle that *the end justifies the means*, 1576
addressed the concept of sovereignty in *La République*.
Bodin, surprisingly less known in the world than his
Florentine counterpart, argued that in the face of the
threat of tyranny and anarchy, absolute sovereignty of
the king was necessary, with one imperative condition:
*the sovereign must uphold justice (the law of God and
Nature)*. This concept emerged after Gallicanism, but
before constitutional law became a science.

THE COUNCIL OF FERRARA-FLORENCE

1439

The council aimed to restore the lost Christian unity of 1054. Each party had different immediate interests: Pope Eugene IV sought prestige, while Patriarch Joseph II sought salvation from the Ottomans. Joseph II died during the proceedings and the desired unity was not achieved.

THE SLAVE TRADE

1441

Slave trading dates back to antiquity, when the defeated became the property of the victor. Only under Emperor Constantine did the first laws emerge, viewing slaves differently: intentional killing of a slave, even by their master, was considered murder and punishable by law, and separating a slave's family was prohibited. Starting from the 11th century, Tatars, Arabs, and Turks took millions of European slaves.

The "European" slave trade was initiated by the Portuguese in 1441. The need for labor force in the American colonies, on plantations, meant that this trade flourished. Slave traders had no moral dilemmas; they forcibly baptized slaves to "save" their souls, then sold them as ready-made Christians. The slave trade was a state monopoly, and traders bought licenses.

Through piracy, the English also entered the slave trade, especially as piracy was supported by the British crown. John Hawkins (a merchant, owner, commander, and shipbuilder, one of the three admirals of the English fleet in the confrontation with the *Invincible Armada* in 1588) captured a Portuguese slave ship in 1562, selling the slaves for his own gain in the Caribbean. He was assisted by Francis Drake. The slave trade business grew exponentially. In 1602, the Dutch established the Dutch East India Company, which competed with and eventually ousted the Portuguese from this trade. Italians, French, Swedes, and Danes also entered the profitable "enterprise". In 1807, Great Britain and the USA banned the slave trade. Britain abolished slavery in the Caribbean in 1834 and in India in 1861; France abolished slavery in 1848.

THE FALL OF CONSTANTINOPLE

The fall of the capital of the Byzantine Empire into the hands of the Turks marked the end of an important **1453** chapter in European history. Many Greek scholars fled to the Italian peninsula, catalyzing the spirit of the Renaissance. Much theological knowledge reached Moldova. With the overland route to India cut off, oceanic explorations were propelled. Constantinople fell, but a few Byzantine state structures went on for some years: Morea (Peloponnese) until 1460, Trebizond (Anatolia) until 1461, and Theodosia (Caffa-Crimea) until 1475.

TOWARDS THE UNITY OF SPAIN

The marriage of Isabella, the heir of Castile, and **1469** Ferdinand, the heir of Aragon, in 1469, led to the unification of Spain, accomplished by their grandson Charles V, Quintus, in 1516.

TU FELIX AUSTRIAE NUBE

After expanding Burgundy to its maximum extent, from Marseille to Amsterdam and annexing Alsace **1477** and Lorraine in 1477, Charles the Bold (1467-1477), Duke of Burgundy, died in the Battle of Nancy. The French king Louis XI the Prudent (1461-1483) took over the Duchy of Burgundy. The other provinces of Charles the Bold came under the possession of the Habsburgs through the marriage of his daughter and heiress, Mary, to Maximilian of Austria. Then, their son, Philip the Handsome (b. 1478 – d. 1506), a Habsburg, married Joanna the Mad (b. 1479 – d. 1555) in 1494, the daughter of the kings of Spain, Ferdinand and Isabella. Through a series of deaths, Joanna became the sole heiress in Spain by 1500. In the same year, a son was born to them, the future Charles V (b. 1500 – d. 1558). Thus, the Burgundian inheritance (the Low Countries, Luxembourg, Franche-Comté) passed to Charles V, King of Spain and Holy Roman Emperor.

THE END OF THE RECONQUISTA

1492

The Emirate of Granada, the last Moorish stronghold in Iberia, fell after a year of siege. Ferdinand of Aragon (1475-1512) and Isabella of Castile (1474-1504) liberated Spain, almost 500 years after the start of the Reconquista and 800 years after the arrival of the Moors. Ferdinand also remained the ruler of Sicily and Naples after a succession dispute with the French kings Charles VII and Louis XII.

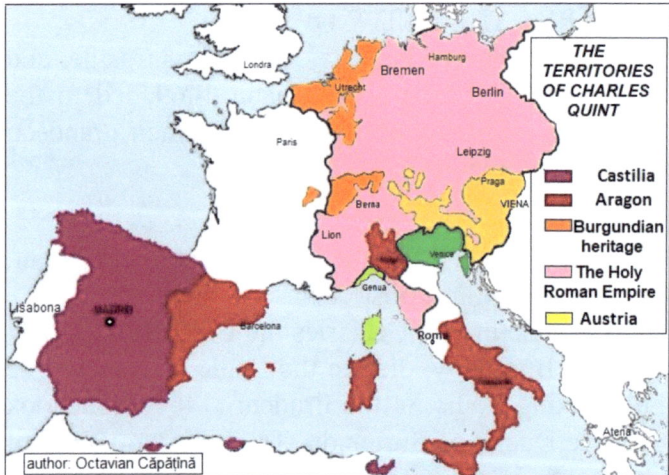

Fig. 19. The European territories of Charles V

132

CHARLES V

Charles I of Spain (1516-1556) was proclaimed Emperor of the Holy Roman Empire in 1519, under the name Charles V (Quint). Spain became the leading European power; under the Emperor's rule were the **1519** Holy Roman Empire, Spain, Sicily, Sardinia, the Kingdom of Naples, the Duchy of Milan, the Low Countries, Central America and a part of South America. Charles held sway over an empire where the sun never set, but also faced a significant problem, the Reformation. In 1530, he convened the Diet of the Holy Roman Empire in Augsburg to seek an agreement with the Lutherans. An agreement was not reached; instead, conflict ensued. His victory over the Protestant princes in 1547 at the Battle of Mühlberg did not restore religious unity in the west. Through the Treaties of Adrianople (1545) and Constantinople (1547), Charles and Suleiman the Magnificent, an ally of France, committed to ending hostilities. Charles V grew weary; at Augsburg in 1555, a peace treaty was signed with the Lutherans based on the principle *Cuius regio, eius religio* (*Whose realm, his religion*). An exception was made for imperial cities where each ruler could practice either the Catholic or Lutheran faith.

THE RISE OF SWEDEN

1523

In 1523, Gustav Vasa (1523-1560), elected as the King of Sweden, established a powerful medieval state by centralizing both secular and religious authority. His first action was to decline Danish sovereignty.

THE GERMAN PEASANTS' WAR

1524

It was a widespread bloody popular revolt that occurred in the German territories from 1524 to 1525. It was suppressed by the aristocracy, which killed around one-third of the approximately 300.000 peasants who had taken up arms. The peasants' demands were both economic and religious. The movement was led by peasants and Protestant clerics. Lacking artillery and cavalry, and due to the movement's democratic nature, it lacked a unified military command structure. It was the largest popular uprising in Europe before the French Revolution. Survivors were severely punished, and few of their demands were met.

FRANCE FORCED TO GIVE UP ITALY

1525

Through his victory at the Battle of Pavia in 1525, over King Francis I of France (1515-1547), Charles V compelled the defeated Francis to relinquish Genoa, Milan (conquered in 1498), and all claims to Naples through the Treaty of Madrid.

THE PASHALIK OF BUDA

1526

1541

1688

After the Ottoman victory at the Battle of Mohács in 1526 and the fall of the fortress of Buda (Ofen) in 1541, the Ottomans, led by Suleiman, transformed Pannonia, the medieval Catholic kingdom known as Hungary, into an Ottoman province, a pashalik. The Ottomans besieged the gates of Vienna; Catholic France consistently sided with the Ottomans.

THE UNION OF BRETAGNE WITH THE KINGDOM OF FRANCE

1532

The conflict between the Duchy of Bretagne and the Kingdom of France, spanning from 1465 to 1491, ended shortly after the death of the Duke of Bretagne,

Francis II, in 1488, as his daughter was forced to marry Charles VIII (1491-1498) of France in 1491. Through this personal union, where Bretagne retained its autonomy, France avoided being encircled by the Habsburgs and became a maritime power. In 1532, the Breton Parliament, partly through intimidation, signed an Act of Union with France in Nantes, which also respected a certain degree of Breton autonomy.

SEPARATION OF THE ENGLISH CHURCH FROM ROME

Henry VIII (1509-1547), initially strongly attached to the Catholic Church, triggered the autonomy of the Church of England when the Pope refused to annul his marriage to Catherine of Aragon. He declared himself the head of the Church, and thus, the *annates* (taxes paid to the Vatican) remained within the realm. This had happened earlier in France in 1438. The Anglican Church is more of an autonomous entity, separate from the Vatican, rather than a Protestant church in the sense developed by Luther and Calvin.

1534 - 1563

THE COUNCIL OF TRENT, THE COUNTER-REFORMATION

The Council of Trent began in 1545, was interrupted and resumed multiple times, with the initial goal of restoring unity to the Western Church. It concluded after 24 years and solidified the definitive rupture between Catholics and Protestants. Not only Luther in 1517 and the more radical Calvin in 1534, but also the separation of the Church of England had become insurmountable challenges for Rome. For former Catholics, now radicalized Protestants, Rome had become synonymous with Sodom and Gomorrah,

1545 - 1569

and any reconciliation was deemed impossible. In contrast, the Council of Trent itself became insurrectional: not to the theory of predestination by Augustine, but to that of Thomas Aquinas, who admitted that reason can operate autonomously within the theological framework, just as man is autonomous in relation to God. The acceptance of Thomistic theory essentially meant the acceptance of Pelagianism, the concept of the "heretic" Pelagius (354–420), long forgotten. The counter-reformation movement, initiated from below, was followed by a radical change in attitude among the higher ranks of the Catholic Church. The indulgence in monasteries was curtailed, strict discipline was introduced, monks cared for the sick and assisted the poor. The place of Popes who collected art or thirsted for power and had relative morality was taken by serious individuals. Ignatius of Loyola, a Basque nobleman and former military man, founded the Jesuit order, based on military discipline, an order that specialized in educating the youth. The order energetically and unscrupulously served the Vatican.

CUJUS REGIO, EJUS RELIGIO

1555

The religious peace of Augsburg between Catholics and Lutherans, which marked the failure of Charles V's religious policy, stipulated that the people should adopt the religion of their ruler. An exception was made for the imperial cities where citizens were free to practice the confession they wished, whether Catholic or Lutheran. The following year, Charles V stepped down from power, leaving his son Philip II of Spain and his brother Ferdinand I as Holy Roman Emperor.

THE UNION OF LUBLIN

1569 The personal union of Krewo in 1395 between the heiress of Poland and the Grand Duchy of Lithuania, whereby the two entities remained separate, no longer corresponded to the present dangers. The Grand Duchy of Lithuania was threatened by Sweden and by the Ottomans. Through a compromise between the Lithuanian and Polish nobility, the Union of Lublin was signed. The treaty provided for the establishment of a common Sejm (parliament) in which the lesser nobility (szlachta) participated, having the same rights as the magnates (higher nobility). The seniorial system changed into a manorial system, in which small landowners, even leaseholders, emerged, while the peasants declined into serfdom, becoming serfs.

LEPANTO, ANOTHER TURNING POINT

1571 The Spanish fleet, assisted by the Venitian fleet and financially supported by the Vatican, completely destroyed the numerically superior Ottoman fleet in the Gulf of Corinth, thus breaking the spell of Ottoman invincibility for the Westerners.

THE RELIGIOUS WARS IN FRANCE

1572 - 1598 The wars between Catholics and Huguenots began with bloody episodes, among which *the Massacre of Vassy* stands out, where over a hundred Protestants were slaughtered by the Duke of Guise. More gruesome massacres followed. Catholic Parisians killed 2.000 to 3.000 Protestants on the night of August 25, 1572, during *St. Bartholomew's Day Massacre*. Massacres continued in major provincial cities despite orders of tolerance issued by King Charles IX (1560-1574). Tens of thousands of Huguenots were slaughtered across France.

After 20 years of religious wars, Henry IV (1589-1610) guaranteed the confessional rights of Huguenots through the Edict of Nantes in 1598. From the beginning of the religious conflict in 1562 until 1598, millions of people fell victim. The Edict of Tolerance from 1598 was revoked by Louis XIV in 1685, leading many Huguenots to emigrate *en masse* to Protestant countries, with many settling in Prussia, particularly in Berlin.

THE PEOPLE TAKE ON THE TOLL OF SOVEREIGNTY

1581

Through the Declaration of Independence of the United Provinces (the Netherlands), established in 1579 through the "Union of Utrecht", Dutch deputies took upon themselves the burden of sovereignty that was once invested in King Philip II (1556-1598) *"by the grace of God."* Under the leadership of William of Orange, the Dutch revolted against Spain, the reigning sovereign power. The Spanish sovereign, Philip II, prepared to punish the rebels. In 1588, the *Invincible Armada* was assembled on large ships. It was destroyed by storms, fog and the skill of the English and Dutch. Thus, the boundless "pride" of the Dutch remained unpunished. The Republic of the United Provinces was officially recognized by Spain only in 1648, at the Peace of Westphalia. Since the pope had lost the prerogative of crowning the emperor and the use of excommunication no longer impressed, sovereigns were directly considered "anointed" by God on Earth, as no one dared to challenge the rights of royalty. This myth, however, began to unravel in 1581, but was only destroyed later: in 1649 with the execution of the King of England, in 1793 with the execution of the King of France, and in 1945 when the Emperor of Japan renounced being considered divine. In the opposite direction, Peter the Great (1696-1725) assumed the prerogatives of an absolute monarch by subordinating the Russian Church Synod, whose decisions required his approval.

SPAIN SETS, ENGLAND RISES

Spain was still the largest continental and maritime power. Maintaining this power required **1588** significant material and human efforts. Spain relied predominantly on the exploitation of resources from the New World. England, drawn by the great riches of Portugal and Spain overseas, capitalized on its maritime vocation. The Spanish royal court watched with unease as Protestant England began to threaten its naval supremacy, inevitably leading to conflict. Furthermore, taking advantage of the vacant Portuguese throne, the armies of Philip II occupied the neighboring kingdom in 1580. Portuguese colonies now pumped resources into Spain. England's response was not far behind; it materialized in the signing of an alliance treaty with the Netherlands in 1585. In 1588, the *Invincible Armada* (consisting of 130 ships) attacked the coasts of England and the United Provinces. Despite being outnumbered, the English and Dutch ships maintained their distance and subjected the Spanish ships to sustained artillery fire. English cannons were of a larger caliber, but their clear superiority lay in their mobile mounts, which provided a higher rate of fire and better firing angles. As bourgeois power rose, feudal power declined.

THE MODERN THINKING

Modern thinking was the product of the European bourgeoisie, which was on the rise, engaged in a struggle against feudal aristocracy to secure political positions from which to consolidate its economic power. The values of this current of ideas, typically bourgeois, are labor, property and freedom. The individual of the Middle Ages was contemplative, while the modern individual became active. Wealth depended on labor, prestige and freedom on wealth. Before Marx, before Hegel, Luther promoted this value – labor. He said, *"The diligent servant who sweeps the courtyard is dearer to me than the fat monk who prays all day."* People aspired to absolute freedom, yet this was limited by the absolute freedom of another individual. The modern idea of a social contract between the people and the ruler emerged: the people relinquished some of their freedom in favor of the sovereign, who in return provided them with personal security. If the sovereign did not uphold the social contract, the people could revoke it. Modernism also referred to the fundamental relationship between humans and nature, with nature being the object of transformative human action. The modern individual realized that in transforming nature, knowledge was necessary – *scientia est potentia*. Modern philosophy rediscovered nature, which scholastic philosophy had neglected as the devil's realm. In contrast to the Middle Ages, whose ideal was *complexity*, the ideal of modernism was *simplicity*. Nature works in the simplest way possible, the modern spirit says (this preconception was later refuted by the extraordinary wastefulness observed in nature). Nature contains a mathematician who optimizes resources to achieve goals and finds the simplest path. The great issue of Modernism was no longer an ontological problem, but a problem of knowledge, that is, the trinomial of God, nature, and man. The pragmatic Francis Bacon wrote, *"Philosophy is stamped with a triple mark: the mark of the power of God, the mark of natural differences and the mark of human utility."* The new concept of *knowledge* was about *nature* as the object and *man* as the subject. The most important representatives of Modernism were Francis Bacon (1561-1626) and René Descartes (1596-1650), the former illustrating Empiricism and the latter Rationalism. Their concepts did not come from a mere rejection of Aristotelian scholasticism, but from a revulsion towards it. Bacon undertook the task of developing a new, suitable method that, in contrast to sterile scholasticism, favored knowledge through investigation and experimentation, with the goal of humans dominating nature: from servant of nature to master of nature. Descartes focused on the qualitative aspect of knowledge, that which doubted: rational knowledge had to be cleansed of all errors.

THE EVOLUTION OF PUBLIC LAW

From the Greco-Roman heritage, medieval thinkers retained the three forms of political organization: the rule of the one chosen by the gods (monarchy), the rule of the good (aristocracy), and the rule of the many (democracy), with their extremes – tyranny, oligarchy, and anarchy. An adaptation was attempted with a view to the religious absolute state of the time. I have already mentioned Jean Bodin, who linked the absolute sovereignty of kings to the sovereign's respect for justice and tolerance towards subjects. John Milton (1608-1674), poet and thinker, clearly defined the source of rights in 1641: *"The power of kings and judges is nothing but a derived, transmitted, and entrusted power from the people, for its common good, which actually retains this power that cannot be taken away without violating its natural birthright."* This laid the foundation for modern constitutional law.

Thomas Hobbes (1588-1679) translated Thucydides' *History of the Peloponnesian War*, from which he derived some ideas.

141

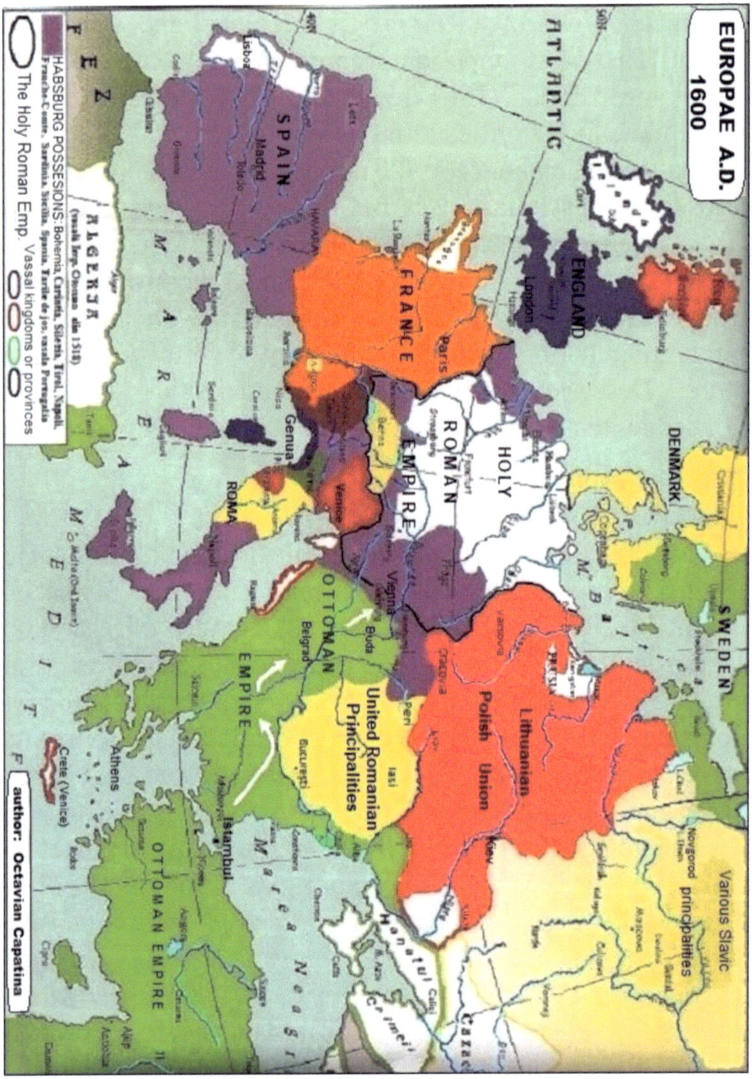

Fig. 20. Political map of Europe in 1600

142

Starting from the observation that a democratic government cannot survive a war, he believed that democracy would be an undesirable form of governance. Much later, in 1651, in *Leviathan*, Hobbes assumed that humans and mankind engage in *bellum omnium contra omnes* (the war of all against all), and he concluded that they must enter into an "imaginary" contract by which individual rights were transferred to the state. The legitimacy of the state also lay in its duty to guarantee the security of its citizens.

In 1690, John Locke (1632-1704) in his work *Two Treatises of Government*, went further and rejected absolutism and the divine right of monarchs, as everyone possesses inalienable natural rights to life, liberty and property. People were differentiated by the sum of their own experiences and observations. The theoretical contemplation of suitable forms of governance concluded with Charles de Montesquieu (1689-1755), who proposed the principle of the separation of powers within the state. In the eastern part, everything remained frozen; in 1721, the Moscow Synod certified that the Tsar was the deputy of God and the Church Synod had to submit to him.

THE FIRST UNION OF THE ROMANIANS

Michael the Brave (1593-1601), the ruler of Wallachia, led the anti-Ottoman uprising in **1600** southeastern Europe immediately after ascending to the throne. Mihai crossed the Danube into the Balkans. Aron Vodă of Moldavia also came against the Turks in Dobrogea. Such a tempest the Turks had never seen coming upon them. The punitive expedition led by Sinan Pasha, the victor over the Persians, resulted in the defeat of the Turks at Călugăreni (1595). Pagans in the front and on the sides, and "Christians" in the rear – Cardinal Bathory, who became the voivode of Transylvania, allied with the Turks. In 1599, Michael the Brave had no choice

143

but to crush the cardinal near Sibiu and enter Alba Iulia as the prince of Transylvania. In May 1600, he also conquered Moldavia, where the boyars were playing into the hands of the Poles, who were allied with the Turks.

THE LIBERATION OF MOSCOW

1612

After some early victories of the Polish-Lithuanian Union over the Muscovites, culminating in the occupation of Moscow in 1610 and the election of the son of Sigismund III Vasa (Swedish), as the prince of Moscow, the positions of the two forces balanced. In 1612, the Poles and Lithuanians were expelled from Moscow, but other territories remained under Lithuanian control. The war ended in 1618 with the Truce of Deulino. The Polish-Lithuanian Union gained minor territorial gains but lost control over Moscow. After the expulsion of Vladislav Vasa (1610-1613), Mikhail Romanov (1631-1645) was elected as the prince of Muscovites.

THE THIRTY YEARS' WAR

1618
-
1648

The fighting camps were formed in the Holy Roman Empire as early as 1608/09: the Evangelical Protestant Union and the Catholic League – but the spark was missing. It came from a fanatical Jesuit, the new king of Bohemia, the Holy Roman Emperor – Ferdinand II of Habsburg (1619-1637), who did not recognize the Peace of Augsburg anymore. He attempted to limit the freedoms of the Hussite and Lutheran subjects. Bohemia rebelled (the Defenestration of Prague) and even brought in a Lutheran king. In the first ten years, the victories were on the side of the imperial forces. The Protestant princes, overwhelmed by the imperial forces, sought help from Denmark, France and Sweden. The intervention of Gustav II of Sweden in 1630 saved Protestantism in the north. France, which sponsored **1634** the war against Austria, effectively entered the war in 1634, alongside the Protestants. After another 14 years of fighting, the war ended through the exhaustion of the combatants. After a century of religious animosity and a bloody war of thirty years, the population of Europe decreased by about a third. The political winner was France; however, it lost around 200.000 productive and inventive citizens who fled to Protestant countries. Many went to Prussia. *The Peace of Westphalia.* After repeated armed interventions by Denmark, Sweden and France in favor of the German Lutheran princes, Emperor Ferdinand III of Habsburg (1637-1657) was forced to respect the terms of the religious peace established at Augsburg (1555), but this time also for Calvinists. Furthermore, he was made to observe the sovereignty of all states within the Holy Roman Empire, and any 1642 remaining imperial privileges had to be approved by the Imperial Diet. The Holy Roman Empire – the main stage of the Thirty Years' War – already a fiction, thus became a confederation of independent states and cities. Switzerland and the Low Countries separated from the Empire and were recognized as independent states. France gained a portion of Alsace, while Sweden acquired Pomerania and Bremen (at the mouths of the Weser, Elbe, and Oder rivers), while Brandenburg (Prussia) expanded.

THE THIRD ROME
After the decline of the South Slavic cultural centres and the fall of Byzantium, *Rome*, the third one,

moved to the Romanian lands (see M. Eliade). Metropolitan Varlaam, Peter Movilă, Dosoftei and the scholar N. Milescu preserved the spirit of Byzantium in Iași for two centuries. While the Muscovites were just liberating themselves from the Poles and Lithuanians, the ruler of Moldavia, Prince Vasile Lupu (1634-1653), held the leadership of the Eastern Patriarchates, a true Byzantine emperor to whom the patriarchs were submissive (see N. Iorga). Vasile Lupu undertook the task of financial administration of the Eastern Church, which was in complete decline and insolvent, in exchange for seeking to be followed and to have control over it. That is to say: 1) metropolitans had to leave Constantinople, where they were only occupied with betrayals and sales, and return to their bishoprics; 2) The new individual tax, *zetia*, added to the old tax, was no longer demanded, and no other collective tax was imposed; 3) The patriarch's management was subject to annual auditing by a committee; 4) the heads of bishoprics were no longer appointed through simony. In return, Vasile Lupu paid the historical and current debts of the Eastern Church. Here are three episodes that Iorga referred to as *Byzantium after Byzantium*.

a) The synod of the Eastern Church held in Iași in 1642 approved the *"Orthodox Confession"* of Metropolitan Peter Movilă of Kiev (1633-1646), which became the normative work for all of Orthodoxy. In 1645, the *"Orthodox Confession"* was translated into Russian by the same author. Years later, the Russian scholar Venelin wondered: *"The question arises, which of the two men named Peter is the audacious reformer of the Russian Empire and who, therefore, deserves the historical title of "the Great": Peter, Emperor of Russia, or the Romanian Peter Movilă?"*

b) In Christian dogmatics, it was important to know whether the spirit of the Savior is present or not in the sacrament of communion. Nicolae Milescu (1637-1708) took part in the dispute between Jansenism and Calvinism in the West regarding the question of transubstantiation through his work *Enchiridion sive Stella Orientalis Occidentali splendens, id est sensus Ecclesiae Orientalis, scilicet graece de transsubstantione Corporis Domini, aliisque controversial... (A Small Book or The Star of the East Shining in the West, that is, the opinion of the Eastern Church on the transformation of the Lord's Body and other controversies...)*, written in Greek and Latin. The work was requested by the French ambassador to Sweden and was published in Latin in 1669, in a volume entitled *La perpetuite de la foi de l'Eglise catholique touchant l'Eucharistie.* 1667

c) Orthodox Ukrainians joined the Reformed view on the issue of transubstantiation. The Russian Church, more lenient, was also perplexed, as it was based on old Slavonic texts that were incorrectly translated from the beginning. At this point, the great Metropolitan Dosoftei intervened, translating from the original Greek into Russian: *Saint Symeon of Thessalonica on the transubstantiation of the Holy Gifts, the Apostolic Constitutions...* While the Moscow Patriarchate was preparing to anathematize Kiev, Dosoftei clarified the error that had occurred to the Metropolitan of Kiev and removed the split. Furthermore, the great Russian culture began with Antiochus Cantemir, the son of Prince Dimitrie Cantemir. 1690

THE IRISH REBELLION

1641   Through the forced introduction of Anglicanism in Ireland, the anti-English movement received vigorous support from the Catholic Church. The anti-English movement was brutally suppressed by Cromwell in 1649, allowing English settlers to establish themselves in Northern Ireland.

Fig. 21. The sculpture of the "Three Hierarchs" church. Iasi 1642

THE ENGLISH CIVIL WAR AND SUCCESSION

The outbreak of war between the Royalists and the Parliamentarians, led by Cromwell, in 1642, ended **1642** with Parliament's victory at Preston in 1648. After the execution of King Charles I Stuart in 1649, England became a republic. Monarchy was restored after Cromwell's death in 1660, but Parliament took care to limit the king's powers through the *Habeas Corpus* 1679 *Act – your body belongs to you (1679)*. According to this document, no Englishman could be imprisoned without being informed of the reasons for his imprisonment, and he had the right to answer to accusations before a court. After the abdication of the last Stuart, James II (1685-1688), William of Orange, the husband of Mary, daughter of James II, was proclaimed king in 1689 under the name William III (1689-1702); thus, constitutional monarchy began through the royal signing of the *Declaration of Rights* and *The Bill of Rights*. According to this document, the king no longer had the right to dismiss judges and could not overturn Parliament's decisions. These 1690 events known as *The Glorious Revolution* represented the complete victory of English parliamentarism. John Locke laid the foundation for the concept of constitutional monarchy in 1690. After Queen Anne Stuart (1702-1714), who had no heirs, on the throne of Great Britain came George Ludwig, Elector of Hanover, the great-grandson of James II, ruled as George I (1714-1727).

DIVIDE ET IMPERA: A NEW CONFESSION

1646

The occupation of Slovak and Ruthenian territories by the Habsburgs after the transformation of Pannonia into a Turkish province in 1540 allowed Catholic missionaries to influence the religious choices of the indigenous people. In 1646, 63 Orthodox Ruthenian clerics were received into the Catholic Church while retaining the Byzantine rite. In 1664, other communities joined the new confession. The new confession gave the faithful the appearance of preserving the old belief. And so a new church, a new confession, the Greek Catholic Church, was created. The "Union" of some of the Transylvanian Orthodox with the Church of Rome was done on contractual terms and with the preservation of the traditional rite, so that the believers would not feel a change. The unification was enforced by the ruling power, Austria, with the aim of controlling the new province based on the well-known principle of *divide et impera*. The future Greek Catholic priests, trained in Rome, became the main forces behind the emancipation of Romanians from all provinces.

1701
-
1744

CHANGING LORDS

1654

The Cossacks, a multiethnic population (Romanians, Tatars, Slavs) from the northern shores of the Sea of Azov, who lived off raids, decided to switch their allegiance from Lithuanian-Polish protection to Muscovy, due to the Polish arrogance, under the leadership of Hetman Bogdan Khmelnytsky. This had significant geopolitical consequences, and the Polish-Lithuanian Union declined.

THE OLD BELIEVERS

1666

Metropolitan Nikon of Moscow (1652-1658), upon realizing that many original religious texts had been falsely translated, began the improvement of texts and religious practices. A significant role was played by the learned Romanian metropolitans Varlaam, Petru Movilă and Dosoftei. Nikon did not sufficiently explain his changes to the hierarchs and faced strong opposition from them and the faithful. Moreover, Nikon anathematized the "rebels". The secular power supported the metropolitans. Entire villages were burned, churches were demolished, books and icons were burned and protesters were sentenced to death. The adherents of the old practices – the Raskolniki (Old Believers) – who survived, fled beyond the territories controlled by Muscovite and canonically separated from the new Muscovite Church in 1666.

A LOST OPPORTUNITY

Vienna was saved from the Turks by the victory at Kahlenberg of Charles of Lorraine (b. 1643 – d. 1690), originally from France, and Jan Sobieski, the king of the Polish-Lithuanian Commonwealth. Thus began the decline of the Ottomans who, until the Battle of Zărnești, in 1690, had only been defeated by the Austrians. The Austrians had occupied the Pannonian Pashalik as early as 1686. The Austrian victory over the Turks at Mohács (on the Tisza River, now in Hungary) in 1687 confirmed the Turks' retreat. It seemed that nothing was stopping the Austrians. The defeatism among the Turks was so great that if the offensive campaign led by Eugene of Savoy, a general in the Austrian army, had continued, the Turks would likely have been pushed beyond the Bosporus. But, France's attack on the Holy Roman Empire in 1688, when the French crossed the Rhine and occupied the Palatinate, and Prince Eugene of Savoy was moved to

1683

1690

the western front, eased the Ottoman situation. In the east, due to the behavior of the Austrian army in Transylvania – looting and offending – even the Saxons opposed them. Under the Turks 10 Transylvanian families (considered to be "a gate") paid a maximum of 22 florins in taxes, while, under the Austrians, the payment abruptly increased to 250. The Austrian intention was to encompass the Romanian principalities within the empire, which were frightened by what the "imperialists" were doing in Transylvania. Even though a part of the Austrian armies were already in Wallachia (Oltenia), Constantin Brâncoveanu decided to confront them near Brașov. The battle took place at Zărnești in 1690. Here, the Austrians suffered their first defeat against the Turks and Wallachians since the beginning of the campaign. With Prince Eugene of Savoy stationed on the western front, Austria halted the offensive. Returning to the eastern, Eugene of Savoy achieved

1697   another victory in 1697 at Zenta (Serbia) against the Turks, a victory that was solidified by the Treaty of Karlowitz in 1699. The Ottomans ceded the Turkish provinces of Hungary, Croatia, and Slovenia to Austria. Transylvania exchanged Ottoman suzerainty for Austrian sovereignty.

THE ENLIGHTENMENT

Sapere aude (dare to know) – we could say in hindsight that this would have been the most fitting motto for that period known as the *Enlightenment*; a time dominated by an ideological and cultural movement that was antifeudal and antidogmatic. Francis Bacon's empiricism, Spinoza's pantheism, Isaac Newton's scientific discoveries, René Descartes' rationalism, and the new theories of governance by Milton, Hobbes and Locke promoted and solidified belief in the laws of nature and confidence in human reason. But it is also important to note that the roots of the Enlightenment are much older and were brought back to European consciousness with the Reformation and Counter-Reformation. Thomas Aquinas (1224-1274), who definitively departed from Augustine's theology of predestination, argued that human freedom, individual autonomy, far from being limited by the relationship with God, were, on the contrary, secured by that relationship. This observation, accepted by the Counter-Reformation, put an end to one of the "errors" of Catholic doctrine. Martin Luther (1483-1546), even though he didn't stray from the Augustinian dogmatic conception of predestination, reimagined the world, which was remarkable and fruitful in itself. In England, the philosophy of reason "inspired" parliamentary resistance to royal absolutism and the beheading of a king, events that propelled English society towards constitutionalism. English ideas spread to the continent, especially to France, the strongest link in despotism and privilege. Descartes' country was also a place of reason's worship, which indicates that the English seed fell on a doubly fertile ground of revolution. Here emerged three significant works that stirred European consciousness: Montesquieu's *The Spirit of the Laws* published in 1748, Buffon's *Natural History* of 1749, and *the Encyclopedia* (29 volumes), coordinated by Diderot and D'Alembert, published between 1751 and 1780. The Enlightenment culminated in the French Revolution; today's world is an inheritance of the Enlightenment. In the Germanic space, both French rationalism and English empiricism flourished, but their synthesis through Herder (1744-1803) was marked by a national element. The ideas of English and French Enlightenment thus penetrated Germany, and Enlightenment flourished under Leibniz's patronage. The *Erklärung* remained within the confines of a rationalistic approach, but marked by strong theological issues that couldn't be disregarded. According to Kant, the

Enlightenment was an era of transitioning from childhood to majority; from Descartes onwards, it was accepted that reason was a faculty possessed by each individual, the problem being that people didn't know how to use this gift; Kant referred to the incapacity to autonomously use this gift as childhood. Kant's mission for the Enlightenment was to generalize critical thinking: everything was to be brought before the judgment seats of reason. From English empiricism emerged what could be termed *English exceptionalism* from all perspectives; unlike the Sun King, who controlled his nobility by quartering them in Versailles, the English monarch sent their lords into the territories to look after their affairs and those of the kingdom.

MUSKOWIA'S AWAKENING

1700   The old Muscovite dynasty, descending from the Viking Rurik, came to an end in 1598. After Tatar Boris Godunov (1598-1605) and the Swede Vladislav Vasa (1610-1613), the Muskowy boyars chose one of their own, the child Michael Romanov, as master. His great-grandson, Peter the Great (1672-1725), ascended to the throne at the young age of 17 in 1689, and he became associated with the effort to Europeanize this Tatar-Slavic country. The terms "Rus" and "Russia" to designate the lands and populations ruled by Muscovy gradually came into force after the reign of Peter. He aimed to transform all of Russia in the shortest possible time. Starting his rule with a lengthy journey through Northern Europe, Peter governed through decrees. He brought officers, craftsmen and engineers from the West. He drained swamps, built roads, cities and canals. He established schools, high schools, universities and hospitals. He developed a new civil code. Since the reforms could not be sustainable as long as the old boyars still had a say in the Moscow Duma, he constructed a new capital, St. Petersburg, on land wrested from the Swedes. In 1722, after the Treaty of Nystad (1721), Peter replaced the position of the patriarch with a Synod of prelates, where he was represented by a layman. Nevertheless, the Synod's decisions required his approval. He made serving the Tsar the sole basis of the social status of the subjects. Sweden, which ruled over territories inhabited by Finns and Estonians, did not view the Russians' appearance on the Baltic coast favorably. War broke out between Russia, Poland, Denmark, Saxony on one side, and Sweden on the other. Initially, the armies of Peter the Great were defeated by Charles XII in the famous Battle of Narva. After that, Charles turned against the others and for 9 years devastated and burned the Danish, Saxon, and Polish villages and towns. In the meantime, Peter brought officers from the West and trained his army. In the confrontation with Charles at Poltava (Ukraine), where Charles was wounded, Russia emerged victorious. Peter left behind a somewhat trained army and a fleet of dozens of ships built by the Dutch and Scots. Russia became a power to be reckoned with in Northern Europe. However, the connection to modernity, as much as could be achieved—a thin layer over the backward Slavic-Tatar entity —was to be achieved by an energetic German princess who became Empress Catherine II (1762-96).

THE RISE OF PRUSSIA

Frederick I (1701-1713) was accepted by the Holy Roman Emperor Leopold I in 1701 through a legal subterfuge, not as the King of Prussia but as the "King

1701

155

In Prussia", a sandy and desolate land situated beyond the borders of the Holy Roman Empire. Both he and his son Frederick Wilhelm I (1713-1740) subordinated all their individual aspirations to the common interest. Then his grandson, Frederick II (1740-1786), continued their work and transformed Prussia from a battleground of Danes, Swedes, Poles, French and Austrians into a new country with good roads, good schools, and a well-trained army. Although he didn't accept advice and all officials were his servants, Frederick II considered himself a servant of his people, and so he was.

THE UNION BETWEEN SCOTLAND AND ENGLAND

1707
After the personal union of the two countries in 1603 under James VI of Scotland, the successor to Elizabeth I on the throne of England, the actual union of the two kingdoms was signed in 1707 under the name of the Kingdom of Great Britain. In 1800, the English, hoping to eliminate Irish distinctiveness, added the Kingdom of Ireland to the Union.

THE TREATIES OF UTRECHT AND RASTADT

1713 - 1714
The end of the War of the Spanish Succession between Austria and France (1702-1704), through the Treaty of Utrecht, confirmed the success of British power-balancing politics. The "Spanish inheritance" was divided. Philip V of the House of Bourbon retained Spain and its colonial empire. Austria held onto the Catholic Netherlands (Belgium), as well as Milan, Naples, and Sardinia. Savoy received Sicily, which was exchanged for Sardinia in 1720. Great Britain obtained Gibraltar.

PRAGMATIC SANCTION AND SUCCESSION

The Salic Law of succession no longer aligned with historical interests. Emperor Charles VI (1711-1740) addressed the "Salic" issue through the Pragmatic Sanction, which allowed for female succession to the throne. After the emperor's death, the War of the Austrian Succession followed, concluding with the recognition of Empress Maria Theresa's succession.

1713

AN UNPARALLELED MARTYR

The martyrs of early Christianity were regarded as saints. Deacon Stephen, a disciple of the Savior, was stoned outside the walls of Jerusalem for professing faith in Jesus, becoming the first martyr and saint of the Church. Then came apostles like Paul and Peter, and many others. But none quite like the voivode of Wallachia, Constantin Brâncoveanu (1688-1714), who, along with his entire family, was taken to Constantinople in April 1714. There, he was tortured to relinquish his vast wealth to the Turks, accused of plotting against the suzerain power. On August 15th, the Feast of the Assumption, before the Sultan, Constantin Brâncoveanu witnessed the beheading, one by one, of his counselor and son-in-law, Ianache Văcărescu, and his sons Constantin (27 years old), Ştefan (25 years old), Radu (23 years old?), and Matei (16 years old). Matei, with his head on the block, addressed his father: *"Let me live my youth. I would rather become a Muslim than die innocent."* The Romanian voivode remained unmoved. Afterwards, he was also executed after refusing clemency. The price of clemency was renouncing the Christian faith and converting to Islam. The martyrs' heads, impaled on spears, were paraded throughout Constantinople.

1714

Their bodies, after being thrown into the Bosporus, were secretly retrieved by Lady Marica Brâncoveanu and given a Christian burial in the country.

THE DIVISION OF STATES

The division of the Polish-Lithuanian Commonwealth. Almost two centuries after Poles and Lithuanians established a prince in Moscow and a century after they saved Vienna from Ottoman siege, the Polish-Lithuanian Commonwealth was divided among Prussia (Frederick the Great), Russia (Catherine the Great), and Austria (Maria Theresa) multiple times in 1772, 1793, and 1795. During the Restoration (Congress of Vienna in 1815), the Duchy of Warsaw, which had been established by Napoleon in 1807, was once again absorbed by Prussia and the Russian Empire.

1772 - 1815

The Division of Moldavia. Grigore Ghica III, who opposed the breaking apart of the country, was assassinated through the intrigues of Austria's Maria Theresa (1740-1780); Austria obtained the Upper Land of Moldavia through bribery in Constantinople. It couldn't obtain it directly due to the resistance of this uncompromising and unbuyable Romanian ruler.

1774

So *tu felix Austriae nube* was just one facet of Austria's expansion over numerous peoples; the other facets are now seen: *bribery and intrigue.*

The second partition of Moldavia. The delegates of Russia had received orders from Petersburg in May 1812 to conclude peace with the Ottoman Empire on any conditions, as Napoleon had invaded Russia. However, an English fleet stationed in the Bosporus forced the Sultan to make peace with the Russians.

1812

The Phanariot Moruzi, a Turkish official bought by the Russians, concluded the peace treaty in Bucharest on behalf of the Sultan. The Ottomans ceded something that did not belong to them, Bessarabia, to the Russians. The Turks were only suzerains, not sovereigns in the Romanian Principalities.

Dividing Eastern Europe.

In Moscow, on October 9, 1944, Winston Churchill proposed to Stalin the division of spheres of influence, which had much more dramatic consequences in Romania. Unlike all the other countries handed over to the Soviet sphere, Romania did not have its own communists and communist parties.

1944

Fig.22. The partition of Moldova and of The Polish-Lithuanian Commonwealth.

In Romania, communism was served by former Horthy supporters and Bolshevik Jews.

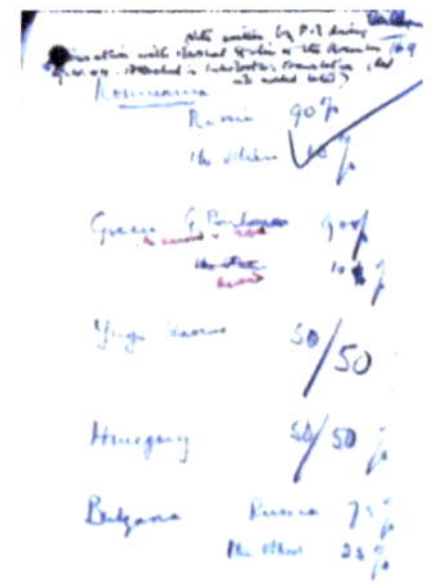

Fig. 23. Division of spheres of influence.
Churchill's proposal to Stalin

THE ERA OF SCIENCE AND TECHNOLOGY

As we have seen, the idea of understanding the world through experiments was old, its birth dating back to the time of Petrus Peregrinus de Maricourt and his disciple Roger Bacon (1214-1294). Leonardo da Vinci (1452-1519), who considered himself an "inventor" and not a "reciter", relied solely on experimentation. Another Bacon, Francis (1561-1626), laid the theoretical foundation for empiricism over centuries. Our senses provide certain knowledge and constitute the source of all knowledge, and true science is acquired through processing sensory data. Francis Bacon, through *Novum Organum* (1620), also laid the groundwork for the inductive method characterized by observation, experiment, comparison, and analysis. *Natural history*, with the vast material collected from Aristotle onwards through Carl Linnaeus, was classified (1735-58). This set the stage for evolutionism. The Scotsman James Watt provided humanity with the first usable steam pump and patented the first steam locomotive in 1784. However, the first locomotive was built according to the plans of Richard Trevithick; it operated in the Welsh mines in 1804. In 1821, the Englishman M. Faraday invented the electric generator, ushering in the era of electric current utilization. Germans Marcus (1864), Benz (1885) and Daimler (1889) separately constructed internal combustion engines, which they used for the propulsion of a tricycle and a carriage, respectively, thereby opening a new technical era. The Romanian Traian Vuia (1872-1950) also achieved the world's first airplane that took off under its own power on March 18, 1906. Prior to that, the Wright brothers' aircraft had taken off in December 1903, but not under its own power; it was catapulted. Between 1906 and 1910, Henri Coandă designed and built the aircraft and the jet engine, after Alex. Ciurcu and Just Buisson had set a boat in motion on the Seine in 1886 using the world's first jet engine. In 1908, Herman Oberth conceived the liquid-fuel rocket, using alcohol and oxygen in 1917 and hydrogen and oxygen in 1920. In 1921, he conceived the multi-stage rocket, and, in 1935, he created and launched the first rocket at Mediaş with liquid propellant (a mixture of fuels capable of strong exothermic reactions).

KANT. THE CLASSICAL GERMAN IDEALISM

Immanuel Kant (1724-1804) belongs to the *Enlightenment*, but he was the starting point of Classical German Idealism. Kant was the culmination, crisis and transcendence of the *Enlightenment*, according to W. Windelbrand. Modernity increasingly claimed the right to subject everything to criticism. Kant wrote the *Critique of Pure Reason* in 1781, starting from the idea that critical reason must be complemented with the critique of reason. The *Critique of Pure Reason* is explained by Vasile Muscă through four key ideas: 1) the Copernican inversion, 2) activism, 3) apriorism, and 4) agnosticism.

Copernican inversion. From Greek philosophy to Kant, the explanation of knowledge started from the object; Kant reverses this relationship, starting from the subject, from the human, as this is the center of the universe and knowledge is a creation of humans. The object depends on the subject, but not in an ontological sense. To avoid misunderstandings, Kant repeats everywhere that the object has an existence independent of humans; humans only create the gnoseological image of objects. From this distinction, Kant speaks of the *"thing-in-itself"* and the *"thing-for-us"*. Schopenhauer considered this demarcation as Kant's most important contribution to philosophy.

Activism. Kant shatters the myth of the *mirror-like consciousness*, which posits that the human intellect reflects reality. According to Kant, when God gave us reason and consciousness, He assigned to reason and consciousness a purpose that cannot be limited to reproducing reality. Reason and consciousness must have an active role and manifest themselves in the act of *knowing*. Ultimately, knowledge is the result of human activism. The idea of activism becomes a fundamental characteristic of Classical German Idealism.

Apriorism. Kant paid attention to the form of knowledge, which has an a priori character, meaning it is given before experience and enables any form of knowledge. Since empirical data is chaotic, it becomes useful when classified and ordered. Classification and ordering occur at the level of the intellect, where we have a priori forms known as concepts.

Agnosticism. The object, the *"thing-in-itself"*, is what has not been subjected to a priori forms. We know the image of the "thing-in-itself" offered by knowledge, and this "thing-for-us" is different from the "thing-in-itself". Therefore, we are condemned to agnosticism.

The Classical German Idealism emerged from Kant and encompassed philosophers such as Fichte (1762-1814), Schelling (1775-1854) and Hegel (1770-1831). Each considered the next as their disciple, but each was original to such an extent that the role of disciple can only be retained in a formal sense and not in terms of creation. All were Kantians, but Fichte adopted only Kant's terminology, just as Hegel adopted only Fichte's terminology. The final relationships between each and the next were marked by egos, leading to the intense enmity between Schelling and Hegel. According to Walter Schulz (Tübingen – see V. Muscă), the apex would be Schelling, not Hegel. Between the first manifestation of Classical German Idealism, the appearance of the *Critique of Pure Reason* (1781), and the publication of Hegel's *Lectures on the Philosophy of Right*, exactly 40 years passed. Historians of philosophy have noted the explosive character of this philosophical phenomenon, comparable only to classical Greek philosophy (Socrates, Plato, Aristotle). According to one interpreter of the phenomenon, it would be based on: 1) the revival of the Hellenic spirit (German culture did not participate in the Renaissance), flourishing in German Neohumanism, 2) the literary-philosophical parallelism, 3) the French Revolution. In fact, Marx referred to Classical German Idealism as the *"German theory of the French Revolution"*.

In response to Kant, Fichte believed that practical reason represents the essence of knowledge in its entirety and thus of humanity. He starts from a principle, the independent and sovereign ego from which all forms of knowledge are deduced. Hegel, on the other hand, departed from Kant's secular vision and deepened, at the same time, the historical Kantian vision of the world. According to Hegel, the model of thought is as follows: the positive thesis is negated by its antithesis, then the two are analyzed, resulting in a synthesis that reconciles contradictions; the synthesis, in turn, becomes an antithesis, and the process is repeated circularly; and the finite as the self-manifestation of God is a part of the infinite. Thought itself presupposes negation and synthesis as constituent parts; this is the dialectical thinking model he proposed. Hegel traced the becoming of human spirit step by step, starting with the subconscious, self-consciousness and rational will, passing through created institutions and human history, and finally reaching art, religion and philosophy; at this point, humans recognize themselves as spirit, as a gift from God. From his revolutionary youth, Hegel turned into a frightened conservative in old age. From Hegelianism emerged a left-wing current exploited by Feuerbach and later by Marx. Schelling believed that the *Absolute* manifests itself in each individual as a unity between the objective and the subjective. According to him, the *freedom* of humanity was real only when both good and evil acted.

FROM FORCED MAGYARIZATION TO GENOCIDE

In 1782, the Enlightenment emperor Joseph II (1780-1790) aimed to replace Latin with German as the official language of the empire. He did so based on the observation that the elites spoke German, while the subjects spoke German, Slavic idioms and Romanian. The census of 1725 showed that about 19% of people in Ofen (now Buda) and Pest knew the Hungarian language, a fact confirmed by the census of 1787. This intention of the emperor triggered the modern phase of Magyarization of the eastern peoples, which primarily targeted the Germans. The Germans were affected the most as they built the cities and held commerce and industry. Magyarization was carried out through schools and churches, but radicals demanded "blood". Indeed, at a certain point, if you spoke German on the street, you could get beaten with a stick, and signs written in German were smashed and so on. The last German-language theater performance in Budapest ended when young Hungarians led by the Slovak Kossuth (1802-1894) stormed the audience and actors with clubs. This is how the culture of hatred developed against anything non-Hungarian, directed towards Slovaks, Germans, Croats and Magyarized Romanians who wanted to be more Hungarian than the Hungarians themselves (see *The Image of the German in Hungarian Literature* by J. Weidlein). Once the culture of hatred was ignited, things progressed naturally towards genocide during opportune historical moments. In 1848, the first genocide in modern Europe occurred in Transylvania. Between 1940 and 1945, the second genocide took place in Transylvania, and between April and June 1944, *the Final Solution* was implemented. Continuous genocide occurred in Hungary and the territories ceded to Horthy by Hitler (see *Culture, Religion, Ethnicity and Race in the Central Danube Basin*). Amidst these tragic historical moments, Magyarization was carried out with a savagery that was difficult to bear, yet hard to ignore. Observers like Gheorghe Barițiu, Ioan Slavici, Stephan Ludwig Roth, Carl Klein, Nicolae Iorga, as well as Franz von Lőhrer, Johann Herder, Lev Tolstoy, Bjorm Björnson, Robert W. Seton-Watson, Bernard Shaw, Milton Lehrer, Johann Weidlein and others all noticed this.

THE REVOLUTION

The Declaration of Independence of the American colonies stated the natural rights to life, liberty and the pursuit of happiness. In 1784, Horea, *Rex Daciae*, the leader of the social uprising in the last feudal state in Europe, Transylvania, demanded the abolition of privileges: *everyone should pay taxes and earn their living through their work.* How could they earn a living through their work and still pay taxes without everyone being equal? The idea of equality, without privileges for some, became increasingly popular.

1776

1784

France was marked by layer upon layer of privileges granted to the nobility, clergy and magistrates. The country was poorly administered and corrupt – public offices were bought. The monarchy had been constantly at war for the past 40 years and was insolvent.

In these circumstances, King Louis XVI (1774-1792) was forced to convene the Estates General, which had not been assembled since 1614. Delegates of the Third Estate (merchants, artisans, peasants) from the National Assembly formed the Constituent Assembly, which decreed on August 4th: 1. All forms of tithe (tax owed to the Catholic clergy) are abolished; 2. The sale of judicial offices is abolished; 3. Justice is free; 4. Feudal courts are abolished; 5. All financial privileges are abolished; 6. Privileges of provinces, principalities, regions, cantons, cities, and municipalities are abolished; 7. Jurisprudence is aligned with common law; 8. All citizens, without distinction, are eligible for all ecclesiastical, civil, or military offices. In a matter of hours, the Constituent Assembly legislated as much as an enlightened century. Hegel, usually reserved in his declarations, noted: *a promising sunrise.* Austro-Prussian armies reached the northern border (July 1792) and threatened the young republic. Prussian General Brunswick demanded the restoration of the monarchy, otherwise offering *an exemplary and memorable military execution to Paris.* The people radicalized, and an army of volunteers faced the Prussians and Austrians, defeating them. France occupied the Catholic Low Countries and the left bank of the Rhine. From the enthusiasm of citizens defending their homeland, a formidable army emerged, feared by all the empires of Europe. For the accusation of complicity with the invaders, Louis XVI was executed on January 21, 1793. This was followed by a fierce competition among the bloodthirsty revolutionaries, each more demagogic than the other, a long period of

Aug. 4 1789

1792

gruesome and widespread assassinations that are difficult to imagine. Mass executions and assassinations were hidden or justified by "republican" historians.

The revolution, the idea of freedom, had a profound effect of awakening to reality among Europeans; from that moment on, they would refer to themselves, to their own lives. And so it has remained from then until today.

A SHOCK DELIVERED TO OLD EUROPE

After seizing power through the coup d'état on 18 Brumaire (November 9/10), the opportunist Napoleon **1799** Bonaparte became the "First Consul", effectively taking all power into his hands. After astonishing victories in Europe, Napoleon crowned himself "Emperor of the French" in the forced presence of the Pope (1804) at Notre-Dame Cathedral. Surrounded by capable young individuals, he reorganized French 1804 institutions. He updated Justinian's civil code (equality before the law, religious tolerance, the right to property, family security). In 1806, when Hegel 1806 saw him entering Jena on horseback, he saw in Napoleon the embodiment of the *spirit of the world*, as great personalities are mere instruments of *the absolute spirit*. After the French victories over Austria (Austerlitz 1805) and Prussia (Jena 1806), the Holy Roman Empire, founded in 962, disappeared. In 1806, Napoleon formed the Confederation of the Rhine from the southwestern German states. After the victories at Jena and Auerstedt (1807), Prussia was occupied. From the western territories previously dominated by Prussia,

Napoleon formed a new kingdom, Westphalia, composed of Hesse, Brunswick and southern Hanover. In 1807, Napoleon created the Duchy of Warsaw, subordinate to Saxony. Great Britain consolidated its maritime supremacy after the naval battle of Trafalgar (off the southern coast of Spain) in 1805. Despite the alliance with Russia (Treaty of Tilsit, 1807), the Continental Blockade was a failure. In 1808, Napoleon faced a guerrilla war in Spain that wore down his troops. After the victory at Wagram

1809 (1809), Austria, Prussia, and Denmark became allies of France, while other countries were either annexed, occupied or dominated. The only remaining enemies were England, Sweden, and Russia. In 1809, the British liberated Portugal. *An indecisive battle, similar to a defeat.* After the campaign in Russia, with the few

1812 surviving troops escaping the harsh conditions, France had to face a coalition of previously defeated Austria, Prussia, and Russia in the so-called "Battle of the

1813 Nations", at Leipzig (1813). The fight ended with heavy losses for both sides, but Napoleon suffered the greater loss, as it became clear that he was not invincible. Allies obtained through force no longer submitted to him, and the Confederation of the Rhine

1814 disappeared. In April 1814, Prussian and Russian armies reached Paris.

THE RESTORATION

After the defeat of Napoleonic France at Waterloo,

1815 the Congress of Vienna had the role of restoring the old absolutist regimes and to remove the consequences of the Napoleonic Wars and the French Revolution in Europe. Austria, Prussia and Russia expanded their territories by annexing neighbouring lands and adopted an aggressive internal policy.

France returned to its borders from 1789. It still had to pay war reparations and host foreign troops on its territory. The United Kingdom of the Netherlands received the Austrian Netherlands (Belgium). The Kingdom of Prussia gained Westphalia, the Rhineland, and Pomerania. Austria was given back Tyrol, Salzburg, and additionally received Lombardy and Venice. Russia was given two-thirds of the former Polish-Lithuanian Commonwealth, which was constituted as an autonomous kingdom with the Russian tsar as its king. From Sweden, Russia acquired Finland and was recognized for the annexation of Moldova up to the Prut River in 1812. The United Kingdom regained the Hanoverian crown and maintained its dominance over the Ionian Islands and the island of Heligoland. Additionally, sovereignty over Gibraltar was recognized. In Spain and the Kingdom of the Two Sicilies, the Bourbons were restored. Sweden received Norway as a result of its support for the anti-Napoleonic alliances. Switzerland's independence and perpetual neutrality were recognized. Also under the auspices of the Congress of Vienna, the 37 German principalities and 4 free cities signed the German Confederation Act (Deutsche Bundesakte). The act did not specify anything concrete regarding a common parliament, unified judiciary, or common internal laws. The act was a declaration of intentions, to be materialized in an uncertain future. Among the signatories, alongside the Emperor of Austria, the King of Prussia and German princes, were the British king, sovereign of Hanover, the King of Denmark, Duke of Holstein, and the King of the Netherlands, the Grand Duke of Luxembourg.

1820

Schleswig and Holstein, which were under the Danish crown, now became part of the German Confederation through the Duchy of Holstein. The Confederation filled the void left by the Holy Roman Empire after its dissolution in 1806. Austria currently held supremacy within the Confederation. The one thing and perhaps the most important thing that couldn't be "restored" was the spirit of freedom and equality that the French had brought among the common citizens of Central Europe. Great Britain, which had developed a powerful naval fleet controlling the most important trade routes, became the global power of the world. The British Empire, despite losing a part of its North American colonies, would control a quarter of the world's population. While autocracies were reestablished across Europe, in Great Britain, the *Reform Act* strengthened the parliament's legitimacy, increasing the number of eligible voters to 650.000.

CHANGES IN THE EUROPEAN POLITICAL GEOGRAPHY

1817

1827

1830

1831

Serbia (a small part of today's Serbia) gained internal autonomy within the Ottoman Empire in 1817. Greek leaders proclaimed independence from the Ottoman Empire and received military aid from France, Great Britain and Russia (1821-1832). With the decisive victory of the Anglo-Franco-Russian fleet at Navarino (1827) over the Turkish-Egyptian fleet, within 10 months, the Turks had to evacuate the Peloponnese and Athens. Greece's independence was recognized in 1830 at the Congress of London. In 1832, the Kingdom of Greece was established. In 1830, the Catholic Netherlands (Belgium), united with the Kingdom of the Netherlands after the Congress of Vienna, rose up in arms against the Union.

They regained independence in 1831 and in 1839, their independence and neutrality were guaranteed by the Treaty of London.

EXISTENTIALISM

Kierkegaard (1813-1855), in direct opposition to the philosophy that came before him, particularly Hegel and Hegelianism, was no longer interested in speculations about *what existence is*. He departed from the idea that *BEING – that which is, the existence –* must be lived, not known or studied. He believed that the individual, not society, should be solely responsible for giving meaning and authenticity to life. These fundamental ideas were later developed by Heidegger and Sartre, forming what came to be known as existentialism. In a different vein, building on Schelling's later work, Kierkegaard proposed, in lieu of rationalistic and abstract philosophy based on speculation, a philosophy of faith.

A CATASTROPHE CAUSED BY FAMINE

Due to a potato disease and unfavorable weather seasons between 1846 and 1848, famine led to the death of around 700.000 people in Ireland and massive emigration of the youth to America.   **1846**

A REVOLUTIONARY WAVE

The "revolutionary" movements of 1848, some of them fanciful, others national, democratic and liberal, began in Palermo in January, followed by events in Paris and Naples in February, Vienna, Venice, Berlin, Milan and Munich in March, Blaj in May, and Bucharest in June. In Budapest, a revolution did not occur except for the uninformed (see David Prodan). The Budapest movement resulted only in the first genocide of modern Europe. In Blaj, philosopher Simion Bărnuțiu posed the issue of self-determination   **1848** for nations, alongside the acute problem of serfdom in the still-feudal Transylvania. As a consequence of the genocide of 1848/49, the feudal servitudes in Transylvania were abolished by the Austrian absolutist regime in 1854. However, from 1867, Romanians again remained at the complete discretion of hungarian chauvinism, *at the discretion (usque ad bene placitum principum ac regnicolarum)* of Hungarian landlords. Overall, the European revolutionary movements of 1848 accelerated the formation of nation-states.

THE EUROPEAN BALANCE – THE CRIMEAN WAR

1853 - 1856

Great Britain viewed with concern the rising power of despotic and backward Russia both in Europe and Asia (Persia). The Crimean War started from a minor conflict. France, protector of Catholic pilgrims in the Holy Land, sought a position there, opposing Russia's pursuit of privileged positions in Jerusalem and Bethlehem through Orthodox monks. As the Sultan leaned toward the West, Russian troops invaded the Romanian Principalities (July 1853), which were under the suzerainty of the Ottoman Empire. Austria did not engage militarily in the conflict, but mobilized its army in the Carpathians, and the Russians withdrew from the Principalities. Then, Great Britain, France and Turkey attacked the Tsarist Empire from the sea, at Odessa (April 1854), after which they landed in Crimea, the new territories obtained by Russia from Turkey a few decades earlier. In 1855, Sardinia and Piedmont joined the Anglo-French forces. Sevastopol fell in September 1855 and peace was concluded in Paris on March 30, 1856. Russia lost the Romanian territories through which it controlled the mouths of the Danube, the right to fortify

172

further, and to maintain a military fleet in the Black Sea. As a consequence, Prussia and Russia improved their relations, a significant factor motivating future wars in Europe.

EVOLUTIONISM

British naturalists Russell Wallace and Charles Darwin published an article in 1858 on the evolution of species through natural selection: *a useful variation is preserved.* In 1859, Darwin's work *On the Origin of Species by Means of Natural Selection* was published, where he presented his theory of natural selection – the struggle for survival had a similar effect to the artificial selection involved in selective breeding, which was well-known at that time. Met with skepticism and hostility, the theory was accepted within scientific circles in just a decade.

NEW NATION-STATES

Johann G. Herder, in his important work *Ideas for the Philosophy of the History of Mankind (Ideen zur Philosophie der Geschichte der Menschheit)*, showed that both natural history and human history are governed by the same laws, and therefore peoples have a natural right to their own nation-state. From here, the idea of nation-states could no longer be stopped by empires. Among the Germans, Italians, and Romanians, it happened that the Romanians were the first to come together, alongside the Italians, and the last in achieving unity. Looking at the German unification, the Germans had the easiest task, emerging from *German Romanticism*; the Romanians had the hardest task due to the presence of empires. But Nietzsche said in about 1870: German culture was defeated by the German state. *Romania.* Alexandru Ioan Cuza was elected in Iași as the ruler of Moldavia and re-elected in Bucharest as the ruler **1859** of Wallachia. He thus unified the two Principalities against the will of the powerful neighbouring empires

173

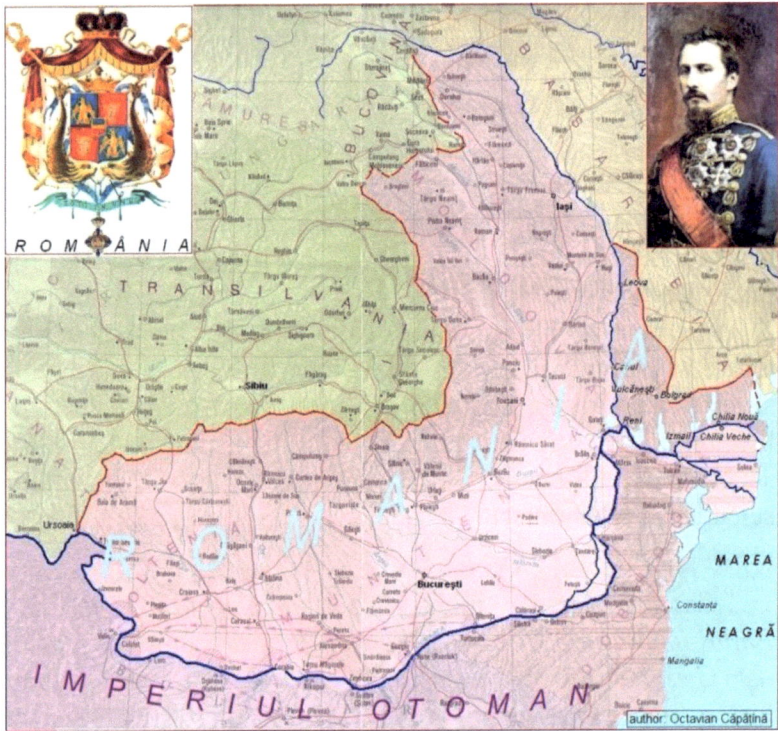

Fig. 24. The Romanian modern state, 1859

(Habsburg, Ottoman, and Tsarist). Romanians from the Habsburg Empire (from the Tisza Plain, Transylvania, and the Upper Country) and from the Tsarist Empire (Bessarabia and Transnistria) remained outside the country, subjected to social, cultural, and economic oppression. They were "captives" of the malevolent medieval autocracies. The three declining and generally antagonistic empires coordinated their efforts on three different occasions to undo the union, but these threats actually solidified the unity. Cuza's response was pre-emptive; he united the two armies.

174

In two years, despite the opposition of the empires, the United Principalities came to have a single parliament, a single government, a single capital, a single customs point, a single administration, and a single public health service. Cuza abolished serfdom, secularized monastic properties and granted land to peasants. He enacted civil and penal codes, established mandatory and free primary education, standardized the metric system, and proclaimed the autocephaly of the national church. He established the Court of Accounts, the Savings and Loan House and more. In other words, he modernized a country in just 6 years, as had never been seen anywhere else.

Italy. The struggle of the Italians for unity lasted half a century. The French and Piedmontese victories at Magenta and Solferino against Austria (1859) aided the Kingdom of Sardinia and Piedmont (House of Savoy) in achieving Italian unity. As a result, in 1860, Modena, Parma, and Romagna, which were part of the Papal State, united with Piedmont. In contrast, Savoy (French-speaking) and Nice (Italian-speaking) passed to France. Around Piedmont and Sardinia, the other small states of the peninsula gathered with overwhelming popular support. The Kingdom of the Two Sicilies (Sicily and Naples) came "home" in 1861, Venice in 1866 when Prussia defeated Austria and Napoleon III extended his hand. In 1870, the Papal State was reduced to the Vatican City, and Rome became the capital of Italy.

1866
-
1871

Germany. The German states and cities, reduced from hundreds to a few dozen by Napoleon and under Austrian hegemony, still remained extremely diverse linguistically, culturally, socially and economically.

1863
-
1864

Cultural unity. The philosopher Herder, who laid the cultural foundations of German nationalism, argued that each nation has its own unique and special soul. Hegel, building on Herder's ideas, argued that individuals fulfill their potential in service to the state. Along with many others, Goethe (1749-1832) and Schiller (1759-1805) decisively contributed to the formation of German cultural unity. *Economic unity.* Through the Prussian customs union (Zollverein), Prussia responded to the need for industrial development in the states of the German Confederation, which were economically underdeveloped at that time. The customs union law greatly simplified the tangle of customs duties. It involved a symbolic tax on raw materials, a tax of 10% for industrial goods, and 20% for luxury items. In 1834, there were 18 states in the Customs Union, and by 1836, it had grown to include 25 German states. *Political unity.* After the victories over Austria at Königgrätz in 1866 and over France at Sedan in 1870, the second German Empire (Reich) was established in 1871.

THE GERMAN WARS

The Danish-German War. The duchies of Schleswig and Holstein were in a personal union with the Danish crown. In 1848, the first war erupted, lasting until 1851, in which the final victory, particularly at sea, belonged to Denmark, but it ended with an armistice. In 1863, Denmark adopted a new Constitution, recognizing Schleswig as an integral part of the Danish Kingdom. Austria and Prussia, with the support of several states in the German Confederation, viewed this step as a violation of previous agreements.

1863
-
1870

Fig. 25. The Second German Empire

As a result, Prussian-Austrian troops occupied the entire Jutland Peninsula. Through the peace treaty, Denmark lost Schleswig-Holstein-Lauenburg to Prussia and Austria.

The German-German War for Supremacy. After the Congress of Vienna, Austria retained supremacy in the German Confederation. The Prussian-Austrian condominium in Schleswig-Holstein led to tensions that escalated into war. Through the decisive victory at Königgrätz (Bohemia) in 1866, Prussia defeated Austria and Saxony, resulting in the Peace of Prague. Austria relinquished its rights over the duchies of Schleswig-Holstein, and the German Confederation, dominated by Austria, was dissolved.

1866

177

Bismarck's Prussia and the northern German states formed the North German Confederation in 1866. The territory of the former Confederation fell under Prussia's control, which truly represented the political and military aspirations of German intellectuals for unity.

1867 *The Franco-Prussian War.* The power dynamics in Europe had shifted, and only the right opportunity was needed to confirm them. The throne of Spain was vacant, and the candidacy of Prince Leopold of Hohenzollern-Sigmaringen presented a suitable occasion for a new conflict, as France couldn't accept being surrounded by hostile states. In France, a strong anti-monarchical sentiment had emerged, making a victorious war a potential salvation for Napoleon III. Initially assuming that Prussia would rely solely on the North German Confederation, France, now the aggressor, was left isolated by Denmark, Austria, and Italy, while the Catholic German states of Baden, Württemberg, and Bavaria joined Prussia. Chancellor Bismarck ensured the neutrality of Russia and England in the future conflict. After the German victories at Metz, Sedan, and the capture of Napoleon III by the Germans, France surrendered and became a republic. France lost Alsace and Lorraine and was obliged to pay war reparations. The Kingdom of Prussia, uniting almost all German states, declared itself an empire. King Wilhelm I was crowned Emperor of the Germans at Versailles.

1867 THE FINAL PHASE OF AN ABSURD EMPIRE
Austria lost its hegemony in the Confederation of German States after Prussia's victory at Königgrätz. It's also important to note the defeats suffered by France and Italy at Magenta and Solferino (1859). In

this situation, Austria believed it could save itself as a major power through a mésalliance with Hungarian landowners, resulting in the creation of Kakania, as Viennese intellectuals called it. Beyond the absurdity of consolidating a half-feudal empire in the heart of Europe, the Austro-Hungarian dualism proved to be the most provocative war-inducing solution.

"DAS CAPITAL" BY KARL MARX

A significant work of the philosopher, social activist and historian Karl Marx (1818-1883), *Das Kapital*, published in 1867 in Hamburg, laid the foundation for the theory of overturning capitalist society and replacing it, out of historical necessity, with a new society. Marx's idea was that proletarians are paid only for a fraction of their labor; the rest, surplus value, goes to the capitalist. Proletarians were paid just enough to reproduce themselves, in order to perpetuate the production of surplus value. Marx stated: *"The growing accumulation of machinery, no longer accompanied by a corresponding diminution of the proportion of living labour [sic] required to keep it in motion, is a symptom of growing accumulation of capital. The greater the progress of capital, the more extensive the machinery employed."* Hence the necessity for revolution. This idea, partially or halfway correct, electrified a portion of the world's proletariat leaders for over a century and materialized into a criminal revolution, known as *The Bolshevik Revolution*, resulting in the emergence of a more autocratic state, more contemptuous of human value than any other known state construction.

SCIENCE UNTIL THE 19TH CENTURY

In broad terms, the fields of mechanics and optics, dealing with directly observable phenomena, had already been clarified. Chemistry, thermodynamics and electromagnetism, phenomena that were harder to track, usually indirectly, were lagging behind. Chemist Antoine Lavoisier (1743-1794) formulated the principle of conservation of mass, defined the chemical element and demonstrated that oxygen and nitrogen are chemical elements. He also explained the role of oxygen in nature. Later, August Kekulé (1829-1896) proposed the hypothesis of chemical valence, and Dmitri Mendeleev (1834-1907) discovered in 1869 the periodic law of the chemical properties of elements. Michael Faraday (1791-1867) experimentally discovered the phenomenon of electromagnetic induction and intuited the existence of lines of force. The laws of the electromagnetic field were theoretically established by James Maxwell (1831-1879). Heinrich Hertz (1857-1894) discovered electromagnetic waves. Ludwig Boltzmann (1844-1906) statistically founded the second law of thermodynamics and defined the concept of entropy. Gregor Mendel, a monk, shifted the paradigm of inheritance theory by merging it into the theory of inheritance through particles. In the new era, our understanding of nature, in the classical sense, was to be expanded in new directions, both towards the macrocosm and the microcosm. However, with the opening of these new windows of science, the limits of classical mechanics also became apparent. The Galilean-Newtonian science could no longer explain the world, nor could it serve to comprehend phenomena occurring at speeds significant in relation to the speed of light, at the atomic level, nor could it even explain the dual nature of light. The first major breach in the Galilean-Newtonian system was made by James Maxwell's theory of electromagnetism, which did not rely on classical mechanics in describing the phenomenon. Later, Planck, Lorentz, Einstein, Bohr, Born, Heisenberg, Schrödinger, Pauli, Dirac laid the foundations of quantum mechanics and the theory of relativity.

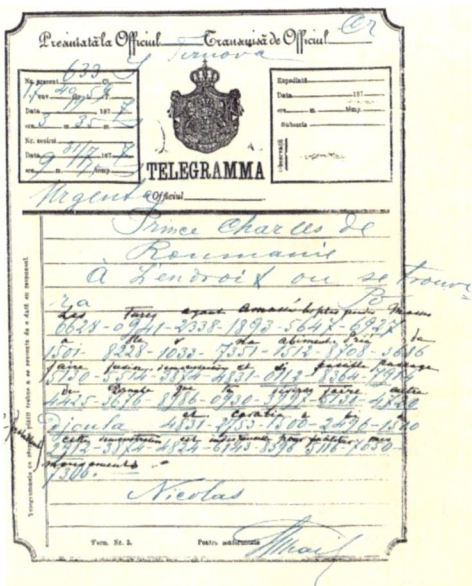

Fig. 26. Telegram from Grand Duke Nicholas of Russia,
1877, requesting urgent military assistance from Romania.

THE RUSSO-TURKISH WAR, WON BY ROMANIANS

In 1875-76, the Russians, with their own gain in mind, came to the aid of the rebellious Serbs, who desired independence and the liberation of new Serbian territories from Ottoman occupation. The Romanians also desired the firmness of "independence", having *de facto* independence since 1862, but not *de jure* (see M. Eminescu). The war began in June 1877, but the Russians were being defeated on the front. Thus, Grand Duke Nicholas, the brother of the Tsar, who was leading the Russian armies south of the Danube, urgently asked Prince Carol for assistance *because the Turks were crushing us* (see the telegram above). After a month of war, Carol took command of the Romanian-Russian armies on the southern Danube

1877

181

	front. As a result of Romania's vigorous intervention, Osman Pasha surrendered to the Romanians. The Romanian army made a strong impression in Paris and London. However, Romania failed to capitalize on the immense sacrifice by bringing home the South Danubian Romanians. Through the Treaty of Berlin, Romania gained Dobrogea but lost control over the mouths of the Danube to the Russians, who, as always, did not honor the agreements they signed, including the one with Romania signed in Bucharest on April 16, 1877. The war also led to the independence of the small Serbia, while the northern half of present-day Bulgaria gained internal autonomy. Although not directly involved in the conflict, Austria occupied Bosnia-Herzegovina, and Britain occupied Cyprus.
1878	

NIETZSCHE. THE COMPLETE BREAK

Nietzsche (1844-1900) simply states that *"God is dead. God remains dead. We have killed him."* Without belief in God, the values of Christian morality cannot be sustained; they disappear. Christian morality is the morality of the weak, the morality of slaves, those who need compassion. In Christian religion, suffering is tolerable and serves as an opportunity for sinners to repent for the afterlife. In Christianity, humility and submission have replaced pride, competition and the freedom of action. Therefore, Nietzsche believed, we are condemned to create our own moral values. Moreover, with the collapse of Christian morality, only the desert of meaninglessness and purposelessness remained, leading to nihilism. Finding purpose in a godless universe was the task he undertook. The French *Revolution* had a profound awakening effect on the contemporary consciousness; from now on, everyone referred to their own time (Zeitgeist), to their contemporary history. Although, initially, the understanding of *the spirit of the age* was somewhat unstable, it did not encompass the ludic fashion that is only a collateral effect. Nevertheless, Fichte's definition of *the spirit of the age* was essentially an eternal spirit, not a spirit of the epoch. In Nietzsche's view, the spirit of his time was a time of the times that would come, and he was ahead of his contemporaries. The paths he pursued were hesitant. He was always dissatisfied, constantly searching for solutions. In the end, would he have been satisfied with where he arrived? We don't know, for his search effort abruptly ended at the age of 35, leaving behind notes that we don't know whether, if he had lived in full mental health, he would have edited or published. Nietzsche also published his ideas in the form of aphorisms; he didn't elaborate a philosophical system, so we can encounter the most diverse meanings in his works. Current and outdated ideas, fruitful ideas and ideas that led nowhere. At one point, related to his shared experience with R. Wagner, Nietzsche believed that overcoming the "lie of millennia" could be achieved through a repetition of Greek tragedy, which combined both good and evil. In *The Birth of Tragedy*, Nietzsche asked how we could overcome nihilism. He found the solution between *happiness,* represented by Apollo*, and the ludic and suffering*, represented by Dionysus. The answer to finding a new world was not so much in the balance of Apollonian and Dionysian elements but in the pre-eminence of the latter. Dionysian attributes were those of the Titans, the barbarians, the opposite of balance, measure and Apollonian harmony. The Dionysian, unbridled passion, suffering, and evil must be accepted in the universal character of existence. For Schopenhauer (1788-1860) in *The World as Will and Representation*, existence was devoid of hope, leading to nihilism and pessimism. The ambiguity of nihilism – both weakness and strength – can lead to decadence, but also to a new beginning. Nietzsche saw life as an instinct for growth and survival, calling this instinct the *will to power*. Nietzsche, a product of his time, was also a decadent, but he recognized it and attempted to resist decadence. He departed from Schopenhauer's nihilism but countered it through self-surpassing, proposing the *Übermensch (the Superman)*. The way out of nihilism lies in self-surpassing. The individual who has the courage to repeat their own life infinitely, with mistakes and suffering, would be the Übermensch. Humanity could avoid degeneration only through the Übermensch, who embodies the universal. The Übermensch does not yet exist, but it would represent the self-surpassing of the current human condition. Nietzsche's Übermensch is more of an abstract and poetic image, like the hypotheses of philosopher L. Blaga.

THE SCRAMBLE FOR AFRICA

The exploitation of Africa (both its people and material resources) was officially acknowledged at the Berlin Conference of 1884. Rival European countries sliced up the African continent "amicably". This was followed by numerous abominable genocides perpetrated by Europeans in Africa. Egypt was under Ottoman rule from 1517 to 1914. In Africa, only Liberia and Ethiopia remained independent.

THE FIRST ZIONIST CONGRESS

1897 After the assassination of Tsar Alexander II (1855-1881) in the Tsarist Empire, pogroms followed one after another. In Basel, in August 1897, nearly 200 Zionist delegates from around the world demanded, for the first time, the creation of a Jewish state in Palestine.

NORWAY'S INDEPENDENCE

1905 The dependency on Sweden was denounced by the parliament in Oslo (Storting) in 1905, and Sweden accepted. The Danish prince, Charles, was elected king of Norway under the name Haakon VII. Also in 1905, Finland obtained a certain autonomy within the Tsarist Empire.

THE DYING EMPIRE ANNEXING TERRITORIES

Austria declared the annexation of Herzegovina and Bosnia, which had been occupied after the Russo-Turkish War of 1877.

BULGARIA'S INDEPENDENCE. THE YOUNG TURKS

In 1908, Bulgaria, specifically its northern half, which had been autonomous since 1878, proclaimed its independence from the Ottoman Empire. At the same time, *the Young Turks* movement compelled the Sultan to reinstate the liberal constitution of 1876 and convene the parliament, which had not been assembled since 1877.

THE BALKAN WARS

Montenegro declared war on the Ottoman Empire. Within a few days, Serbia, Bulgaria and Greece joined in, motivated by the mistreatment of the Christian populations in the Balkans. On 8 November 1912, the Ottomans surrendered in Thessaloniki. They retained a strip of land around Constantinople. Bulgaria acquired the historic provinces of Thrace and Macedonia, securing its access to the Aegean Sea. In June 1913, Bulgaria attacked Serbia and Greece, prompting a military response. Romania declared war on Bulgaria, and when the Romanian army approached Sofia, Bulgaria surrendered. Ottoman troops occupied Adrianople (now Edirne, Turkey). The Treaty of Bucharest concluded the conflict. Serbia and Greece divided Macedonia between them, Turkey expanded its European territory, and Romania acquired a strip of land in southern Dobruja , inhabited by Turks, Romanians and Bulgarians.

STEPPING BEYOND THE BORDERS

As early as the 19th century, the wavelengths of spectral lines, the temperature dependence of specific heat in certain substances, the photoelectric effect and the intensity of thermal radiation could no longer be explained within the framework of the Galileo-Newtonian view, nor could they be understood based on common sense or the visible cause-effect relationship. When Max Planck (1858-1947) proposed the idea of discontinuous energy variation, his colleagues hardly took notice, as the idea seemed so fantastical. According to the old theory, the emission of light and heat occurred in a continuous flow, but Planck deduced from experiments that energy was radiated in discrete units (quanta) or packets of quanta. He calculated a new universal constant, h, which is used to compute energy levels and is named after him. The first application of this new concept was made by Albert Einstein (1879-1955) when he explained, in 1905, why the energy of electrons is independent of the intensity of the light that releases them (a discovery made by Philip Lenard in 1902). This explanation could not arise from wave theory. Also in 1905, Einstein developed the theory of special relativity, necessary for understanding concepts of space, mass and energy in the case of atomic and subatomic particles. In 1915, through the generalized theory of relativity, Einstein made the birth of modern cosmology possible. The second major use of this new concept, that of *quanta*, was by Niels Bohr in 1913, when he improved Rutherford's atomic model by admitting discrete energy levels for electrons, values that were integer multiples of Planck's constant. The atomic model was further refined by A. Sommerfeld in 1916, who introduced ellipses as orbits of electrons. At this point, the Rutherford-Bohr-Sommerfeld atomic model contained a systemic error because it explained electron orbits based on Newtonian mechanics, while most orbits calculated using quantum physics were excluded. In

1924, Louis de Broglie demonstrated that, on an atomic scale, subparticles exhibit both wave and particle characteristics simultaneously. In 1926, Erwin Schrödinger (1887-1961) published the equation that forms the basis of wave mechanics. Instead of treating the electron as a particle, Schrödinger regarded it as a wave. Particle or wave? Here, Max Born (1882-1970) first intervened, understanding that the electron is neither a precisely localized particle nor a three-dimensional wave. Born introduced the concept of particle probability. One year later, W. Heisenberg (1901-1976) formulated the uncertainty principle. As a conclusion of quantum physics, we could say that a subatomic or atomic event has a probability of occurring within a certain time interval. At this point, quantum physics could explain and calculate electron displacement at slow speeds, but when electrons moved at speeds close to the speed of light, the calculations went astray. Enter Paul Dirac (1902-1984), who, in 1927, employed the theory of special relativity to describe particles uniformly across all velocities, leading to a field theory that describes the interaction of light with matter. In 1928, he discovered an equation for predicting electron behaviour and predicted the existence of the positron, which was subsequently detected in 1932. The adventures stemming from stepping beyond borders, beyond limits, began with Planck, but did not conclude with him. Planck, who witnessed this tumult he had set in motion, attempted to build a bridge between Newtonian and quantum physics. He did not succeed. Mathematician Octav Onicescu (1892-1983) proposed a "bridge" in his work *Invariant Mechanics*, represented by the equations $p_1 = m_1 * v_1 + \mu * v_2 + h_1 * \upsilon * r$ and $p_2 = m_2 * v_2 + \mu * v_1 + h_2 * \upsilon * r$, where p_i is the momentum, v_i is the velocity of two masses m_i at a distance r, and μ and υ are the masses of gravitational and repulsive interaction, respectively.

THE GREAT WAR

1914 Imperial tensions between the Anglo-French and the Germans sought the fabrication of a pretext. On February 18, 1914, the Reich Finance Ministry requested the opening of bank branches in the US, Denmark, Sweden and Russia, which could be necessary *under certain circumstances.* On June 9, 1914, the German Great General Staff (GGGS) ordered all industrial enterprises to comply with the mobilization plan within 24 hours. The stories of *The Great War,* however, begin with the assassination on June 28, 1914. The Habsburgs, Hohenzollerns and Romanovs ruled over millions of subjects in the name of divine right. The Habsburgs and Romanovs abused, in a discretionary feudal manner, various ethnicities and religions. The divergent economic interests between the old empires and the new German Empire, the racist madness of a so-called "vital living space", and the warrior mentality of leaders and politicians solidified the provocative attitude of many nations at the beginning of the last century. Among the leaders who fanned the flames, leading to the outbreak of the First World War, stood out the Prime Minister of Hungary from 1913 to 1917, István Tisza (1861-1918), hence also known as the "Butcher of the Balkans". He fuelled the war frenzy of the monarchy and was the shadowy will behind this massacre, constantly inciting violence in the not very intelligent Viennese emperor. The assassination in Sarajevo of the Habsburg heir to the throne, whether arranged or accidental, provided the German capital and the chauvinists in Budapest with the opportunity to push for a "war of honor".

On one side, Austria, Germany, Turkey, Italy (until 1915) and Bulgaria participated, and on the other side, Serbia, Russia (until June 1917), France, Britain, Italy (since 1915), Romania (since 1916), and Greece. The major belligerents skilfully "worked" their adversaries through propaganda. The Habsburg Empire funded the "Russian revolutionaries" before the war began. The conflagration began with Serbian victories. On September 9, 1914, on the Marne River, *the lightning war* based on the Schliessen Plan, aimed at the swift annihilation of France through the blow struck over neutral Belgium, was definitively blocked. Here, on the Marne, the legend of German invincibility melted away. This was followed by the concentration of German forces on the Eastern Front. In the east, Austrian troops were defeated on all fronts, and the Tsarist army occupied Polish and Ruthenian territories. To limit Austrian losses, the German army intervened. In February, I.L. Gelfand, a Jew from near Minsk, offered the German Foreign Ministry a plan for removing the Tsarist Empire from the fight and dismantling it through a "revolution". The plan was accepted and financed.

The first mass killing attack with toxic gases (168 tons of chlorine gas) took place near Ypres (Belgium) 1915 on April 22, 1915, carried out by the German army. On May 23, 1915, Italy left the alliance with Germany and Austria and joined the Entente. Bulgaria entered the war alongside Germany and Austria on November 6, 1915. In September 1915, Lenin, through the double agent Keskula from Estonia, transmitted his program to the Reich, which included at point 5) the withdrawal from the Entente and a separate peace with Germany, without annexations and reparations. The German assault on Verdun, launched in February and ending in December 1916, left both sides approximately in the same positions, with a slight gain of ground for the French, but around 335.000 Germans and 360.000 French dead. On the Somme, facing the British, the Germans also gave way. The "revolutionizing" of the Tsarist Empire shifted from the Foreign Ministry to the German Great General Staff (GGGS) starting in the spring of 1916. Romania entered the war alongside the Entente on August 15, 1916 (by the Julian calendar), mainly due to the complete lack of rights for Romanians in Austro-Hungary. Romania entered the war even though neither the Franco-English (at Salonika) nor the Tsarist Empire (in Dobrogea) upheld their commitments. The Romanians fought in both camps since about a third, if not more, of the cannon fodder in the K&K army were Romanians, and there were many Romanians from Bessarabia in the Tsarist army. The faithful Germans, adhering to their military doctrine, now favored by Russian weakness, brought troops from the Russian front and from France and rushed upon Romania. The Romanians were led by politically promoted officers. On November 23, 1916, the Germans occupied Bucharest. Two vital resources for the continuation of the war fell into their hands: cereals and oil. Plundering was practiced by both the army and the German and allied officers and soldiers. By the end of the year, St. Petersburg was in revolutionary chaos, from which it would not emerge for years. In 1917, Germany and Austria unleashed total submarine warfare, *à outrance*. On April 9, the German train with Lenin and 32 other revolutionaries left Zurich bound for St. Petersburg.

The GGGS notified the German Foreign Ministry that Lenin had arrived in Petersburg on April 14, 1917. The Russian army on the Eastern Front in 1917 was engulfed in Bolshevik anarchy, financially supported and logistically aided by the secret services and the German army. The soldiers of the Tsar no longer obeying officers' orders abandoned the front, and looted whatever they could in retreat. On March 15, 1917, Nicholas II (1894-1917) abdicated. The German army established the first mass extermination camps in Europe in Alsace and Lorraine for Romanian prisoners. On April 6, the United States declared war on Germany due to the German maritime blockade, which affected global trade and Germany's dealings with Mexico. On July 17, at Kronstadt (north of Petersburg), representatives of the GGGS (General Max Hoffmann) and the Bolsheviks met; they established the next steps of their collaboration there. At the same time, the armies of Germany and the Austro-Hungarian Empire, led in Romania by Generals von Falkenhayn (former chief of GGGS) and von Mackensen (front breaker) were halted at the gates of Moldova in the summer of 1917: at Mărăști, Mărășești and Oituz. Their new plan to eliminate the Eastern Front in order to focus exclusively on the Western Front was postponed. Taking advantage of the dissolution of the Russian armies, the Germans decided to deliver the "coup de grâce" to the Russians and on September 3, 1917, they captured Riga. Politically, they supported the Bolshevik anarchy with money, officers and troops. The Duchy of Finland, through its local parliament, proclaimed its independence from the Tsarist Empire, the empire of

Romania joins the Entente (1916) for the liberation of 3.5 million compatriots barely tolerated on their land.

A British cartoonist from «Punch» imagines a dispute like: Hindenburg is on my side said Wilhelm II of Germany! King Ferdinand of Romania replies: but on my side freedom and justice fight.

Fig.27. After a British cartoon

evil paralyzed by the Bolshevik revolution. Finland had been acquired by Russia from the Swedes in 1809; now two divergent processes were unfolding in Finland: Russification and national awakening. The two sides clashed, and the national spirit emerged victorious. On December 15, the Bolsheviks separately signed an armistice with Germany at Brest-Litovsk, after which Russo-German fraternization along the former front line became widespread.

However, each side pursued its own goals. On the Romanian front, its former ally, Russia, became the most dangerous enemy; for example, the 49th Russian division was completely disarmed, and Austrian officers found in the Russian division were arrested.

On March 16, 1918, the Bolsheviks signed the peace imposed by Germany at Brest-Litovsk and received in return millions of gold rubles, advisers, officers and German soldiers to perfect the "revolution". Russia renounced Poland, Lithuania and Courland and acknowledged Ukraine's autonomy. The cacophony of the Entente, which added to the already voluminous dossier of betrayal and inter-Allied incoherence on the Eastern Front, took increasingly absurd forms (the expression belongs to Count de Saint Aulaire, who experienced it firsthand): the British also supported the Russian revolution, and the Americans financed it, the socialists in Paris believed that the new regime would organize a Russian Valmy – in practice, everyone played into Germany's hands. Romania, completely isolated and surrounded, signed a subjugating peace on May 7, but it was not ratified by the sovereign. As a result, 70 German divisions from the east were sent to the front in France. GGGS believed it had victory in hand. But the third German assault on the Western Front in 1918 marked the beginning of the disaster for the Germans. The head of GGGS, Erich Ludendorff, wrote that August 8 was the start date of their collapse. Finally, in September 1918, after more than 2 years, the Allied offensive on the Salonica front began. On September 30, Bulgaria signed the armistice, on October 31, Turkey did, and on November 3, the K&K army signed the armistice with Italy.

1918   The Habsburg Empire disappeared. On November 9, Wilhelm II abdicated, and on November 11, a representative of the Weimar Republic signed the armistice with the Allies.

Fig. 28. WWI. Eastern front. 1917-1918

THE INTELLECTUALS AND ATROCITIES

Examples. Viennese writers such as St. Zweig, H. Hofmannsthal, A. Schnitzler, R. Rilke fuelled popular enthusiasm in Austria at the outbreak of the war in 1914. In Budapest, there was delirium, even if the prime minister didn't appear in public for several days. Starting from August 25, 1914, in the city of Leuven and its surroundings, the German army retaliated against Belgian partisans: in 4 days, killing about 6.000 civilians and destroying the city along with its art monuments and the university. These actions led to a wave of disgust and rebellion against the Reich. 93 German intellectuals came to the aid of the authors of this barbarity, issuing a *Call to the Cultural World (Aufruf an die Kulturwelt)*, denying the deeds. Among them were Max Planck, Conrad Poengen, Emil Fischer, Wilhelm Ostwald, Eduard Buchner.

After Panait Istrati published on October 1, 1929, in France, his chapter *The Rusakov Affair or USSR Today*, in which he exposed Bolshevik atrocities, Romain Rolland wrote: *"Nothing written in the past ten years against the USSR by its most bitter enemies has done as much harm as these pages will do."* Not only Romain Rolland, but almost the entire French leftist intelligentsia was aligned with Soviet Russia. For them, the truth did not matter; the utopia was important.

THE PEACE AMONG SOLDIERS

On the Galicia front in October 1914 and during Easter in 1915 (March 22, 1915 old style), Transylvanian and Bessarabian brothers, some serving in the Habsburg forces, others in the Russian forces, shook hands, tended to each other's wounds and shared sweet bread. On the French front, English and German soldiers "fraternized" for a few hours on Christmas night, 1914; they exchanged gifts and sang together.

SOLDIERS OR POLITICAL LEADERS?
SELF-DETERMINATION, FROM DECLARATIONS TO RIGOROUS VOTING

The program transmitted by Lenin through the double agent Keskula to Germany, in September 1915, which at point 4 provided for the autonomy of nationalities within the future Russia, remained secret and did not reach the public, therefore it had no consequences and cannot be considered in this matter.

Romanian soldiers from Serbia shouted across the Danube to the Romanians in the K&K army, in July 1914: *"Hey, brothers, haven't you had enough? Forget about the emperor and go home."*

On the Galicia front from the K&K side, there was only foolishness, racism and swagger on command. Only Romanians were at the frontline as troops; the "Magyarized" ones hadn't seen the front line yet except as reserves in December. The erosion of dynastic loyalty among the Transylvanians was becoming more evident: 26.200 Transylvanian Romanian soldiers deserted, more than in 1914, thus *voting* for self-determination. After August 15, 1916, when Romania declared war on Austria-Hungary, tens of thousands of Transylvanian Romanians in America voted for self-determination by presenting themselves at American recruitment offices. As at that time non-American citizens couldn't be enlisted in the U.S. – some of these Romanians voted for self-determination by crossing the border into Canada and enlisting in the Canadian army. Other tens of thousands of young Transylvanian Romanians voted for the unity of all Romanians by enlisting in the Romanian army. The temporary Russian provisional revolutionary government led by Prince Gh. Lvov declared on March 27, 1917, that it *"wants a peace based on the self-determination of nations."* In April 1917, in Odessa, the Congress of Soldiers, Educators, and Craftmen (with around 10,000 participants) demanded autonomy, national organizations, education in the Romanian language and the Latin script. Before American President W. Wilson called for "autonomous development", the *Darnytsia Memorandum* (Kiev, Ukraine) was published on April 26, 1917 by Transylvanian Romanian prisoners of war, affirming the right of peoples to self-determination. After a year and a half, Robert Lansing, the Secretary of State, on behalf of the U.S., called for autonomy for all peoples. On May 10, 1917, troops formed from Transylvanian Romanian prisoners and refugees, gathered in Kiev, took the *Oath of Allegiance* to Romania in Iași. After a law (May 18, 1917) authorized the U.S. government to recruit a national army from volunteers, over 17.000 Transylvanian Romanians voted for self-determination by presenting themselves at American recruitment offices. On July 9, 1917, the German Parliament, at the initiative of the Social Democrats, adopted a resolution speaking of the right of the peoples within the Russian Empire to self-determination. On December 4, 1917, the Parliament of Bessarabia, *Sfatul Țării*, comprised of representatives of nationalities, confessions, professional associations, and counties, proclaimed the independence of Bessarabia. On January 8, 1918, President W. Wilson enunciated the 14 principles for the regulation of peace, including autonomous development for the peoples of Austria-Hungary. On January 24, 1918, Sfatul Țării unanimously voted for the independence of Bessarabia. On March 10, 1918, 150.000 Transylvanian Romanian Orthodox Romanians represented at *the National Assembly of Romanians in America* held in Youngstown, Ohio, decided to sever all ties with the Habsburg Empire. The Parliament of the new independent Moldovan Democratic Republic voted for Union with Romania on March 27, 1918. On October 12, 1918, the Romanian National Council issued *the Declaration of Self-Determination for Romanians in Transylvania, Banat, Crișana, Ugocea and Maramureș*, which was read in the *Diet of Budapest* after 6 days. Emperor Charles' proposals from October 16, 1918, to offer extensive autonomy to the peoples and even to federate Cisleithania, were rejected by Secretary of State Robert Lansing with the memorable words *"the autonomy for the nationalities is no longer enough."* On October 28, 1918, the Czech National Committee declared autonomy for the Czechs in Prague. The Slovak politicians joined the *Declaration of Prague* the next day. On October 29, 1918, in Zagreb, the Southern Slavic State was proclaimed by representatives of the majority of South Slavic political factions, organized in the National Council. Over 33 days, this self-proclaimed state joined the Kingdom of the Serbs, forming the Kingdom of Serbs, Croats, and Slovenes. After the formation of *the Central Military Senate* of officers and soldiers in Vienna, all Romanian soldiers pledged allegiance to the "Romanian nation and King Ferdinand". 50.000 Romanian soldiers maintained order in the chaos-stricken Vienna; the anarchized K&K divisions in Vienna were disarmed by Romanian troops. On November 1, 1918, the Hungarian National Council proclaimed the Hungarian People's Republic. On November 9, 1918, the Central Romanian National Council in Arad requested that 26 counties from Transylvania, Banat, Crişana and Maramureş (including Bichiş, Cenad, and Ugocea) be handed over to the local Romanian National Councils for administration. The date of November 11, 1918, is considered the date of the re-establishment of Poland, the second republic, when J. Pilsudski took over military leadership in Warsaw in the Polish state formed by the German occupiers in the Russian zone, a puppet state. Even in those days, retreating Hungarian soldiers, driven by the *"holy war of the Turanian race",* committed countless crimes against civilians in Transylvania. On November 15, 1918*, the Central Romanian National Council* decided that, based on the vote in each locality, the Romanians from the former empire would unite with the Kingdom of Romania. The decision included regulations for the election of deputies who would vote for the Union in accordance with the Hungarian electoral law of 1910, by constituencies, in all designated localities to be election centres. The number of deputies: five per electoral constituency; the way of the election: an open universal vote. On November 28, 1918, the *General Congress of Bukovina* decided to unite this province with Romania, taken by the Habsburgs through annexation in 1774. On December 1, 1918 (November 18), in Alba Iulia, 1,228 deputies with signed ***Resolutions***, some by heads of families, others by all inhabitants (universal suffrage), and with the ***Credentials*** (*minutes, mandates, plenipotentiaries, protocols, attestations*) of local communities, in the presence of over 100,000 people, proclaimed the *Union* with Romania. The only province from the former empire to separate based on the rigorous vote of the overwhelming majority of its citizens. Paradoxically, it was not the political leaders who from the beginning shook off the damaging loyalty to the K&K charade, which concealed the most base chauvinism and primitivism, but the youth on the front lines. In the end, even the political figures were activated. As known from the cultural history of humanity, new ideas and the crossing of mental thresholds were achieved by the youth and by moving groups. Just as in Transylvania, Bukovina, Maramureș, the Tisza Plain, Bessarabia and Transnistria, the detachment from the feudal mystique of blind subservience to an emperor "anointed by God" was accomplished by the youth in motion.

THE BOLSHEVIK-GERMAN REVOLUTION

After the abdication of the Tsar on March 15, 1917, the Duma and the Petrograd Soviet contested **1917** each other for power. A compromise was reached, and the government of G. Lvov (March-July) was formed, followed by the socialist government of the woeful Kerensky (July-November), who carried out a 1918 "socialist" revolution, but maintained commitments to the Entente. This became a reason for Germany's vigorous intervention alongside the Bolsheviks, providing financial, propagandistic and military support against the socialist government. The initial Bolshevik actions aimed to dismantle the Tsarist army. Lenin returned to Russia with the assistance of the German secret service, German money and officers, seizing power from the socialist government under the banner of *Peace and Bread*. Soviet Russia signed an armistice with the Central Powers on December 15, 1917. On January 12, 1918, *the Intelligence Bureau* (of espionage) of the *German Great General Staff (GGGS)* requested the *Commissar for Foreign Affairs* to manipulate the Central Executive Committee to re-elect individuals like Trotsky, Lenin, Zinoviev, Kamenev, Peters (head of CEKA) etc., in other words, those under German influence. On March 3, 1918, at Brest-Litovsk, Soviet Russia signed a separate peace treaty with Germany, receiving in return millions of gold marks, German officers, and government advisors, forming a true German-Bolshevik symbiosis. In the ensuing civil war, the Red Guards were either advised by German officers or directly led by them. Often, the Red Guards included not only officers, but also German soldiers. However, ironically, even the German soldier was not immune to Bolshevik propaganda. After Lenin's death in 1924, Stalin gradually seized power in the Soviet Union. He turned the class struggle, the fight against "deviationist Bolsheviks", and the fight against "fascists" into governing principles. He unleashed terror. The "Deviationists" and "fascists" were Bolshevik citizens who stood in his way. The fear stemming from countless assassinations was part of the plan for absolute power conquest. The intensity of the terror only began to diminish in 1956, three years after Stalin's death.

TERRORISM, COMMUNISM, FASCISM, NAZISM

1917

The "Dictatorship of the Proletariat", which was effectively a pathological form of leadership within the former Tsarist empire, began on November 7, 1917, with the arrest of the socialist government of Kerensky. And the terror against the peoples of the empire has not stopped until today, with the break between 1985-1992.

The first national-fascist regime was established in Hungary, a fierce dictatorship based on forced labor and extermination camps (see the Diary of Eva Heyman). This regime politically supported Hitler's rise in Germany for his revisionist ideas. 1920

On October 30, 1922, Mussolini and his fascists, through demagogy, blackmail, and terror, seized power in Italy. They invested in infrastructure, fought against the Mafia and began to establish a colony. 1922

In June 1923, in Bulgaria, Alexander Tsankov took over the government through a military coup and suppressed his opponents (communists and agrarians). 1923

There was a military coup, backed by General Pilsudski, to "cleanse" Polish political life. From this moment until its dissolution by Hitler and Stalin, Poland was ruled exclusively by the military. 1923

King of the Serbs, Croats, and Slovenes, Alexander I, dissolved the parliament and political parties, assuming executive power. He was assassinated in 1934. 1926

The Chancellor of Austria, E. Dollfuss, dissolved the parliament and established an autocratic regime. 1929

On January 30, 1933, Hitler was appointed Chancellor by the President of Germany, Paul von Hindenburg. After Hindenburg's death in 1934, Hitler took on the role of President as well, effectively becoming the "leader" as per his own slogan, *"ein volk, ein reich, ein führer."* 1933

King Carol II dissolved the parliament and political parties, effectively taking control of Romania's governance; the governments were merely his tools. 1938

At the end of the civil war, Francisco Franco began a dictatorship marked by a period of repression against 1939 political opponents, forced labour camps, and executions (resulting in over 30,000 deaths).

NEW STATES ON THE MAP OF EUROPE

1919 The unconditional signing of the armistice with the Entente powers and the revolt of its own citizens and soldiers lead to the disappearance of the Austro-Hungarian Empire and the emergence of new states: Czechoslovakia, Austria, Hungary, Poland.

THE SPREAD AND REBUTTAL OF BOLSHEVISM

1919 The Bolshevik state under NKVD member Bela Kuhn (1886-1937?), in coordination with Bolshevik Russia, attacked Czechoslovakia and Romania. The Romanian army defeated the Hungarian army and occupied Budapest on August 4th. On November 14, 1919, the Romanians handed over Budapest to right-wing politicians in Szeged, future Hungarian fascists and nationalists. Simultaneously, the Romanian army repelled the Soviet attack on the Dniester. Toward the end of 1919, a clear front formed between Ukrainians (led by Petliura) and Poles (led by General Pilsudski) against the Bolsheviks. Border clashes escalated into a full-fledged war when the Poles launched a major offensive within Ukrainian territory in April 1920. The Bolshevik counterattack pushed back the Polish

1920 armies all the way to the outskirts of Warsaw. To aid Poland, the Interallied Commission in Poland was established, a diplomatic mission of the Entente. In August 1920, the Poles achieved an unexpected victory against the Bolshevik armies. Faced with the rapid Polish advance, the Soviets requested a ceasefire in October 1920 and signed the Treaty of Riga on March 18, 1921, in which they divided a part of Ukraine between them. After a 3-year civil war between the White and Red Guards, the Bolsheviks emerged victorious, gradually conquering Georgia, Eastern Ukraine, Armenia, Azerbaijan – states that had declared independence after the Treaty of Brest- 1922 Litovsk. The USSR, the so-called *first state of workers and peasants,* was, even from its foundation in 1922, a formidable machine of crime and repression, a prototype of all the totalitarian regimes of the 20th century.

THE PEACE TREATIES

The disintegration of the Central Powers was confirmed by the peace treaties signed in 1919/20. The Treaty of Versailles with Germany, the Treaty of Saint-Germain with Austria, the Treaty of Trianon with Hungary, the Treaty of Neuilly with Bulgaria and the Treaty of Sèvres with Turkey. France regained Alsace and Lorraine, Denmark obtained Schleswig, Hungary was recognized as a state, Poland reemerged as a nation. From the ruins of the former Austro-Hungarian Empire, Czechoslovakia emerged and the South Slavic Kingdom was unified. Between historical rights and the rights of nations, due to the ignorance of political leaders, the arbitrariness of peace emerged. Two million Germans from the former Austro-Hungarian Empire were ceded to Czechoslovakia (the Sudetenland). Romanians lost the most at the negotiating table – half of Banat and Crișana; they relinquished Transnistria and Timoc out of ignorance. Two-thirds of Maramureș were ceded to Czechoslovakia by the Romanian government in an act of friendship. Aromanians, Macedonians and Kutso-Vlachs were divided among Greeks, Albanians, Bulgarians and Yugoslavs.

AN UNCHANGED CHURCH

Predestination and justification or salvation? The Orthodox Church, in general, an unchanged church circumstantially (see *filioque*), without tribulations (Augustinian predestination, followed by Thomistic repudiation of predestination), and unburdened by unnecessary florilegia, has experienced throughout history the humility of the powerful of the day, but has remained within the original framework of the Nicene-Constantinopolitan dogma. The salvation of man in the vision of the Church of the East was established by the apostles and the holy fathers of the Church. The Apostle Paul says: *"All things are lawful for me, but not all things are helpful; all things are lawful for me, but I will not be dominated by anything."* Therefore, the fathers of the Christian Church believed they relied on the Gospels when they asserted that man was not created perfect by God, but through freedom, man, aided by divine grace, can attain perfection. Saint Macarius the Egyptian (295-392) affirmed: *"Divine grace has ordained things in such a way that each person participates in their spiritual growth according to their choice, according to their own will, their own effort, in proportion to their faith and zeal."* Saint Gregory of Nazianzus (330-390), from Cappadocia, said that *through Christ, the integrity of nature was restored, because He represents in archetype what we are.* In other words, the free person must work themselves towards their salvation and communion with God. In this self-driven pursuit, man is not alone; he cooperates with the holy grace. St. Gregory of Nyssa (335-395), the brother of Saint Basil the Great from Cappadocia, wrote: *"The One who created man with the purpose of tasting all His gifts certainly could not deprive him of the most precious thing: to be independent and free."*

TWO DISTINCT CHURCHES

The Anglican Church is neither Protestant nor Catholic; it is somewhat unique. Canonically, it is very close to the Romanian Orthodox Church, which in turn distinguishes itself with its spirit of tolerance, in opposition to its Slavic "sisters".

EURO-ASIANISM

Professor Nikolai Trubetzkoy, a White Russian refugee in Sofia in 1920, formulated the theses of Euro-Asianism as an alternative to Bolshevism and Tsarism. These theses were: 1) a bipolar world; 2) the significant role of Mongolian influence on Russian history and culture and 3) the importance of the interaction between Slavs and Turanians (Uralic-Altaic, Turkic peoples). The historian Lev Gumilev (1912-1992), who revived the concept in the USSR, also recognized the symbiosis between Turanians and Russians. According to these theses, which are strongly endorsed today by Putin, Russian civilization is not solely European or Asian, but rather something distinct.

A NEW IDEOLOGY – POLITICAL CORRECTNESS

Antonio Gramsci, who believed that *"as long as workers have a Christian soul, the Revolution will not be possible"*, and Georg Lukacs, a Cominternist who wondered *"Who will save us from Western (non-European) civilization?"* are considered the founding fathers of Cultural Marxism, the totalitarian ideology known today as Political Correctness. In 1923, the Frankfurt School was established, which founded the new, yet old ideology. In 1933, the School moved to New York, from where it infiltrated American universities, causing havoc among thousands of students who were completely ignorant about the cultural patterns of various civilizations.

TERRITORIAL RECTIFICATIONS

1921

Upper Silesia, populated by both Germans and Poles, was formally part of Germany, but was under provisional administration by the Allies. Both Germany and Poland had laid claim to it. In a referendum organized with international assistance in 1921, over 59% of the population voted for remaining part of Germany.

Polish locals initiated a revolt (the Korfanty Uprising), leading to an interethnic conflict. After lengthy negotiations at the League of Nations, the province was divided between Germany and Poland, with the larger and industrialized southeastern part being given to Poland.

1922
After World War I, the western coast of Anatolia was returned to Greece. However, the Greek army advanced into the interior of Anatolia, providing an opportunity for the Turks, led by Mustafa Kemal Atatürk (1881-1938), to launch an offensive against them. The Greek army surrendered without a fight in Smyrna (now Izmir). Consequently, the Greeks left the western coast of Asia Minor after nearly three millennia of inhabiting and contributing to the civilization in that region.

A NEW SPIRIT WITH NEW TREATIES

1925

1928
The Treaty of Locarno between Germany and the Allied countries recognized the borders established at Versailles, and Germany was admitted to the League of Nations. The Briand-Kellogg Pact (signed by the foreign ministers of France and the USA) in 1928, endorsed by 62 states, outlawed war as a political instrument. Japan, Italy and Germany, among the signatories, repeatedly violated it from 1931 onward.

THE GREAT DEPRESSION

The stock market crash of 1929 in New York marked the beginning of a global recession that lasted for years and led to mass unemployment, a significant decrease in the standard of living and a lack of confidence in the future. The recovery from the crisis was slow and difficult, achieved only through massive public investments in infrastructure.

THE SPANISH CIVIL WAR

In 1931, the parliamentary elections in Spain were won by the Republicans (leftists). King Alfonso XIII abdicated and the republic was proclaimed. Alcala Zamora, a leftist, was elected president by the parliament. Zamora maneuvered to keep the right-wing out of power, even though the elections in 1933 were won by the right. Meanwhile, the economic situation worsened, strikes occurred and the separatist actions of the Basques, Catalans and Galicians further complicated the situation, with entire regions on the brink of civil war. In 1934, in Galicia, worker militias declared a socialist republic, engaging in assassinations and looting. After a left-wing Popular Front coalition of Republicans, Socialists and Communists won the elections in February 1936, large-scale assassinations and unrest followed, as well as plundering and the seizing of property. Number two in the government was a Soviet NKVD agent. In these circumstances, the army launched an offensive against Madrid. The Republicans armed the trade unions. International brigades were formed, on both sides, composed of volunteers and mercenaries supported by the USSR, Germany and Italy.

1931

1933

1936

THE NATIONAL SOCIALISTS IN POWER

Even though Hitler's party suffered a relative defeat in the elections of November 1932, President Paul von Hindenburg (1847-1934) appointed Hitler as Chancellor on January 30, 1933. Hitler immediately abolished the Parliament, dissolved all professional and cultural organizations and conditioned the practice of professions on membership in the new organizations, all controlled by the National Socialists (DAF – German Labor Front, RNST – Class of Rural

1933

Producers, RKK – Reich Chamber of Culture). Upon Hindenburg's death in 1934, Hitler combined the presidency with the role of Chancellor and declared himself *Führer*. Through the racial laws of 1935, German Jews became second-class citizens. On *Kristallnacht* (Night of Broken Glass) on November 9-10, 1938, a new peak was reached – synagogues and Jewish shops were destroyed, and around 30.000 Jews were temporarily arrested. Of the 500.000 Jews in Germany, approximately 260.000 had left the country by the start of the war in 1939, paying an emigration tax.

IRELAND'S INDEPENDENCE

1937 The Constituent Assembly proclaimed independence in 1919, but ultimately accepted the status of a dominion in 1921. This triggered an internal crisis and a civil war. Ireland declared itself fully independent in 1937.

THE END OF EUROPE?

In 1936, philosopher Lucian Blaga (1895-1961), in his *Trilogy of Culture*, extracted the philosophy of culture from the pitfall into which Spengler, Riegl and Frobenius had led it, describing world cultures through the morphology of the spaces in which they were born. Russian culture was characterized as the culture of the steppe, the European culture as three-dimensional, the Arab culture as that of caves and so on. Later, Arnold Toynbee also adhered to this explanation. Their conclusion regarding historical evolution was that Europe was undergoing a pronounced cultural decline. And if it wasn't already finished, it would soon be "terminated". Blaga noted that there are many other elements and latent potentials that can define cultures. Cultures differ from one another through the axiological emphasis placed on the image of humanity, through their anabatic/catabatic or neutral attitude toward the moral space, through their formative aspirations and through the way in which the temporal and spatial horizons are arranged in variable constellations, ultimately imprinting the specificity of each culture. Therefore, not a debatable spatial factor, nor the morphology of the terrain, but a multitude of factors, taking into account the unconscious, produced the diverse cultural individualities of the world. Blaga observed that, in general, the style of an era is reflected in various spiritual domains. For example, Impressionism in painting has its equivalent in music, architecture, mathematics, philosophy and so on; similarly, classicism, romanticism and so on. However, this phenomenon is neither homogeneous, nor linear. The painter Grünewald, an expressionist, lived during the Renaissance, not contemporaneously with Van Gogh.

WORLD WAR II

Act 0. France and Great Britain directed Germany's expansion eastward (Austria, Czechoslovakia, etc.). **1938**

The 1ˢᵗ Act: Stalin and Hitler. In August 1939, Germany and the USSR concluded a partially secret treaty, in which they divided Eastern Europe. Based on this treaty, the USSR occupied parts of Finland, Poland, Romania and the entire Baltic countries in the years 1939-1940. Germany invaded western Poland in September 1939; after the invasion of western Poland, Great Britain and France declared war on Germany. Leaving aside the treaty with the USSR, Germany occupied the west part of continental Europe in May-June 1940, except for Great Britain, which resisted with exemplary determination under W. Churchill's leadership and the solidarity of the British people. The French Communists welcomed the occupation of France. Hungary, secured by Hitler, occupied southern Slovakia, northwestern Romania, and historic Maramureș. **1939**

1940

Germany achieved brutal hegemony in continental Europe. The ethnic Germans in Hungary were sacrificed by Hitler in favor of an alliance with Horthy. The Hungarians outdid the Germans in the savagery of collective killings and deportations against Romanians, Slovaks, Ruthenians and Jews.

1941   On June 22, 1941, after a delay of several months due to operations in Greece requested by Italy, and in Yugoslavia suggested by Hungary, the Germans invaded the Soviet Empire. Romania joined them to recover Bessarabia, the eastern half of Moldova, occupied by the Soviets under an agreement with Hitler. On December 7, Japan attacked the United States, and the next day the U.S. declared war on Japan. On December 11, Germany declared war to the

Fig. 29. "Blitzkrieg" in the West. May-June 1940

United States. Thus, America entered the war on the side of Great Britain and the USSR.

However, for a somewhat attentive observer, the Eastern Blitzkrieg had already failed, not in the face of the Red Army, but against the determined residents of Moscow who were ready to play their part. From here on, nothing was simple for Nazi Germany. According to other observers, the turning point was the Battle of Stalingrad (Nov. 1942 – Feb. 1943).

1942

The Red Army, armed by the USA, achieved increasingly significant victories. In Italy, Mussolini was deposed in July 1943, and in September, Italy signed an armistice with the Allies. Hungary also began tentative negotiations with Moscow in 1943. Moreover, from 1943, the aerial supremacy of the Allies forced Germany into a continuous retreat, leading to eventual surrender.

1943

On June 6, 1944, the Americans and the British landed in Normandy. Germany was caught in a vice from which it could not escape. The events of August 23, 1944, are not even mentioned by W. Churchill in his work *The Second World War*. But here's what the Chief of the Armed Forces High Command, General Wilhelm Keitel, and the Chief of the Army High Command, General Heinz Guderian, wrote to the Führer immediately after its outbreak: *"In addition to the immediate military consequences, it simultaneously caused an extremely dangerous front reversal that will lead to the loss of territory not only for Romania but also for Bulgaria, Yugoslavia, and Greece, endangering the entire German army in the Balkans."*

1944

June

Aug.

Objectively speaking, along the 46th parallel, from Cetatea Albă to Beba Veche in western Romania,

211

there are over 800 km along which the Red Army did not fight, but only "requisitioned". The detachment from the Axis through the arrest of the "leader" had four precedents in which Germany betrayed Romania: on August 23, 1939, in Moscow; on November 13, 1939, in Berlin; on June 15, 1940, in Berchtesgaden; and on August 30, 1940, in Vienna.

1945 *The last act*: Churchill, Roosevelt, and Stalin at Yalta. The meeting (February 4-11, 1945) of the three allies established the main lines of the future peace: 1. The USSR retains eastern Poland, compensated by the extension of the western border through the forced relocation of millions of Germans. 2. Germany and Berlin are divided into four zones of military occupation (including a French zone). 3. The Soviet Union joins the United Nations on the condition that the permanent members of the Security Council have veto power (thus giving the USSR control over the entire globe). 4. The countries occupied by the Red Army remain in the Soviet sphere of influence. Stalin emphasized that his demands were non-negotiable. All this because as early as February 20, 1943, the American president had offered the Kremlin dictator a *vast field of expansion in the small countries of Eastern Europe*.

Until the peace treaties, the Potsdam Conference divided Germany into four occupation zones and moved the truncated Poland under Soviet control westward to the Oder-Neisse rivers line.

1946 The last pogroms took place in the Soviet-occupied countries of Hungary, Czechoslovakia and Poland (Kielce).

THE ANTI-COMMUNISM RESISTANCE IN ROMANIA

The Sovietization of Romania has two characteristics that clearly differentiated it from the other countries in the East with Soviet troops on their national territory. Romanians did not have indigenous communists, but they formed resistance outposts in the mountains against communism, a resistance that lasted for 13 years (1944-1957). The process of imposing communism was carried out with leaders brought in on Soviet tanks and by appealing to the mass of Horthy supporters in Transylvania (over 600.000, according to the philosopher Gaspar Tamaş), who overnight transformed from Horthy supporters to communists and anti-fascists. The resistance involved young idealists, officers, soldiers, intellectuals, peasants – strong personalities with high morality who could not conceive of their country being communized. They awaited the "Americans", armed and ready, for the final battle against the red cancer. Due to the torture of mountain village inhabitants by the new security forces built by NKVD advisors from Romania, survival resources became increasingly scarce for resistance fighters. Infiltration of agents into partisan groups diminished the number of resistance members year after year. This phenomenon lasted for 12 years until the main groups were eliminated by the security forces.

THE AROMANIANS

Just like after World War I, one of the oldest peoples in the Balkans remained without their own state. Aromanian groups were divided among Greece, Albania, Bulgaria and Yugoslavia (North Macedonia).

THE MYTH OF THE DICTATORSHIP OF THE PROLETARIAT

In June 1953, in East Berlin, Dresden and Magdeburg, the first workers' strikes, and large-scale demonstrations took place in the Soviet bloc as a response to the authorities' intention to increase work

1953

213

quotas for the workers. Three thousand workers were arrested by Soviet troops, and 13.000 by the East German militia. In February 1956, the leader of the Bolshevik Party, Khrushchev (1894-1971), himself a former collaborator of Stalin's, condemned Stalinist terror and attempted to end the cult of Stalin. In June **1956**, in Poznan, nearly 100.000 Polish workers demanded better working conditions and took to the streets. They were met with tanks and 10.000 soldiers. Almost a hundred workers were killed.

1956

In June 1956, the ideologue of the USSR, Mikhail Suslov, sent a message to the Hungarians: there are too **1956** many Jews in the leadership of the Hungarian communist state. On October 23, 1956, students in Budapest initiated a nationalist demonstration, demanding *a government without Jews and Schwabs* (see Johann Weidlein, a witness). Tens of thousands of people joined them. After Hungarian security forces opened fire on the demonstrators, the protest quickly turned violent. Imre Nagy (1896-1958), a former member of the team that assassinated the Romanov family and a former Cheka member, was reinstated as prime minister on October 24. The government formed at that time included bourgeois politicians as well. On November 1, 1956, Nagy announced Hungary's withdrawal from the Warsaw Pact and its neutrality. Three days later, the Soviet army intervened and suppressed the movement. Loss of life was estimated at around 2.500 Hungarians and 700 Soviet soldiers. Another approximately 200.000 citizens, many of them agents of Hungarian and Soviet services, left Hungary and sought refuge in the West.

After the uprising, the communist regime established in Budapest by the Soviets became the most loyal, but also the "freest" within the Eastern Bloc.

THE EUROPEAN COMMUNITY

With the aim of strengthening the economies of France, Benelux, Italy and the Federal Republic of Germany, which was created in the western area of occupation, the Coal and Steel Community (Benelux, **1952** France and FRG), established in 1952, evolved into a customs union – the European Economic Community – in 1957. Over time, it also assumed political **1957** objectives. In 1973, the Community expanded with the accession of Denmark, Ireland and the United Kingdom, followed by Greece in 1981, and Spain and Portugal in 1986. After the fall of communism, Austria, Finland, and Sweden joined in 1995; in 2004, Cyprus, the Czech Republic, Estonia, Hungary, Latvia, Lithuania, Malta, Poland and Slovakia; in 2007, Romania and Bulgaria; and, in 2013, Croatia. The United Kingdom left the EU in 2020.

THE BUCHAREST SPRING

The above phrase belongs to American professor Larry L. Watts, who studied thousands of archival documents regarding Romania's split from the Soviet bloc. Similar to the United Kingdom or West Germany, Romania was a target, not an ally, of Soviet intelligence services. Romania engaged in international relations based on principles rather than interests, a stance that caused unimaginable losses to the Soviets in Egypt, Israel, Vietnam, China and Angola. The separation of Romania from the Soviet bloc was unquestionable for experts; in August 1968, when the Soviet bloc's intervention in Prague became evident even to the uninformed, the split was undeniable. The dictator from Bucharest had been so "processed" in the West by the

Soviet services and their satellites (Hungary, Bulgaria, Czechoslovakia, East Germany, Poland, Yugoslavia and Finland) that, not comprehending what was happening, his only reaction was to tighten his grip. External independence was coupled with a repugnant internal dictatorship, based on the secret police – the *Securitate*.

KONRAD LORENZ, A LUCID MIND

Lorenz, the father of ethology, in a synthesis of the 20th century titled *Civilized Man's Eight Deadly Sins*, observed the causal interdependencies between certain ongoing processes today that threaten not only our culture, but also humanity as a species. The scientist's past affiliation with the "National Socialist" movement may have somewhat relativized his highly reasoned and grave warning at the same time. The processes highlighted by Lorenz in today's world include: i) overpopulation, ii) the destruction of the natural world, iii) the perpetual competition of humanity beyond its limits, iv) the disappearance of emotions, sentiments and increased intolerance to the slightest sensation of discomfort, v) genetic decay and degradation, vi) the destruction of tradition, vii) decreased cultural immunity to indoctrination. These are interconnected and mutually aggravating. Some of these processes are easy to understand and notice, while others are prove to be more a challenge. The doctrine that asserts that only cultural and material "conditioning", to which a person is subjected throughout their life, determines their social and moral behaviour, completely excluding the most intimate organization that stems from phylogeny, is pseudoscientific. Proponents of this doctrine claim that humans are born as a blank slate and all their consciousness, knowledge and feelings are the result of "conditioning". From this contemporary fallacy that all people are born equal stems the current politics. The only valid conclusion should be that everyone should have equal chances for development. Lorenz further believes that ignoring innate behavior is not only entirely wrong, but also has apocalyptic consequences for the human species.

REVIVAL AND REGRESSION

Pope Paul VI (1963-1978) renounced the *filioque*, accepting the creed of Nicaea: *"the creed of the immortal tradition of the Holy Church..."*

1968

French youths, inspired by Maoist leftism, wanted "something else", even if they themselves didn't know what exactly, and imposed their desire for change in France.

The Soviets, however, didn't accept the new political directions; they intervened militarily, alongside satellite states, in Czechoslovakia, which believed in and desired a "humane socialism".

THE FALL OF COMMUNISM

Karol Wojtyla was elected pope in 1978. Nine months later, he told the Poles, "Don't be afraid." After a year, the "Solidarnosc Union" appeared, and the monopoly of communist power disappeared forever.

1978

"Transparency" was the new policy of Mikhail Gorbachev, the General Secretary of the Communist Party of the Soviet Union. The Soviets supported the "reformist" communists in the satellite countries of Europe (Poland, Czechoslovakia, East Germany, Hungary and Bulgaria) through their satellite intelligence services. In Romania, which was not a Soviet satellite (see Larry Watts), things progressed slowly. An agreement with the Americans and a "tourist" invasion by the Soviets were needed to initiate change. In the Soviet plan, there was a massacre of 60.000 people, which, when attributed to the dictator, would justify the intervention of French and Hungarian armies. Gorbachev didn't accept overt intervention. As

1985

1989

Romanians mobilized unexpectedly against the dictatorial regime, 162 people were killed before the dictator fled. Afterward, six times more people were killed. One scenario was staged and another played out, even if partially. The German Democratic Republic, with Soviet bases on its territory, reunified with the Federal Republic through the will of the citizens, Chancellor Kohl's skill and Gorbachev's acquiescence.

NEW STATES ON THE MAP OF EUROPE

1991 The Communist Party of the Soviet Union, which aimed to reform the USSR, lost power in Moscow and in all the union republics. These republics declared independence one after another: the Baltic states, Ukraine, Moldova, Belarus, Russia, the Caucasian republics and the Central Asian ones in 1991.

THE BLOODY BREAKING APART OF YUGOSLAVIA

1991 Against the backdrop of long-standing disagreements and differing levels of economic development among the federation's republics, fratricidal war was fuelled and sustained from outside. Religious intolerance also played a significant role. The Ten-Day War or the War of Independence of Slovenia was the first civil war in a series that followed *the Declaration of Independence of Slovenia* on June 25, 1991. It was fought by local Slovene defence formations against the Yugoslav army and lasted from June 27 to July 7, 1991, when an agreement was signed, by which Belgrade recognized Slovenia's independence. The majority of Croats desired independence and supported leaving Yugoslavia, while 1992 ethnic Serbs in Croatia backed Serbia and opposed secession. Many Serbs aspired to a new Serbian state within the Yugoslav federation encompassing all areas predominantly inhabited by them in Croatia and Bosnia and Herzegovina. This marked the beginning of the Serbo-Croatian War. Each side sought to gain as much territory as possible. The ceasefire was established in 1992, but Croatia continued military operations until 1995, also participating in the war in Bosnia. In 1995, Croatia launched *Operation Storm* with the aim of capturing Krajina (eastern Croatia), populated by many Orthodox Christians. In the Republic of Macedonia, a referendum for independence held on September 8, 1991, resulted in 95,26% of the population voting for independence and leaving the Yugoslav federation. Independence was proclaimed on September 25, 1991. Macedonia was the first former federation member to gain sovereignty without resistance from Belgrade. The former republic of Bosnia and Herzegovina declared independence on March 3, 1992. After numerous incidents involving Slavs, Muslim Slavs, or Catholics, the actual war began on April 6, 1992, and ended on December 14, 1995. The main military actors were the Muslim forces of the former Republic of Bosnia and Herzegovina, the self-proclaimed entities of the Bosnian Serbs and Bosnian Croats. Many civilians also participated in the violent ethnic cleansing actions. *Kosovo.* The West failed, diplomatically **1999** speaking, to secure the withdrawal of the Serbian army from the province of Kosovo and to remove Milosevic, the President of Serbia, in order to allow the Albanian refugees in Albania and Greece to return home. NATO launched air strikes against Serbia on March 24, 1999. The air raids involved the USA and Germany. After 79 days of bombing, the Serbian army withdrew from Kosovo. The province of Kosovo received assistance from European organizations until 2008. International peacekeeping forces, KFOR, with a contingent of 50.000 soldiers, were deployed in the province to maintain order. In 2008, Kosovo self-proclaimed independence. The legal framework through which independence was achieved is fragile and beneficial to Russia. The "unseen" architects of Kosovo's independence were not hindered by legal grounds and geopolitical consequences Montenegro, inhabited by Slavs and Orthodox Slavized peoples, left the federation with Serbia through a referendum and became independent. Serbia did not intervene militarily.

MOLDOVA'S STRUGGLE FOR INTEGRITY

In Transnistria, the space between the Bug and Dniester rivers, the Russians came after 1792, the entire province being inhabited by Moldovans and a few Tatars, a fact confirmed by a Tsarist conscription from 1793: *between the Dniester and Bug rivers, out of 67 villages, 49 were exclusively Romanian, and the rest were mixed with Tatars*. Because in 1918 the Transnistrians remained under the influence of the Soviets and were undergoing Russification, Stalin established a new republic, the Moldavian Autonomous Soviet Socialist Republic; in 1934, it covered an area of 8.434 square kilometers and had a population of 615.500, of which 80% were Romanians. Furthermore, even after the "census" conducted by the criminal authorities in Tiraspol in 2004, the majority of the locals were Moldovans (50,3% in rural areas). Stalin ceded the southern part of Bessarabia and northern Moldova to Ukraine and annexed a small portion of the Moldavian Autonomous Soviet Socialist Republic on the left bank of the Dniester to Soviet Bessarabia. This new Moldova declared its independence from Russia after the Moscow coup in 1991.

Even before the Moscow coup, the law enforcement agencies of the USSR, directly instigated by the President of the Soviet Union, Lukyanov, became involved in the Republic of Moldova. This involvement became increasingly aggressive after the former Soviet republics declared their independence from Moscow. The Russians sent officers from the special forces OMON, discharged soldiers, convicts, volunteers, thugs, and Cossacks to Moldova, who incited, terrorized, and killed the locals. Russia successfully conducted misleading campaigns through the press, radio and television. Their agents in Germany did their duty. Here's a fragment from a letter from the residents of Dubăsari, in Transnistria, addressed to the President of Moldova, Mircea Snegur, the President of Russia, Boris Yeltsin, the President of Ukraine, Leonid Kravchuk, the President of Belarus, Stanislav Shushkevich, and the Mayor of St. Petersburg: *"The residents of the city of Dubăsari - Moldovans, Ukrainians, Jews, Russians, Bulgarians - address you. Life in the city has become unbearable for us; the separatists of Transnistria deprive us of the basic human rights: the right to life, to work, to exist on this land. Those who support the legal authorities, and the independence of Moldova are constantly persecuted and blackmailed. Our houses are set on fire, peaceful population is shot at directly, those who support the legal Power of the Republic of Moldova are taken prisoners. They are taken to basements... All of this is done by the so-called National Guard of Transnistria, which accepted newcomers from the entire USSR, common criminals, mentally ill individuals, minors."* Mihail Bergman, a participant, and commander of the Russian army in Transnistria, tells us about the activities of the special OMON forces of the Soviet empire: *"These individuals, acting under orders from their leader, carried out the dirtiest tasks. They eliminated unwanted individuals, initiated actions to incite separation, created diversions on their own territory (for example, blowing up*

221

electricity poles), provided documents from the KGB archive of the Moldavian SSR." Moldova did not have an army in 1992. The combat formations were hastily assembled during the aggression, composed of volunteers and equipped with leftover Soviet supplies. Some political leaders were connected to the KGB and betrayed or conducted business with the separatist leaders. Even under these circumstances, the volunteer army, armed with makeshift equipment, managed to shock the Russian army. When a warlike general took command of the 14th Army in June 1992, this theoretically neutral force intervened with artillery, aviation and infantry units on the side of the criminals from Tiraspol. Tens of thousands of houses and buildings were destroyed, and hundreds of thousands of Moldovans fled the conflict zones (80.000 from Tighina alone).

Fig. 30. The refuge of Moldovans from Transnistria in 1992 [14].

The Moldovan politicians reached a ceasefire agreement with the criminals from Tiraspol. The military intervention of the Commonwealth of Independent States (Russia and Ukraine) was supposedly "seeking peace". This is what Russia wanted, at least for the moment – an opportunity to "pacify" the conflict it had generated. What happened in Transnistria is characteristic of the operating methods of the "Russians". They provoke, engage in acts of sabotage and even mass assassinations, and then appear with peacekeeping troops to resolve the unbearable situation.

MOLDOVA

Territories across the Dniester, ethnic map (2004) drawn by the occupation authorities

a) mediul rural

16,7% 50,3% 26,5%

Total rural 177680

Raionul Camenca
Raionul Ribniţa
Raionul Dubăsari
Raionul Grigoriopol
Oraşul Tiraspol
Tighina
Raionul Slobozia
RÎBNIŢA
CAMENCA
DUBĂSARI
GRIGORIOPOL
TIRASPOL
TIGHINA
SLOBOZIA

LEGENDĂ:

Romanian
Ukrainian
Russian

state border
district boundaries

Map processed by Octavian Căpăţînă

Partile estice ale Moldovei	Total	romani	rusi si rusificati	ucraineni si ucrainizati	evrei	altii
Teritoriu controlat de rusi	555347	177382	168678	160060	1259	47959
	100,00%	31,94%	30,37%	28,82%	0,23%	8,64%
Teritoriu revendicat de rusi	588308	205146	179745	160874	1269	48275
	100,00%	34,99%	29,12%	27,44%	0,22%	8,23%
Teritoriu din stanga Nistrului	461715	168413	117599	140664	876	34163
	100,00%	36,48%	25,47%	30,47%	0,19%	7,40%
Unitatile admin. din stanga Nistrului controlate de rusi	439977	147877	117017	140172	867	34044
	100,00%	33,61%	26,60%	31,86%	0,20%	7,74%

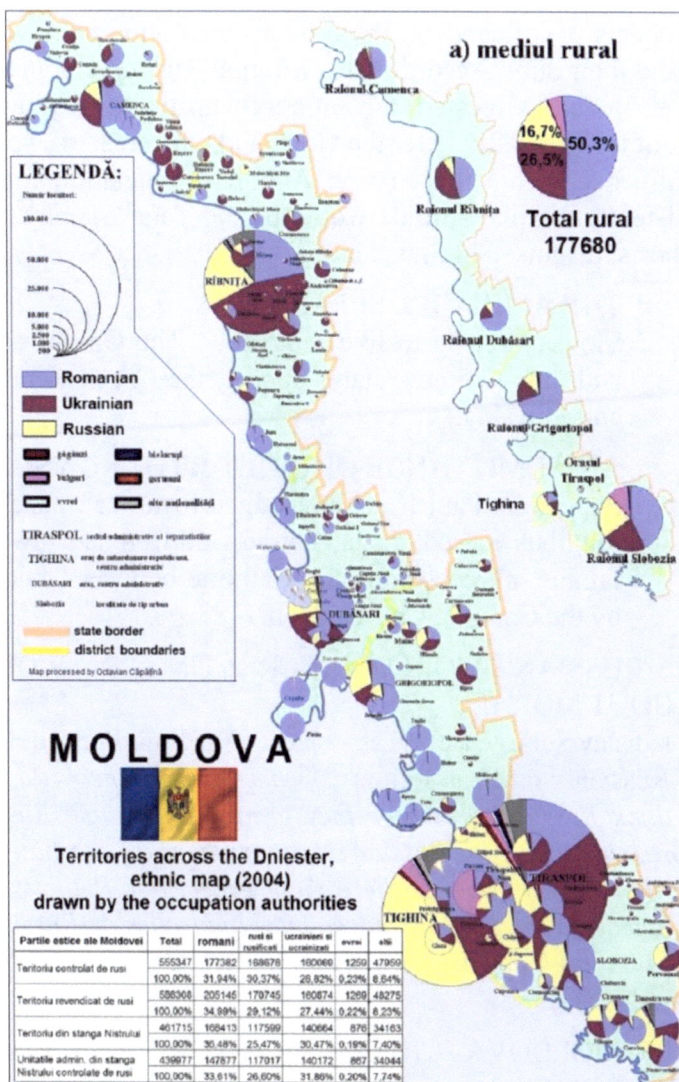

Fig. 31. Ethnographic map drafted by the criminal regime in Tiraspol. The indigenous population, those from rural areas, are predominantly Romanians.

223

The agents of influence in the foreign press and on television also did their duty. According to N. Iorga, Russian colonialism was attributed to Western adventurers who took refuge at the court of the tsars after Peter the Great and who created a sphere of influence within the empire. Another explanation for the consistently warlike attitude would be the Tatar-Slavic ethnic synthesis, disguised in Slavic attire.

1993 THE AMICABLE SEPARATION
Slovaks decide to live separately. The Czechs agree and thus two new states appear, the Czech Republic and Slovakia.

2000 AN ADMITTANCE OF GUILT WITH NUANCES
Pope John Paul II acknowledged historical mistakes: religious hatred, racial hatred, indifference towards famine, all committed by Catholic believers, but *not* by the Catholic Church itself.

THE RUSSIAN WORLD – CREATING A WORLD WITHOUT MORAL

Vladislav Surkov, a close associate of Vladimir Putin, defined "the Russian world" as follows: *"where people speak Russian and think Russian, or where they greatly appreciate Russian culture, where they see Russian development as an alternative to what they have at home, where they respect our Putin, where people fear our weapons – any country that relies on Russia for protection and defence is part of the Russian world"* (see Armand Goşu).

AFTER MOLDOVA, CHECHNYA, GEORGIA - CRIMEA AND DONBASS

After the fall of Constantinople, Crimea fell to the invading Turks. The envoy of Stephen the Great (1457-1504) to Venice, in May 1477, addressed the Senate of the Republic, saying: *"It is of the utmost importance that Moldova, which is the defensive*

224

barrier of Poland and Hungary, not be abandoned, at least now when the Turks are preparing to attack Chilia and Cetatea Albă, which are most important for Moldova, the key to regaining Crimea..." Not only Transnistria, as seen before, but also the mouth of the Dniester River, the western proximity to Crimea, were ethnically Romanian, and Moldova defended the area against the Tatars. The Tatars became increasingly aggressive under the Ottoman Empire's rule. In 1783, Crimea passed from Ottoman suzerainty to Russian suzerainty, with the new suzerains promising to respect its autonomy. However, Russia did what it knew best. It generated internal conflicts that weakened the Khanate and then fully subjugated it. After World War II, the Tatars were deported by Stalin. In 2014, the majority of Crimea's population was Russophone, with the other part consisting of Ukrainians and indigenous Tatars. There were also families of Russian military personnel stationed there. According to the bilateral agreement between Russia and Ukraine in 1997, the Russian Federation had the right to a military presence in Crimea of no more than 25,000 soldiers. Under the cover of this agreement, Russia transferred an additional 9,000 soldiers in March 2014 without specifying the purpose and without anyone identifying them. In a tense and threatening atmosphere, local authorities supported by Moscow "organized" a local referendum for annexation to the Russian Federation, following Stalin's doctrine – *it doesn't matter who votes or what they vote for, only who counts the votes*. The result was that all of Crimea wanted to join Russia. The Kremlin immediately granted their "wish" and annexed the province. How the Tatars and Ukrainians voted, if they voted at all, remains a mystery.

Maskirovka is the Russian doctrine by which they create the fire and then come to extinguish it, never actually leaving once the job is done. Emboldened by their success in March 2014 in Crimea, in April they intervened with *insigniae*-less soldiers in the Russian-speaking Donbass region of Ukraine. This was followed by a civil war fuelled by Russia, as seen in Moldova, Georgia, Chechnya and everywhere else for the past three centuries. A century ago, intellectuals were bought from France; now, companies, organizations, parties, governments are instead bribed and bought.

THE INVASION OF UKRAINE. THE GENOCIDE

The conflicts between Moscow and Moldova (1992), Chechnya (2000), Georgia (2008) and Ukraine (2014) didn't "awaken" the free world, not even its leaders, such as the US and the UK. Here are some ideas about Russia in, from one of the most knowledgeable individuals on the planet on this matter, the Russian Gary Kasparov:

Hitler and Stalin invaded Poland, and now Putin has invaded Ukraine; there's no real difference. In particular, Obama and Merkel were not only paralyzed by Moscow's aggression (1992-2014), but their inaction encouraged the dictator in Moscow. Paradoxically, so many Western politicians seem more like clowns, while a former comedian has become a leader. Meanwhile, Germany and France sold military equipment to Russia. At the very least, economic sanctions should have been imposed before the invasion (February 24, 2022), not after, as sanctions can only play a preventive role. The liberation of Ukraine, including the recovery of Crimea, would put an end to three centuries of Russian invasions. Ukraine's victory will mark the beginning of freeing Russia from the imperial virus and fascism, enabling it to become part of the civilized world.

The genocide in Ukraine highlighted the failure of the UN, which should be left to die (or vegetate), and a new organization should be established in its place, based on new principles where the moral condition of its members is mandatory. The only G7 governments that rose to the occasion after the invasion on February 24, 2022 were the Anglo-Saxon ones.

Fig. 32. The Russians passed through Irpin (Ukraine) - 2022. Net public source

Fig. 33. The Russians passed through Harkyiv (Ukraine) – 2024. Net public source

A few years before, Samuel Huntington was artificially inventing, bookishly, a conflict now contradicted. In reality, it is a battle between civilization and barbarism. Barbarism or Euro-Asianism, here, means the denial of the individual, which is the essence of the European spirit. Petro-Dollars (Yuan) of Moscow are successfully used to buy journalists and press   agencies, politicians, parties and governments. And not just from developing countries, but even from EU member states.

THE EUROPEAN WORLD OUTSIDE EUROPE AND THE UNITED NATIONS

At least the United States, Canada, Australia etc. carry on the spirit of Europe with great vigour. This doesn't mean that these "European" countries outside of Europe aren't faced both with real and invented problems. Japan and South Korea, with original cultures vastly different from those of Europeans, politically speaking, have been "Europeanized" as well.

Today, the democratic world is balanced against the totalitarian world (China, Russia, Iran, etc.). China excels in science and technology and has become the second-largest economy after the US. In this geopolitical context, the UN has become not only an insignificant and practically useless organization, due to the veto power in the Security Council (US, UK, France, Russia, China). Therefore, totalitarian states like Russia and China, regardless of their actions or intentions, will never be condemned by the UN. The genocide in Ukraine won't be condemned by the UN Security Council. The world witnessed horrifying events during World War I and World War II, events that seemed impossible to repeat. Just as a figure from the 19th century, Erich von Ludendorff, laid the foundation for Nazi revenge, another figure from the 20th century, now completely outdated, started the genocide in Ukraine. But now, the new administration installed on January 20, 2025 in Washington raises big question marks.

A NEW WORLD ORGANIZATION BASED ON ETHICS

Totalitarian states cannot be part of such an organization, nor can client states or states that lack the minimal decency to condemn the genocide in Ukraine. Such an organization must be able to intervene effectively in cases like those in Moldova (1992), Chechnya (2000), Georgia (2008), or Ukraine (2014, 2022).

NATURE AS AN INDIVISIBLE WHOLE (ECO-HUMANISM)

We've seen that Stoicism aimed at achieving happiness through virtue. And, by virtue, in the broadest sense, they also meant living in harmony with nature. Virtue, to them, was rational, in contrast to passion, which was irrational. The Renaissance, in contrast to scholasticism, discovered that man is the measure of all things. From there, it was only a small step, two centuries ago, until Kant and then the Romantics established that reason and conscience should have an active role to play. Since then, the brutal and unbalanced intervention of man upon nature has accelerated and intensified. With a syncope at the dawn of the modern era, with their pantheistic-naturalistic ontology Giordano Bruno, Lucilio Vanini, Hieronymus Cardano and Baruch Spinoza saw man as part of nature and not above nature. This conception was harshly rejected by the Catholic church and the idea died. The Renaissance and Romantic idea of man as the measure of all things has since "shaped" the unbalanced intervention on nature. Not even Hegel, who believed that modern philosophy should start from Spinoza, could rehabilitate the natural ontology. Perhaps the ideas of Edmund Husserl (1859-1938), the founder of phenomenology, who tried to bridge the gap between empiricism and rationalism, can succeed in rehabilitating natural ontology today.

BIBLIOGRAPHY

1. P. Anonymus, *Cronica notarului Anonymus*, București, ISBN 973-9182-34-5
2. Jessikka Aro, *Trolii lui Putin*, 2021, ISBN 978-6069-68216-6
3. Adolf Armbruster, *The Romanity of Romanians*, ISBN 978-973-45-0660-6
4. George Barițiu, *Părți alese din istoria Transilvaniei*, 1993, Brașov
5. Lucian Blaga, *Izvoade*, ed. Minerva, Bucharest, 1972
6. Lucian Blaga, *Romanian Thinking in 18th Century Transylvania*, Bucharest, 1966
7. Lucian Blaga, *Experiment and Mathematical Spirit*, Bucharest, 1969
8. Lucian Blaga, *The Trilogy of Culture*, Bucharest, 1969
9. Stelian Brezeanu, *The History of the Byzantine Empire*, 2007, ISBN 978-973-7839-20-6
10. Jean Carpentier, *The History of Europe*, ISBN 978.2.7578.4982.5
11. N. Cartojan, *The History of the Old Romanian Literature*, Bucharest, 1940-1945
12. Octavian Căpățînă, *Culture, Confession, Ethnicity, and Race in the Middle Basin of the Danube*, 2024, ISBN 978-1-0364-0874-9
13. George Ciorănescu, *Bessarabia, a Disputed Land*, ISBN 973-9155-17-0
14. Ion Costaș, *Transnistria 1989-1992*, 2012, 978-606-609-330-9
15. Stephane Courtois, *Cartea neagră a comunismului*, 2024, ISBN 978-6306-543-849
16. Florian Curta, Sorin Paliga, *Slavii în perioada migraților*, 2023, ISBN 978-606-537-584-0
17. Sergiu Pavel Dan, *Scipio's Dream - The History of Rome*, Cluj-Napoca, 1983
18. Ovidiu Drâmba, *History of Culture and Civilization*, Bucharest, 1984-2010
19. Mircea Eliade, *From Zamolxis to Genghis Khan*, Bucharest, 1980
20. Mircea Eliade, *The History of Religious Beliefs and Ideas*, Bucharest, 1986
21. Mihai Fătu, 1985, *Biserica românească din Nord-Vestul țării sub ocupația horthistă*, București
22. Jacob Field, *The History of Europe in Bite-sized Chunks*, ISBN 978-606-33-4152-6

23. Traian Golea, *Transylvania and Hungarian Revisionism*, Miami Beach, 1988, ISBN 0-937019-08-9

24. Armand Goşu, *Russia – A Complicated Equation*, 2022, ISBN 978-973-468931-6

25. Armand Goşu, *Putin against free-world, 2023*, ISBN 978-973-46686-4

26. Nicolae Gudea, *Christiana Minora*, 2011, ISBN 978-606-543-126-3

27. Nicolae Gudea, Ioan Ghiurco, 2002, Din istoria creştinismului la romîni, Cluj-Napoca, ISBN 973-647-074-1,

28. Bogdan Petriceicu Haşdeu, *The Critical History of Romanians*, Bucharest, 1984

29. Elisabeth Heresch, *The Secret Parvus Documents*, ISBN 978-606-910-089-9

30. Eva Heyman, *I Lived So Little*, 1991, ISBN 973-9011-02-0

31. Take Ionescu, *Memories, Speeches*, 2005, ISBN 973-8434-66-1

32. Nicolae Iorga, *Byzantium After Byzantium*, Bucharest, 1972

33. Simon Jenkins, *A Short History of Europe*, ISBN 978-606-33-4527-2

34. Gordon Kerr, *A Short History of Europe*, ISBN 978-606-535-682-5

35. Milton G. Lehrer, *Transylvania, A Romanian Region*, 1991, ISBN 973-29-0010

36. B.P. Haşdeu, Istoria Critică a Românilor, Bucharest, 1984

37. H. Kinder, W. Hilgemann, *Atlas of World History*, 1978, ISBN 0-14-051054-0

38. G. Popa-Lisseanu, *Fontes Historiae Daco-Romanorum*, 2020, ISBN 978-606-17-1702-6

39. Oliver Lustig*, Distortions and Forgeries* ..., Bucharest, Mag.Istoric, 1985

40. Karl Marx, *Notes on Romanians*, Bucharest, 1964

41. Anton Moraru, *Bessarabia under the Colonial Yoke of Russia* ..., Chişinău, 2007

42. Vasile Muscă, *A Course on the History of Philosophy, 2018-2020*, Carpatica Foundation

43. Gelu Neamţu, *Documents for the Future Regarding the Anti-Romanian Genocide in Transylvania*, ISBN 978-973-109-169-3

44. Mihai Netea, *An (Incomplete) Genetic History of Romanians*, ISBN 978-973-5075712, 2022

45. Jean Nouzille, *The Calvary of Romanian Prisoners of War in Alsace-Lorraine 1917-1918*, Bucharest, 1997

46. M. Oppermann, *The Thracians between the Carpathian Arch and the Aegean Sea*, Bucharest 1988

47. S. Paliga, Al. Comşa, *An Anthropological Perspective*, ISBN 978-973-728-703-8

48. Teodor V. Păcăţian, 1904-1915, Cartea de aur, Sibiu

49. Vasile Pârvan, *Epigraphic Contributions to Daco-Roman Christianity*, Bucharest, 1911

50. Adrian Poruciuc, *The Prehistoric Roots of Romanian Traditions*, 2018, ISBN 9789736423710

51. David Prodan, *Transylvania and again Transylvania*, 1992, ISBN 973-9132-52-9

52. Ion Iosif Russu, *The Ethnogenesis of Romanians*, Bucharest, 1981

53. Cont. de Saint Aulaire, *The Notes of a Diplomat ...*, 978-973-50-5292-8

54. Ioan Slavici, vol.8, *Historical and Ethnographic Writings*, ISBN 978-973-637-158-5

55. R. W. Seton-Watson, *Racial Problems in Hungary*, Midleton, DE, USA, 2012, ISBN MOD 1005462344

56. Alexandru Şafran, *An Ember Torn from the Flames*, 1996, ISBN 973-97375-6-0

57. Gheorghe Şincai, *Chronicle of Romanians and ...*, BPT, Bucharest, 1978

58. Ion Taloş, *Emperor Trajan and the Romanity of Romanians*, 2021, ISBN 978-606-797-739-4

59. Octavian C. Tăslăuanu, *With the Austrian Army in Galicia*, first published in 1919, 2019, ISBN 4 444000 34073 9

60. Dominique Venner, *The Shock of History: Religion, Memory, Identity*, ISBN 978973736361-9

61. Larry L Watts, *Misapprehending Romania: The Impact of Cognitive Bias, Organizational Pathologies and Disinformation on US assessments of Romanian policy and behavior during the Cold War*,

62. Johann Weidlein, *Investigations into Hungary's Minority Policy*, Schorndorf, 1990

63. Johann Weidlein, *The Image of the German in the Hungarian Literature*, 2002, ISBN 973-577-257-4

64. Johann Weidlein, *Hungary's Revisionist Policy and the Decline of the German Empire Reflected in Hungarian Documents*, rev. Der Donauschwabe

65. Johann Weidlein, Der Aufstand in Ungarn un das ungarlandische Judentum, 1957, Schorndorf
66. Moshe Carmilly Weinberger, *The History of Jews in Transylvania*, Bucharest, 1994, ISBN 973-45-0090-2

List of figures

Fig. 2. The gradual advance of HOMO SAPIENS (97,5%) in Europe

Fig. 2. Neolithic artifacts from the Lower Danube. Cucuteni culture. Sources: Muzeul Arh. Cucuteni, Muzeul de Istorie Iaşi, Muzeul de Istorie Naţională Bucureşti.

Fig. 3. The gradual advance of Indo-Europeans

Fig. 4. Europe, 1000 BC. Between the Thracians and Celts there existed an area of interference

Fig. 5. The provinces of Asia Minor

Fig. 6. Marc Aurelius Source: free image from the internet

Fig. 7. the 5 emperors chosen on merit. (author composition)

Fig. 8. The Roman Empire at the time of Trajan

Fig. 9. Fragment, depicting the middle Danube region according to an old Carolingian map.

Fig.10. The expulsion of the Jews from Western Europe

Fig. 11. The 3 famous Flavius: Tribonian, Iustinian, Belisarius (author composition)

Fig. 12. The Roman Empire at the time of Justinian

Fig. 13. The division of the Frankish Empire

Fig. 14. Map of Europe in the year 1000

Fig. 15. The Soviet deportations in Besserabia between 1940-41 and 1944-52

Fig.16. The detachment of Italian painting from the Byzantine hieratics took centuries. (author composition)

Fig.17. Renaissance, Renewal of Europe - Venus (drawing by Lucian Şoit inspired after S. Botticelli)

Fig. 18. Renaissance, Renewal of Europe - Mars (drawing by Lucian Şoit after St. Catterson)

Fig. 19. The European territories of Charles V

Fig. 20. Political map of Europe in 1600

Fig. 21. The sculpture of the "Three Hierarchs" church. Iasi 1642 (author photo)

Fig.22. The partition of states: Moldova (Romanians) and of the Lithuanian-Polish Union

Fig. 23. Churchill's proposal to Stalin, Source: https://en.wikipedia.org/wiki/Percentages_agreement

Fig. 24. The Romanian modern state 1859

Fig. 25. The Second German Empire

Fig. 26. Telegram from Grand Duke Nicholas of Russia, 1877, requesting urgent assistance from Romania.
Source: Album de documente, 1981, Arhivele Statului Bucureşti

Fig.27. After a British cartoon (redrawn by the author)

Fig. 28. WWI. Eastern front.1917-1918

Fig. 29. "Blitzkrieg" in the West. May-June 1940

Fig. 30. The refuge of Moldovans from Transnistria in 1992 Source: Public, 1992, Chişinău

Fig. 31. Ethnographic map drafted by the criminal regime in Tiraspol, 2004. Source: Public, Census, Md

Fig. 32. The Russians passed through Irpin (Ukraine) - 2022.

Fig. 33. The Russians passed through Harkyiv (Ukraine) - 2024.

Aetius; 73; 74
Alaric; 72
Albert of Buxhoeveden; 42
Albert the Great; 85
Alexander I, king of Serbs, Croats and Sloven; 201
Alexander II, pope; 92
Alexander II, tsar; 184
Alexander the Great; 26; 28
Alexander V, pope; 125
Alexander VI, pope; 126
Alexios III, emperor; 98
Alexios Komnenos; 92
Alfonso III; 96
Alfonso XIII; 207
Ambrose, bishop; 54; 65
Andrew II, of Hungary; 91
Anne Stuart; 149
Anselm of Canterbury; 85
Anthony the Great; 57
Apolodorus of Damascus; 44
Archimedes; 32
Ariosto; 122
Aristarchus; 33
Aristotle; 23; 24; 25; 26; 28; 29; 31; 32; 52; 85; 95; 112; 119; 160; 163

Armbruster, Adolf; 51; 231
Aron Vodă; 143
Atatürk, Kemal; 206
Augustine; 41; 54; 112; 136; 153
Augustine of Canterbury; 41
Averroes; 28; 95; 112
Babeș; 48
Bacon Roger; 111; 160
Bacon, Francis; 23; 140; 152; 160
Baldwin of Flanders; 99
Barițiu, Gheorghe; 165
Bărnuțiu, Simion; 171
Basil II, emperor; 64; 80; 84
Batu, khan; 110
Bayezid Ildirim; 126
Belisarius; 75; 76; 77
Benedict of Nursia; 57
Benedict VIII, pope; 55
Benz Karl; 161
Berengar II; 89
Bergman, Mihail; 221
Bernard of Clairvaux; 92
Bismarck; 178
Björnson; 165
Blaga; 16; 17; 111; 184; 208; 231

Boccaccio; 119; 122
Bodin, Jean; 122; 129; 141
Bogdan Khmelnytsky; 150
Bohr; 180; 186
Boltzmann; 180
Boniface VIII, pope; 114; 128
Boris, khan; 63; 80; 85
Born, Max; 180; 187
Bosch, Hieronymus; 122
Botticelli; 122
Brahe, Tycho; 34
Brâncoveanu, Constantin; 152; 157; 158
Briand-Kellogg, pact; 206
Brunelleschi; 122
Brunswick, general; 166
Buisson Just; 161
Burckhardt; 118
Caesar; 37; 59; 77
Calixtus II, pope; 95
Calvin; 65; 101; 124; 135
Cantemir
    Antiochus; 147
    Dimitrie; 147
Caracalla; 51
Carol I of Romania; 181
Carol II of Romania; 201
Catherine of Aragon.; 135
Catherine the Great; 155; 158
Catiline; 37
Celestine III, pope; 90
Chain, Ernst; 48

Charlemagne; 41; 81; 82
Charles I Stuart; 149
Charles III of France; 82
Charles IV – Wenceslaus; 117
Charles IV of France; 115
Charles IX of France; 137
Charles Martel; 79; 80
Charles of Lorraine; 151
Charles the Bald; 82
Charles the Bold; 131
Charles V, Quint; 129; 131; 132; 133; 134; 136
Charles VI, Habsburg; 157
Charles VII of France; 129; 132
Charles VIII of France; 135
Charles XII of Sweden; 155
Childeric; 80
Churchill, Winston; 159; 160; 209; 211; 212
Ciurcu Alexandru; 161
Cleisthenes; 20
Clement V, pope; 90; 114
Clement VII, pope; 125; 129
Clement XIV, pope; 59
Clodius Pulcher; 37
Clovis; 63; 74
Coandă Henri; 161
Columbus; 33; 113
Conrad III; 92

Conrad von Marburg; 97
Constantine the Great; 43;
51; 53; 59; 60; 61; 63;
75; 130
Constantine VII, emperor;
50
Copernicus; 34; 112
Cornelius Sulla; 36
Cornil; 48
Costaș, Ion; 108; 231
Crassus; 37
Cromwell, Oliver; 148
Cucuteni; 14; 15; 17
Curta, Florin; 19; 231
Cuza, Alexandru Ioan;
173; 174; 175
Cyril; 42; 54; 66
D'Alembert; 153
Daimler Gottlieb; 161
Dante; 117; 119; 122
Darwin, Charles; 173
de Broglie, Louis; 187
Decebalus; 44
Decius; 43
Democritus; 23; 30; 36
Descartes; 33; 46; 111;
141; 152; 154
Diderot; 153
Diocletian; 43; 57; 59
Dionysus; 41; 183
Dioscorides; 40; 88
Dioscorus; 54
Dirac; 180; 187
Dollfuss; 201

Dominic, monk; 58
Domitian; 43
Donatello; 122
Donatus Magnus; 54
Dosoftei, Metropolitan;
146; 147; 151
Drake, Francis; 130
Duke of Guise; 137
Dürer, Albert; 122
Edward III of England;
115
Einstein; 180; 186
Eliade, Mircea; 16; 17; 68;
146; 231
Elizabeth I; 156
Eminescu, Mihai; 181
Empedocles; 21
Epictetus; 31
Epicurus; 23; 30; 36
Erasmus of Rotterdam.;
122
Eratosthenes; 33
Euclid; 32; 111
Eugene IV, pope; 130
Eugene of Savoy; 151;
152
Eugenius III, pope; 100
Eva Heyman; 107; 201;
232
Falkenhayn, Erich; 103;
104; 191
Faraday; 160; 180
Ferdinand I of Romania;
198

Ferdinand I, Holy Roman
Emperor; 136
Ferdinand II, Habsburg;
144
Ferdinand III, Habsburg;
145
Ferdinand of Aragon; 131
Fichte; 162; 163; 183
Fischer, Emil; 195
Flavius Heraclius,
emperor; 78; 92
Flavius Tiberius, emperor;
77
Fleming, Alexander; 48
Florey, Walter; 48
Fra Angelico; 122
Fracastoro; 47
Francis I of France; 134
Francis II, duke of
Brittany; 135
Francis of Assisi; 58
Franco; 201
Frederick I of Prussia; 155
Frederick I, Barbarossa;
92; 97
Frederick II, Barbarossa;
51; 94
Frederick the Great; 156;
158
Frederick Wilhelm I; 156
Frobenius, Leo; 208
Gabor Pesti; 68
Gaius Marius; 36
Galen; 47

Galerius, emperor; 43; 57;
59
Galileo Galilei; 23; 112
Galina Andreevna; 108
Gallienus, emperor; 43
Gelfand, I.L.; 189
George Ludwig; 149
Gimbutas; 17
Gimbutas, Maria; 16
Giordano Bruno; 101; 121
Giotto; 122
Giovanni Benedetti; 112
Godunov, Boris; 154
Goethe; 47; 176
Gorbachev, Mikhail; 217
Goşu, Armand; 224
Gracchus; 35; 37
Gramsci, Antonio; 205
Gregory I, pope; 41; 51;
71; 77; 91
Gregory IX, pope; 97
Gregory XI, pope; 122;
125
Grigore Ghica III; 158
Grünewald, painter; 209
Gudea, Nicolae; 49; 232
Guderian, Heinz; 211
Gumilev, Lev; 205
Gustav II, Vasa; 145
Gustav Vasa; 133
Gutenberg; 122
Hadrian, emperor; 43; 45;
75; 76
Hannibal; 77

Harald I; 82
Haşdeu, Bogdan; 56; 232
Hawkins, John; 130
Hegel; 47; 140; 162; 163;
    166; 167; 171; 176
Heidegger; 171
Heisenberg; 180; 187
Henry II of England; 97
Henry III of England; 109
Henry IV of France; 138
Henry V, emperor; 95
Henry VI of England; 116
Henry VIII; 135
Heraclitus; 21; 24
Herder; 153; 165; 173;
    176
Herodotus; 49
Hertz, Heinrich; 180
Hieronymus; 66; 122
Hindenburg; 201; 207;
    208
Hippocrates; 32; 47
Hitler; 105; 165; 201; 207;
    208; 209; 211; 226
Hobbes, Thomas; 141
Hoffmann, Max; 191
Hofmannsthal, Hugo; 194
Homo sapiens; 13; 14
Horea, rex Daciae; 165
Horthy; 108; 160; 165;
    210; 213
Hugh Capet; 89
Hugues de Payens; 90
Huntington, Samuel; 227

Hus, Jan; 66; 123
Iancu de Hunedoara; 126
Ignatius of Loyola; 58;
    136
Innocent II, pope; 90
Innocent III, pope; 94; 99;
    100; 109
Innocent VIII, pope; 101
Ioan Asan II; 99
Ion Vodă; 126
Ioniță Caloian, emperor;
    98
Iorga; 146; 165; 224; 232
Isaac II, emperor; 98
Isabella of Castile; 131
Istrati, Panait; 195
Iustinianus; 75
Jadwiga of Poland; 126
Jagiello; 126
James II Stuart; 149
James VI; 156
Jan Hus; 101
Jean Le Bon; 66
Jean Nouzille; 104; 232
Jesus Christ; 38; 39; 40;
    53; 54; 62; 109
Joanna the Mad; 132
John I of England; 109
John I of Portugal; 66
John of Damascus; 54
John of Sultanyeh; 51
John Paul II; 55; 224
John XII, pope; 89
John XXII, pope; 123

Joseph II
  Habsburg; 164
  patriarch; 130
Kamenev; 200
Kant; 46; 85; 153; 161;
  162; 163
Kasparov, Garry; 226
Keitel, Wilhelm; 211
Kekulé; 180
Kepler; 33; 34; 112
Kerensky; 199
Keskula; 195
Khrushchev; 214
Kierkegaard; 23; 171
Klein, Carl; 165
Koch, Robert; 47; 48
Kohl, Helmuth; 218
Kossuth; 103; 164
Kravchuk; 221
Kuhn, Bela; 202
Ladislaus the Cuman; 100
Lansing, Robert; 196
Lavoisier; 180
Lehrer, Milton; 165
Leibniz; 23; 46; 111; 153
Lenin; 189; 190; 191; 195;
  199; 200
Leo III, pope; 55; 79; 80;
  81
Leo IX, pope; 91
Leonardo da Vinci; 112;
  122; 160
Licinius; 43; 59
Linnaeus, Carl; 160

Locke, John; 143; 149
Lőhrer, Franz; 165
Lorenz, Konrad; 216
Lothair; 82
Louis IV of Bavaria; 115
Louis IX of France; 95
Louis the German; 82
Louis VII of Aragon; 96
Louis VII of France; 92
Louis XI of France; 131
Louis XII of France; 132
Louis XIV; 102; 138
Louis XVI of France; 166
Lucius III, pope; 97
Lucretius; 23; 30; 36; 119
Ludendorff, Erich; 193;
  228
Lukacs, Georg; 205
Lukyanov; 221
Lustig, Oliver; 108; 232
Luther; 55; 65; 67; 118;
  120; 124; 135; 140; 153
Lvov, Gheorghi; 196; 199
Machiavelli; 122
Mackensen, August; 104
Magellan; 113
Maimonides; 28
Marcian; 54
Marco Polo; 113
Marcus Aurelius; 31; 57
Marcus Siegfried; 161
Maria Theresa; 157; 158
Marsilio Ficino; 119
Martin V, pope; 101; 125

Marx; 140; 163; 164; 179; 232
Maximian; 57
Maximinus, Valerius Daza; 59
Maximus; 54
Maxwell; 180
Mehmed II; 126
Mendel; 180
Mendeleev; 180
Metodius; 42
Michael I
    emperor; 81
    patriarch; 91
Michael III, emperor; 42
Michael the Brave; 126; 143
Michelangelo; 122
Mieszko; 63
Mikael Agricola; 68
Mikhail Romanov; 144
Milescu; 146; 147
Milton, John; 122; 141
Mircea the Elder; 126
Mojimir I; 63
Montesquieu; 143; 153
Moraru, Anton; 105; 232
Moruzi, Phanariot; 159
Muscă, Vasile; 24; 29; 85; 161; 163; 232
Mussolini; 201; 211
Nagy, Imre; 214
Napoleon; 21; 59; 158; 167; 168; 175

Napoleon III; 178
Neagoe Basarab; 122
Neanderthals; 13
Nero; 40; 43
Nerva; 43
Nestorius; 54
Newton; 33; 111; 152
Nicetas Choniates; 99
Nicetas, bishop; 41
Nicholas II, tsar; 191
Nicholas of Cusa; 111
Nicholas, duke of Russia; 181
Nicolae de Modrusa; 51
Nicolas Oresme; 111
Nicolo Malermi; 67
Nietzsche; 118; 119; 120; 173; 182
Nikephoros II, emperor; 84
Nikon, Metropolitan; 150
Oberth Herman; 161
Octavian Augustus; 129
Odoacer; 74
Ogedei, khan; 110
Olaf I; 64
Olaf Skötkonung; 64
Olahus, Nicolaus; 51
Omar II; 79
Onicescu; 187
Osman Pasha; 182
Ostwald, Wilhelm; 195
Otto III, emperor; 64
Otto the Great; 87; 89

Ottokar the Great; 87
Ovid; 30; 37; 119
Palade, George Emil; 48
Paliga, Sorin; 19; 231; 233
Parmenides; 21; 24
Pârvan; 40; 49; 233
Pasteur; 47; 48
Paul VI, pope; 217
Paul, apostle; 38; 39; 57;
    157; 204
Paulescu, Nicolae; 48
Pauli; 180
Pelagius; 55; 65; 136
Pepin; 80; 81
Peregrinus; 111; 160
Pericles; 20
Peter Movilă; 146; 151
Peter the Great; 102; 139;
    154; 155; 224
Peters
    head of CEKA; 200
Petliura; 202
Petrarch; 119; 122
Petre Tutea; 39
Petru and Asan; 98
Philip II of France; 92
Philip II of Spain; 136;
    138; 139
Philip IV of France; 90;
    114; 128
Philip Moldovan; 67
Philip of Marnix; 68
Philip the Good of
    Burgundy; 116

Philip the Handsome; 132
Philip V of Spain; 156
Philip VI of France; 115
Pilsudski; 198
Pius II, pope; 49
Pius IX, pope; 128
Planck; 180; 186
Planck, Max; 195
Plato; 22; 24; 25; 26; 28;
    31; 45; 52; 119; 163
Plotinus; 52; 85; 119
Poengen, Conrad; 195
Pompey; 37
Porphyry; 85
Poruciuc, Adrian; 16; 17;
    233
Prodan, David; 128; 171;
    233
Putin; 205; 221
Pythagoras; 32
Rabelais; 122
Rahman III; 88
Raphael; 122
Ratislav; 42; 63
Recared; 63
Renaud de Châtillon; 92
Richard the Lionheart; 92
Riegl, Alois; 208
Rilke, Rainer; 194
Roger I; 82
Rollo; 82
Romain Rolland; 195
Roth Stephan Ludwig;
    165

Roy Medvedev; 104
Rurik; 63; 82; 154
Rutherford; 186
Saladin; 92
Sallustius; 34
Sancho the Great; 89
Sartre; 171
Savonarola; 123
Schelling; 162; 164; 171
Schiller; 176
Schnitzler, Arthur; 194
Schopenhauer; 162; 183
Schrödinger; 180; 187
Sebastian del Cano; 114
Seton-Watson; 165; 233
Shakespeare; 122
Shaw, Bernard; 165
Sigismund III Vasa; 144
Sigismund of
    Luxembourg; 123
Sinan Pasha; 143
Slavici Ioan; 64; 165; 233
Smirnov; 108
Sobieski, Jan; 151
Socrates; 22; 24; 29; 39;
    45; 163
Solon; 19; 20
Sommerfeld; 186
Spengler, Oswald; 208
Spinoza; 46; 152
St. Andrew; 49
St. Augustine; 65; 70
St. Basil the Great; 204
St. Cyril; 70

St. Gregory of Nazianzus;
    204
St. Macarius, the
    Egyptian; 204
St. Martin; 41
St. Patrick; 41
Stalin; 104; 105; 159; 160;
    200; 201; 209; 212;
    214; 220; 225; 226
Ștefan Dușan; 116
Stephen I of Moldavia; 88
Stephen II, pope; 81
Stephen Langton; 109
Stephen the Great; 126;
    224
Subutai, khan; 109
Suleiman the Magnificent;
    133
Surkov, Vladislav; 224
Suslov, Mikhail; 214
Sviatoslav; 63; 84
Syagrius; 74
Sylvester II, pope; 64
Tamaș, Gaspar; 213
Tarquinius Superbus; 20
Tasso; 122
Thales; 21
Theodoric; 73
Theodosius I, emperor; 68
Thomas Aquinas; 23; 28;
    55; 65; 85; 96; 112;
    136; 153
Thomas More; 121; 122
Thucydides; 141

Tisza, Istvan; 188
Tolstoy; 165
Toynbee, Arnold; 208
Trajan; 43; 44; 233
Trevithick; 160
Tribonianus; 75
Trotsky; 200
Trubetzkoy, Nikolai; 205
Tsankov; 201
Tzimiskes, emperor; 56;
    84
Ulfila; 41; 53; 61; 66
Urban II, pope; 92
Urban VI, pope; 125
Valens, emperor; 72
Valerian, emperor; 43
van der Weyden, painter;
    122
van Eyck, painter; 122
Van Gogh; 209
Varlaam, Metropolitan;
    146; 151
Vasco da Gama; 113
Vasile Lupu; 146
Vercingetorix; 38
Vesalius; 47
Vlad the Impaler; 126

Vladimir I of Kiev; 63
Vladimir of Suzdal; 110
Vladislav Vasa; 144; 154
Vuia Traian; 161
Wagner, Richard; 183
Wallace, Russel; 173
Watt, James; 160
Watts, L. Larry; 215; 217;
    233
Weidlein, Johann; 102;
    164; 165; 214; 233; 234
Wilhelm I; 178
Wilhelm II; 194
William of Orange; 138;
    149
William, Duke of
    Normandy; 82
Wilson, Woodrow; 196;
    197
Wycliffe; 66; 117; 122;
    123
Yeltsin, Boris; 221
Zachary, pope; 81
Zamora, Alcala; 207
Zeno of Citium; 30
Zinoviev; 200
Zweig, Stephan; 194